Very
important
Reads

Must Read   catb.org   — F

— B   language

* en.tldp.org/HowTo/Unix.... → load   co-tos
    → good one on Linux Backspace/

Raspberry Pi IoT In C

* scriptoriumdesigns.com → tutorial on embedded programming
                              generally useful — some good basics
                              on interrupts.

Harry Fairhead

I/O Press
I Programmer Library

Harry Fairhead, Raspberry Pi IoT In C

ISBN Paperback: 978-187196246-8

First Edition
First Printing, 2016
Revision 0

Published by IO Press   www.iopress.info

In association with I Programmer   www.i-programmer.info

and with I o T Programmer   www.iot-programmer.com

The publisher recognizes and respects all marks used by companies and manufacturers as a means to distinguish their products. All brand names and product names mentioned in this book are trade marks or service marks of their respective companies and our omission of trade marks is not an attempt to infringe on the property of others.

In particular we acknowledge that Raspberry Pi is a registered trademark of the Raspberry Pi Foundation.

Preface

The Raspberry Pi has had a revolutionary impact on computing. It is both cheap and powerful and since its original launch in 2012 over 10 million Pis have been sold.

The Pi, and in particular the compact and low cost Pi Zero, is ideal for the star role in the Internet of Things, be it for monitoring the Smart Home or controlling a robot. However, to realize its full potential as an IoT device it we need to use a language that gets us close to the hardware.

While we normally associate the Pi with Python or with Scratch, it is also capable of being programmed in C, which gives you full access to its features and to external devices. The main reason for choosing C is speed, a crucial factor when you are writing programs to communicate with the outside world and, what is more, C isn't much more difficult than any programming language.

This book isn't an introduction to the Pi or Linux and it is assumed that either you are already familiar with it or can get up to speed with the many existing introductory resources. It is also expected that you know how to program in some language, not necessarily C, and that you have a rough idea about electronics. You don't have to be an expert before you begin reading but by the end book, if you build some of the projects for real, you should have acquired a reasonable degree of skill.

The main idea in this book is to not simply install a driver, but to work directly with the hardware. This approach frees you from dependence on the current Linux configuration and isolates you from the restrictions of the drivers. Perhaps more importantly it ensures you understand what is going on and are in complete control. Similarly on the hardware side no HATs or other off-the-shelf expansion boards are used. Simple and direct electronics are often all that is needed and finding out how to do it means that you can understand how the expansion boards do their job.

After a quick tour of the Raspberry Pi ecosystem, we introduce NetBeans, used as the behind the scenes programming environment for this book and write a first C program. Next, in the context of GPIO (General Purpose Input Output) we meet the bcm2835 library, which will continue to use throughout, and use it write "Blinky" a program to flash an LED, which is the traditional first program for IoT. Now we are ready to discover how to control the Pi's I/O lines and explore the basics of using the GPIO. Working directly with the raw hardware we'll also master memory mapping, pulse width modulation and other more sophisticated bus types.

From here we can start connecting sensors, which is a core requirement for IoT. First we'll meet the ubiquitous I2C bus, next we'll implement a custom protocol for a one-wire bus, and eventually we'll add eight channels of 12-bit AtoD with the SPI bus, which involves overcoming some subtle difficulties.

We look at the traditional serial interface next and how to use it to communicate with other devices. This paves the way for getting the Pi on the web – after all this is a book about the Internet of Things. In the final two chapters we first look at using a USB WiFi adapter and sockets and then explore the low cost ESP8266, which is particularly useful with the Pi Zero which has only one USB port. We see how to create both a web client and a web server and get them to exchange information.

This is not a projects book, although there isn't much left for you to do to round out the embryonic projects that are used as examples, but an understanding and skills acquisition book. The hope is that by the end of the book you will know how to tackle your own projects and get them safely to completion without wasting time in trial and error.

For updates, errata, links to resources and the source code for the programs in this book visit its dedicated page on the IoT Programmer website:

http://www.iot-programmer.com/index.php/books/PiTheIoTinC

Table of Contents

Preface

Chapter 1

Why Pi for IoT?

The Raspberry Pi has changed the computing world in more ways than one. It isn't a particularly powerful device, but it is so low cost that it introduces an era of almost disposable computing. This isn't quite true. Even the lowest cost Pi, the Pi Zero, actually costs more than its $5 raw cost to get into a usable state, but it really lowers the financial barrier to using advanced computing devices to do all sorts of creative and useful things.

In this short chapter we will take a look at the range of devices that are available and the reasons for selecting one rather than another to do particular jobs. As this book is about using the Pi to connect to the outside world, it is the Pi as microcontroller or embedded IoT device, that interests us the most.

The Pi versus the Microcontroller

Compared to the Pi, the Arduino and any similar microcontroller is a very low power computer. The basic Arduino isn't capable of running Linux, which is a full operating system. It simply runs the one program you have written for it. However, the Arduino and similar devices have a big advantage – they have dedicated I/O lines and usually analog I/O lines. The Pi doesn't have the same variety of I/O lines, but it has enough for many jobs and it can be easily expanded with the use of standard expansion boards called HATs (Hardware Attached on Top) because of the way they plug in.

To make the difference plain you can use a Pi for almost any job that a desktop computer can do, including any server role. An Arduino, on the other hand, isn't up to this sort of work. Sometimes the fact that the Pi is full computer makes it even more suitable for low-level jobs. For example, you want a new door bell? Why not use a Pi and have it say hello using a voice synthesizer.

In short the Pi gives you more computing power for less money.

Everything isn't perfect with the Pi and the IoT. In particular, the use of Linux means that you can no longer pretend your program is the only program running. Linux is a multitasking operating system and it can suspend any program at any time to give another program a chance to run. If you are familiar with microcontroller programming then it will come as something of a shock that you do not have complete control of the machine. What is more, Linux isn't the easiest operating system to get to grips with if you are a beginner.

All of these problems and more can be overcome with a little work and it is worthwhile. The Pi is a fast and capable IoT computer and would still be a good choice even if it cost a lot more.

Which Pi?

As far as the IoT goes, while you can use an early Pi 1 model A or B to do any of the tasks described in this book it is much better not to. The modern range of Pi 2 and Pi 3 devices is so much better suited to the task because they are more powerful.

The Pi 2 is a quad core ARM processor running at 900MHz with 1GB RAM. It has four USB ports and a network port. The fact that it has four cores makes it very suitable for fast interfacing tasks. You can expect your program not to be interrupted by the operating system as there are three other cores it can use to run system programs. The multiple USB ports also makes it easy to add a WiFi dongle.

Pi 3 – the latest full-feature Pi

The Pi 3 is the replacement for the Pi 2. This has a 1.2 GHz 64 bit quad core ARM processor and built in Bluetooth and WiFi. It is faster than either the Pi 2 or the Pi Zero and it has four USB ports and a network port. This is the Pi to use when your application needs a quad core processor. The built in WiFi makes things much simpler. The only down side is that it needs plenty of power to run the WiFi and Bluetooth and it tends to run hot.

The Pi Zero is a very attractive device for IoT work simply because it is small, low power and very low cost. It has a single core ARM processor running at 1GHz and puts in a performance very similar to the Pi 2.

The big difference is that it has only one core which means your program will be interrupted by the operating system to keep the device working. In many applications this doesn't matter. If it does upgrade to a Pi 2/3. Another negative is that it only has a single USB port and no network port. This can make it difficult to get started with. While it is easy to connect a USB WiFi dongle via an adapter this does spoil the overall narrow form factor. One solution is to use an ESP8266 as explained in Chapter 19.

Pi Zero – small and low cost

In this book the target devices are the Pi Zero, the Pi 2 and the Pi3. In general the Pi Zero and the Pi 2 work at roughly the same speed and the Pi 3 is a few percent faster. All three devices are capable of much the same sort of work.

No HATS Needed

The basic Pi can be easily expanded with the addition of a HAT plugin board or an earlier non-HAT expansion board. Some of these expansion boards are so commonly used that they are considered more or less standard. In this book HATs and expansion boards of any kind are not used. The reason is simply that the focus is on the Pi as it comes. There is also a tendency to use an expansion board when in fact all that is needed is a few cents worth of additional electronics or better still just some clever software.

The popular sense HAT adds a range of sensors and an LED display

What To Expect

There are no complete projects in this book – although some examples come very close and it is clear that some of them could be used together to create finished projects. The reason for this is that the focus is on learning how things work so that you can move on and do things that are non-standard.

What matters is that you can reason about what the processor is doing and how it interacts with the real world in real time. This is the big difference between desktop and embedded programming. In the desktop world you don't really care much about when something happens, but when you are programming a physical system you care very much.

This is a book about understand the general principle and making things work at the lowest possible level. This knowledge isn't always necessary when you are working on a relatively slow system in say Python, but it is always useful to help understand what is going on when things go wrong. When you are working directly with the hardware, speed matters and so does knowing what is happening.

User Mode - No Drivers

In most of books on using the Pi you will find that a lot depends on using Linux drivers to access the hardware. Indeed, if you are using a language such as Python, you have no choice but to install suitable drivers as the language isn't fast enough to work in any other way. However, if you have to install a driver or otherwise configure the operating system to make your program work then you have the problem of making sure that any other system it runs on is set up in the same way.

There is also the problem of what happens when the OS is updated. Just recently Raspbian was updated to make use of systemd as its init system and this caused many programs that made use of the hardware to stop working until the system was reconfigured. Changes in Python or other high level language implementations also cause the same sort of problems, causing programs and libraries that did work to stop working.

For this and many other reasons the programs developed in this book are based on user mode access to the hardware and hence don't use drivers. The only exception is the serial port in Chapter 18 where the Linux serial port driver is so standard and unchanging that not to use it would be to do extra work for no reason.

As a result all of the programs in this book are fairly self contained and once compiled they should just run on any Linux system with minimal additional configuration.

Put simply, the approach used in this book is to write low-level C programs that run under Linux but make minimal use of the operating system to access the hardware and require minimal configuration to make them work. This approach makes installation easy and isolates the program from changes in the OS.

What Do You Need?

If you are going to follow the examples you will need either a Pi Zero or a Pi 2/3. You can use an earlier Pi as long as you make allowances for the difference in pin assignments and other minor hardware changes.

You need to have the Pi setup with Raspbian and you need to know how to connect to it and use it via a serial console. You also need to be comfortable with Linux in the sense that you might not know how to do something but you know how to look it up and follow the instructions.

It is also assumed that you are able to program in a C-like language – Java, C#, Python are all C like and, of course, so is C++. There isn't space in this book to teach C programming, but the programs are easy enough to follow and any out of the ordinary coding is explained.

A solderless prototype board and some Dupoint wires

As to additional hardware over and above the Pi you will need a solderless prototype board and some hookup wires – known as Dupoint wires. You will also need some LEDs, a selection of resistors, some 2N2222 or other general purpose transistors and any of the sensors used in later chapters.

A Low Cost Logic Analyzer

You don't need to know how to solder, but you will need to be able to hook up a circuit on a prototyping board. A multimeter (less than $10) is useful, but if you are serious about building IoT devices investing in a logic analyzer (less than $100) will repay itself in no time at all. You can get small analyzers that plug in via a USB port and use an application to show you what is happening. It is only with a multichannel logic analyzer can you have any hope of understanding what is happening. Without one and the slight skill involved in using it, you are essentially flying blind and left to just guess what might be wrong.

Finally, if you are even more serious then a low-cost pocket oscilloscope is also worth investing in to check out the analog nature of the supposedly digital signals that microcontroller put out. However, if you have to choose between these two instruments the logic analyzer should be you first acquisition.

It is worth noting that the Pi can generate signals that are too fast to be reliably detected by low-cost oscilloscopes and logic analyzers which work at between 1MHz and 25MHz. This can mean that working with pulses much faster than 1 microsecond can be difficult as you cannot rely on your instruments.

Safety In Numbers

There is one final word to say about the Raspberry Pi and its ecosystem –
there is safety in numbers. At the time of writing the Pi has sold 10 million
units and while these aren't all exactly the same device they are all
compatible enough to ensure that your programs have a good chance of
running on any of them.

The large numbers of Pis in the world means that you have a good chance of
finding the answer to any problem by a simple internet search, although it
has to be said that the quality of answers available vary from misleading to
excellent. Always make sure you evaluate what you are being advised in the
light of what you know. You also need to keep in mind that the advice is also
usually offered from a reasonably biased point of view. The Python
programmer will give you an answer that suits a system that already uses
Python and electronics beginners will offer you solutions that are based on
"off the shelf" modules when a simple cheap solution is available based on a
few cheap components. Even when the advice you get is 100% correct, it still
isn't necessarily the right advice for you.

The large numbers of Raspberry Pis in circulation also means that it is
unlikely that the device will become obsolete. This isn't something you can
assume about other less popular single-board computers. It is reasonable to
suppose that any programs you write today will work into the foreseeable
future on a device that might not look like today's Raspberry Pi's but will be
backward compatible.

In short the Raspberry Pi provides a secure and non-threatening environment
for your development work.

Chapter 2
Getting Started With NetBeans

There are lots of ways to program the Pi. Popular choices range from Scratch, to Python and you could even choose assembler. Each language has its advantages and disadvantages but there are times when subtle arguments aren't necessary. If you want to program the Pi in a way that extracts the maximum efficiency and without any limits then C is the obvious choice. It is easier to program in C than in assembler and the results are almost the same in terms of speed.

You can describe C as a machine independent assembly language and hence when you learn it you get deeper into the system than with other languages and discover what is really going on. This makes it a good way to improve your understanding of computers and computing in general.

Sometimes you don't need speed, even in an IoT application. For example, if you just want to flash a few LEDs or read a temperature sensor in a human time scale, then you can write in almost any language. However, if you want to directly interface with other systems and control externally connected hardware at its full speed, C is your best choice. If timing is critical, then C is the only way to go. Put simply if you can't make your application work fast enough in C then you probably can't in any language.

With C being so "low level" it makes it easy to access the underlying hardware. In this book most of the peripherals are accessed directly and Linux drivers are mostly avoided. The reason is that, even if a driver is available, it has to be installed and this makes the setup for your program more complex. Also driving the hardware directly isn't that difficult and it means you can modify how it behaves and correct for defects in software. This is the advantage of working with C instead of a language that is so slow that drivers are essential for speed.

You might be worried that you are some how trapping yourself in a low level language and will be unable to take advantage of sophisticated programming practices. Your get out clause is that C is a subset of C++ and you can break out of C anytime you feel like it and start writing code that has objects and all the trimmings of a modern language. Of course, the code you write might not be quite as efficient as the C code you have had to give up, but it is still fast.

There is also the point that C leads on naturally to C++, a full object-oriented extension of C. In this book C is used rather than C++ simply to make the programs easier to understand. In practice many of the functions created would be better off integrated into a suitable object. Equally for the sake of simplicity, the code presented is the simplest that will do the job. This means that we ignore error handling and factoring code into headers and other libraries – everything is as simple as possible and as self contained as possible. After all, the point is to understand what is going on not present production ready code.

Put simply C is a great language for any interfacing, IoT or embedded program and it leads on to C++ and more sophisticated languages.

So C is worth learning.

How do we get started?

Getting Started In C

You can program in C in many different ways. All of the software you need to run a C program is already installed on a standard Pi running Raspbian. You can use an editor on the Pi to create your program and then compile and run it using the command line. However there are easy to use IDEs that make programming in C fast and painless and they provide debugging facilities that make finding bugs much quicker.

You could use Genny or Eclipse they are both open source but in practice NetBeans is the most powerful and this is the approach we are going to use. If you want to use one of the others. or just a text editor and the command line. you can and everything described will work - but NetBeans is worth a try because the help it gives you with generating code and debugging will save you a lot of time in the long run. It is also open source and free to use.

There are two distinct ways you can work with NetBeans and the Pi:

- You could install NetBeans on a Raspberry Pi and work with it via the GUI desktop i.e. directly on the Pi. In this case you are using the Pi as if it was a full desktop computer and it is your development and test machine.

- You could connect the Pi to a desktop machine and make use of remote development features of NetBeans. In this case you are using the Pi as a Build Host and the desktop machine as the development environment.

In both cases the Pi does the compiling and the running of the program. In practice the remote development approach tends to work better because the desktop machine has the power to run NetBeans fast.

It also means that you can change the Pi that you are testing the code on very easily with all of the code stored on the desktop machine. This is very useful because you can try your program out on a range of Raspberry Pis and swap machines simply by changing the build host used for the project.

The desktop machine can be a Windows, OSX or even another Linux machine.

Before we can get down to work we need to find out how to set up NetBeans in both modes of use.

NetBeans On Raspberry Pi

NetBeans is a Java program that will work on any machine that supports a Java Virtual Machine (JVM) and the Pi comes with a JVM already installed as part of Raspbian. As NetBeans is fairly demanding it would have to be a Raspberry Pi 3, or a 2, to run it directly in desktop mode.

As this isn't a complete beginner's book, it is assumed that you have your target Pi set up with Raspbian and you either have a monitor, keyboard and mouse connected or you have an SSH connection. If you haven't reached this stage there are lots of introductory tutorials.

Getting NetBeans working is fairly simple. From the desktop first run a browser and navigate to netbeans.org. Find the download page and select: OS Independent Zip and the language you want to work in.

Click the download button of the version of NetBeans you want to work with. I recommend that you select the specific C/C++ version. The download is smaller and you don't get a lot of confusing additional features which have nothing to do with programming in C. You can always add additional language support at a later date.

After the download is complete you have to extract the files in the zip to a suitable directory. If you are the only person going to use NetBeans then your home directory is suitable. Extract all of the files into the directory.

Navigate to your home directory and then to netbeans/bin and run the file netbeans - this is a shell script that the first time it is run installs NetBeans and subsequently runs the IDE. Run it in a terminal, accept the license agreement and wait while it installs. The other files in the directory are to install NetBeans on a Windows or OSX machine.

At this point you will have a working NetBeans IDE ready to create your first C program.

Optionally you can add NetBeans to the Programming group in the menu. All you have to do is select Preferences, Main Menu Editor. Then select the Programming group and select New Item. Fill in the dialog that appears as shown:

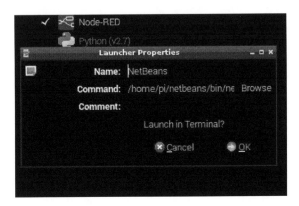

The command is:

```
/home/pi/netbeans/bin/netbeans
```

adjusted to reference your home directory rather than that of user pi if necessary. After this you can run NetBeans from the menu.

NetBeans On A Remote Machine

Although installing NetBeans on Raspberry Pi is easy and it works very well, there are good reasons for installing on a desktop machine and using the Pi as a remote build server. The most obvious advantage is that the desktop machine is likely to be more powerful than even a Pi 3. In addition you can use the same code base and machine to program multiple Pis. All you have to do is change the IP address of the remote build server.

It is assumed that you have your target Pi set up with Raspbian and connected to a network, a wired connection works best because it is faster, but a WiFi connection works. It is also assumed you also know the IP address of the Pi you want to work with.

You also need to make an SSH (Secure SHell) connection to the Pi. You can just make the connection using NetBeans but, under Windows, it is better to use an SSH client such as PuTTY. If you can't make an SSH connection to the Pi then you aren't going to get NetBeans working remotely with it. So check that you can open an SSH terminal.

The first step is to install NetBeans on the desktop machine you want to work with. You can do this by selecting the download that targets the correct OS - Windows, Linux x86/x64 or OS X. Again you can install one of the distributions that supports other languages, but just using the C/C++ version has the advantage of simplicity.

Once downloaded simply run the installer and you should have a fully working version of NetBeans on the desktop machine.

Making the connection between the desktop installation and the Pi acting at the remote build server is described in the next section.

Your First C Pi Program

At this point it is assumed that you have NetBeans installed either on the Pi or on a desktop machine. It is also assumed that the Pi is correctly setup and, if you are using remote development, it is connected to a network and you know its IP address and can SSH to it.

In general before starting work with C it is necessary to setup the details of where the C compilers are located. The Pi comes ready setup with the GCC compilers as standard so there is no need to do anything at all if you are running NetBeans on the Pi. In this case NetBeans will have automatically detected the compilers and set up localhost as the build server.

If you are running NetBeans on a desktop machine then localhost, i.e the desktop machine, will have been setup as the build server, but this is only useful if the necessary compilers have been installed. In the case of Windows this is unlikely unless you have specially installed them.

Remote Build Server

For remote development you have to set up the Pi as the remote build server. You can skip this step if you are using NetBeans on the Pi itself, but it is a good idea to follow the instructions to confirm that you do have the GNU compilers set up correctly.

To do this use the menu command:

    Window,Services

and drop-down C/C++ Build Hosts in the window that appears.

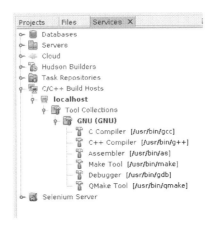

If NetBeans is running on the Pi when you expand the localhost entry you'll see all of the compilers and other software needed to compile a C program:

In this case there is nothing more to do.

If you are running NetBeans on a Windows desktop machine then the chances are that under localhost you will see:

    None(No Compilers Found)

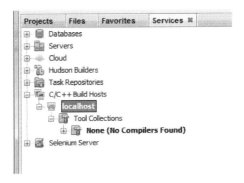

To work remotely we need to add the Pi as a build server. To do this right-click on C/C++ Build Hosts and select Add New Host:

The dialog box that appears lets you set the identity of the build server.

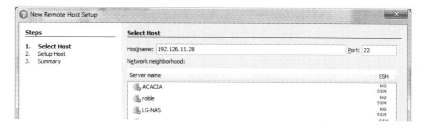

In most cases you will have to supply the IP address of the Pi unless you have set up SAMBA on it. There are advantages to doing this, but not when you are just getting started.

The next dialog box that appears lets you type in a user name and specify how authentication will proceed. You can use a key file, but in the first instance just use a password. You can use the default log in details of user name 'pi' and password 'raspberry'. Notice that these are both case sensitive. You will be asked for the password when you first connect to the Pi. This, of course, is the password that the user you specified needs to log into the Pi. This may seem obvious, but with so many users and passwords involved in setting things up, it can be confusing.

There are advantages to using a user name with root privileges and this will be explained later.

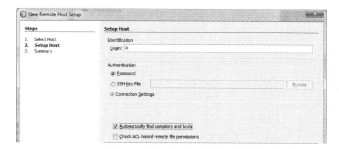

The final dialog box presents you with a summary of what you have set up:

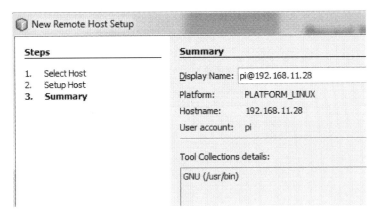

NetBeans should have found the C compiler and linker you are going to use as part of the GNU Collection. In a more general situation you might have to tell NetBeans where the compiler is or select which set of tools you want to use. In the case of the Pi and Raspbian you can leave the defaults as they are.

First Project

Time to write your first C program.

Select File.New Project and select C/C++ Application in the New Project dialog box that opens:

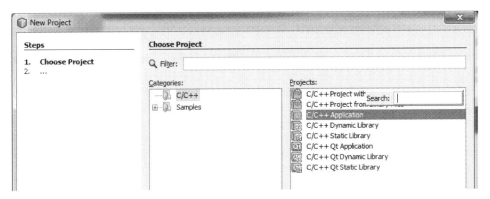

The next dialog box is the one where you customize the project.

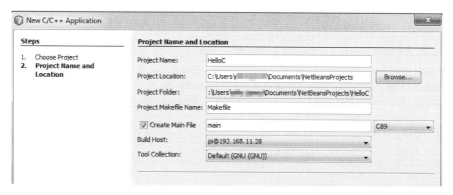

You can give the project any name you like and HelloC is reasonable for this first example. You need to select the dialect of C you are working in and C89 is the most common choice. However, C99 has the advantage that you can use single line comments of the form //comment, a feature which is well worth having, and hence C99 is what we will be using in the rest of this book.

You can generally leave the rest of the entries at their defaults but if you are working remotely you might have to set the Build host to the Pi you set up as the build host earlier. If you are working with NetBeans on the Pi then the Build Host will be Local Host. This is really the only difference between the two methods of working in terms of getting things setup but notice that the project files are stored on the local system and copied to the remote system to be built and for testing.

By default NetBeans uses SFTP (SSH File Transfer Protocol) which will work as long as the SSH connection to the Pi works.

NetBeans takes a few seconds to set up the project. When it is finished you will find a C file, main.c, ready with the start of a program:

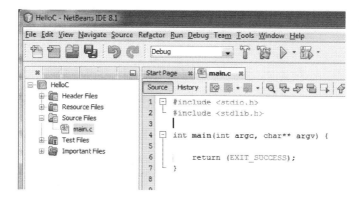

Change the program to read:

```
#include <stdio.h>
#include <stdlib.h>
int main(int argc, char** argv) {
 printf("Hello C World");
 return(EXIT_SUCCESS);
}
```

Yes it's a "hello world" program! What more do you need to test the compiler and linker?

All you have to do now is run the program, either by clicking the green "play" icon or using the menu command Run,Run. If you look at the Output window at the bottom of the screen you will see messages about how the compile is going. If you are working with the Pi as a remote build host the files that have changed will be uploaded and then the compiler will be run using **make.**

If you have entered the program correctly it should compile, link and run. If there are any problems you will see error messages in the Output window. You will see the Hello C World message in a new Output window tab that opens automatically. The printf function always sends its output to the Output window and this is very useful for status and debugging messages while you are developing the program.

It is worth knowing where NetBeans stores your project files.

If you are using the Pi or a Linux desktop to run NetBeans then your projects are stored in:

/home/*username*/NetBeansProjects

If you are using a Windows desktop machine to run NetBeans then your projects are stored in NetBeansProjects in your Documents directory and when you run the program the project's files are copied to the Pi to the

/home/*username*/NetBeansProjects

The two directories on the different machines are kept in sync by the system and sometimes NetBeans will inform you that a file on the Pi has been changed and offers you a chance to copy it back to the desktop machine. In general this isn't necessary because the changes aren't important for editing the project, only for running it.

Troubleshooting

Of course, in practice things go wrong.

There isn't much that can go wrong if you are running NetBeans on a Pi. If you have any problems then the best advice is to use a fresh installation of Raspbian and install NetBeans again.

The main things that can go wrong if you are using the Pi as a build host is that it fails to connect. This can be only because you have the IP address wrong, the user name wrong or the password wrong. There is a small probability that you might not have SSH enabled on the Pi, but this shouldn't happen unless you explicitly turned it off. Again the best advice is to install a fresh copy of Raspbian.

If you have any trouble connecting make sure you can connect using an SSH terminal such as PuTTY.

Summary

- C is a very good language to learn for any IoT project. It is fast and efficient and close to the machine. There are lots of other languages that have it as their ancestor, so it is worth learning.

- You can write programs in C using just an editor and the command line compilers, but NetBeans makes it much easier to create and debug programs. It is free to download and is open source.

- There are two ways to use NetBeans with a Raspberry Pi. You can install it on the Pi or you can install it on a desktop machine and use the Pi as the build host.

- There are lots of advantages to using a desktop machine to edit the programs in NetBeans and using the Pi as the build host to compile and run them.

- All you have to do to use the Pi as a build host is to make sure it is correctly set up, know its IP address and be sure that SSH is enabled. You can then set the Pi up as a build host in NetBeans.

- When you create a new project NetBeans creates the files you need to get started in the NetBeansProjects directory, which is either in your home directory on Linux or your Documents directory under Windows.

- When you run your project, NetBeans will first upload the files to the NetBeansProjects folder if you are using a remote build host and use the compilers specified to run the program.

Chapter 3
Introduction to the GPIO

In this chapter we take a look at the basic operations involved in using the Pi's General Purpose Input/Output (GPIO) lines with an emphasis on output. How fast can you change a GPIO line, how do you generate pulses of a given duration and how can you change multiple lines in sync with each other?

While there are other, more direct, ways that we will examine later, the easiest way to do this is with the bcm2835 library which is designed to make it easy to access the hardware. It has the advantage of being open source and doesn't need any Linux drivers.

In this chapter we take a first look at using bcm2835, how to install it and how to control the GPIO pins as basic input output lines. Later on we will look at how the library works and how to avoid using it if you really need to.

Setting Up bcm2835 With NetBeans

Exactly how to set up the library is a tiny bit trickier than most because it has to run as root to be able to access all of the GPIO facilities. It is also a little puzzling how to set up the library if you are using a remote build server - where do you copy the library for example? As it turns out the answer to this is easy.

First we need to set up a password for the standard root user and allow the root user to log in using SSH. To allow root to log on with a password we have to assign a password, so log in as user pi and give the command:

```
sudo passwd root
```

you will be prompted to type the new password twice. Next use a text editor of your choice, e.g. nano, to edit the ssh.config file to allow root to log on via SSH:

```
sudo nano /etc/ssh/sshd_config
```

Find:

```
PermitRootLogin without-password
```

and change it to read:

```
PermitRootLogin yes
```

Reboot the system to make the changes take effect or restart the SSH agent using:

```
sudo service ssh restart
```

Check that this works by logging on via an SSH console, such as PuTTY, using the user name **root** and the password you supplied earlier.

If you are using NetBeans on the Pi then simply log in as root whenever you are working with it.

If you are using NetBeans with the Pi as a remote build host then you need to create a new build host with the user name root and the password you specified. This might have the side effect of moving the location where projects are created to root's home directory.

With these changes made, check that you can create and/or run a project with the new build host.

If you find that a project is simply failing to run and returns a -1 status with no reason given, the chances are you are not running the program as root.

The final step is to download the bcm2835 library from:

```
http://www.airspayce.com/mikem/bcm2835/
```

At the time of writing this is at version 1.50 and works with all versions of the Raspberry Pi including the Zero and the Pi 3.

To install the library you need to download it into root's home directory. You can do this from the command line using:

```
sudo wget "http://www.airspayce.com/mikem/bcm2835/
                          bcm28351.50.tar.gz"
```

You may need to change the URL to reflect the latest version. The wget command as given will download the tar ball into the current directory.

Then use the following commands:

```
tar zxvf bcm2835-1.xx.tar.gz
cd bcm2835-1.xx
./configure
make
sudo make check
sudo make install
```

where xx is the version number, 50 at the moment. When these commands are completed you will have a bcm2835-1.xx folder which contains copies of the library, the header file and all the source code.

The library and header file that you are going to use will have been installed in /usr/local/lib and /user/local/include where NetBeans will find them automatically. Notice that NetBeans will find them automatically even if you are using the Pi as a remote build host. That is, you do not have to install the library on the machine running NetBeans, only on the build host.

To make use of the library in your program you have to do two final things. First you have to include the header file:

```
#include <bcm2835.h>
```

This ensures that NetBeans will not only find the header on the remote build host it will also let you work with it as if it was a file within the project.

Second you have to specify the name of the library that you want the linker to add to your program. To do this right click on the project and select properties. Select Build,Linker in the dialog box that appears, click the three dots in the Libraries section, click Add Library and specify bcm2835. Don't make the mistake of trying to add a Library File.

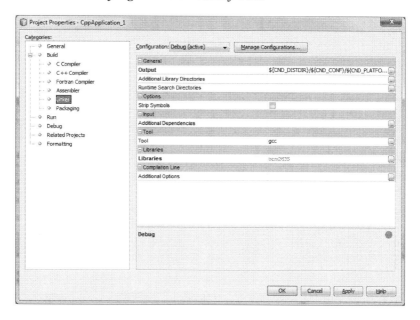

Note you don't have to specify where the library is stored or its version number as NetBeans will work it out.

Now you are ready to write your first IoT program which is nearly always to flash an LED – usually referred to as the "Blinky" program.

A First IoT Program

This purpose of this program is to just let you check that everything is working; the functions used will be explained in detail later.

Start a new project, call it Blink, and make sure you add the bcm2835 library to the linker options. To do this right click on the project and select properties, select Build,Linker in the dialog box that appears, click the three dots in the Libraries section, click Add Library and specify bcm2835.

Then enter the program:

```
#include <bcm2835.h>
#include <stdio.h> int main(int argc, char **argv) {
 if (!bcm2835_init())
   return 1;
 bcm2835_gpio_fsel(RPI_GPIO_P1_07,
                   BCM2835_GPIO_FSEL_OUTP);
 while (1) {
  bcm2835_gpio_write(RPI_GPIO_P1_07, HIGH);
  bcm2835_delay(500);
  bcm2835_gpio_write(RPI_GPIO_P1_07, LOW);
  bcm2835_delay(500);
 }
 bcm2835_close()
 return 0;
}
```

Don't panic when NetBeans initially shows you lots of errors. If you build or run the project NetBeans will take notice of the header files and stop worrying about identifiers like bcm2835_init(). Once the project has been built NetBeans knows all about the new library and will syntax check and offer code completion hints.

Even though you don't know much about the library just yet it isn't difficult to understand what is going on in the program. First we try to initialize the library. If this works, GPIO pin 7 is set to be an output and then the loop turns it on and off (high voltage then low) with a dearly of half a second. The library uses physical pins rather than logical GPIO numbers so RPI_GPIO_P1_07 is pin 7 on connector P1.

RPI_BPLUS_GPIO_xx

? RPI_GPIO_P1_07 ——

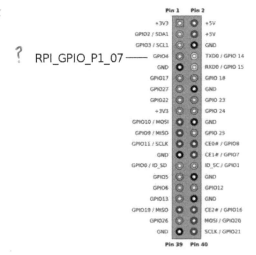

If you want to connect an LED to see the "blinking" for real then this is easy enough, but you do need a current limiting resistor - 270Ohm is a good choice.

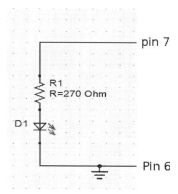

How you build the circuit is up to you. You can use a prototyping board or just a pair of jumper wires.

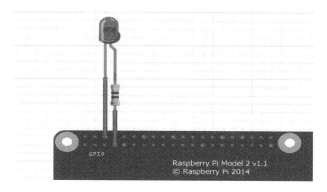

If you can't be bothered to go though the ritual of testing "blinky" with a real LED then just connect a logic analyzer to pin 7 and you will see one-second pulses.

Running Programs On NetBeans

All you have to do to run the program is click the Run icon or press F6. This downloads the program to the Pi that is the Build Server for the project and then runs it on the same Pi. If you try this with Blink you will see the LED blink or the Logic Analyzer will show the output pulse train.

The next question is how do you stop the program. If the program isn't in the form of an infinite loop it will terminate naturally and you don't have to do anything to stop it. Blink is an infinite loop which never ends so you do need to have some way of stopping it. If you click the run icon a second time a second copy of the program will be created and will start to run. This clearly isn't a good idea for programs that are interacting with GPIO lines.

You have to explicitly stop the program before you run it again. To do this simply click the red stop button in the output window:

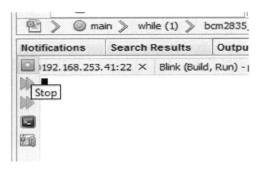

You can also see that there is a program running from the status bar at the bottom of the window:

If you do run multiple programs, either by design or accident, you can stop any of them by double clicking on the run status at the bottom of the window. Notice that the message to the right tells you how many programs are running. You can stop any or all by clicking on the corresponding stop buttons.

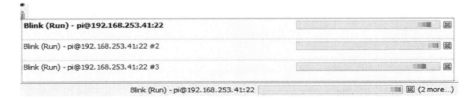

This is the minimum you need to know to run a program using NetBeans. The important topics of debugging and creating templates will be discussed in a later chapter.

Pin Numbering

The one thing that drives every programmer mad are the different ways of referring to the numbering of the GPIO pins. There is the physical pin number, i.e. the number of the pin on the physical connector, and the logical GPIO number, which is assigned deep in the hardware.

Another problem is that different generations of Pi have modified the pin layout slightly and there was an extension in the move from Pi 1 to Pi 2 and 3. In most cases the changes are slight and if you stay within the first 26 pins of the GPIO connector then you don't even have to worry if your program is running on a Pi 1, 2 or 3.

The standard 26-pin connector for a late generation P1 is:

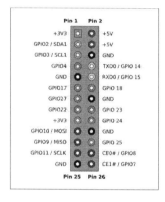

For a Pi 2 or 3 there are additional pins using a 40-pin connector:

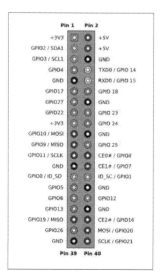

The bcm2835 library works in terms of the GPIO numbers defined by the processor. However, it also provides an enumeration which allows you to work in terms of the physical pins. For example in the blink program the instruction:

```
bcm2835_gpio_write(RPI_GPIO_P1_07, HIGH);
```

sets the GPIO line connected to pin 7 on connector P1 high. If you look at the code for the enumeration you will discover that RPI_GPIO_P1_07 is defined to be 4 corresponding to GPIO 4, which is indeed connected to pin 7.

You could have used:

```
bcm2835_gpio_write(4, HIGH);
```

to set the same GPIO line high.

It is up to you which way you choose to specify pin numbers - by logical GPIO number or physical pin number. In most cases the physical pin numbers are more direct because they specify what you are actually connecting wires to. Notice, however, that you do need to specify the model of Pi that you are working with. For example, the library defines three types of pin 3:

RPI_GPIO_P1_03 which is the Pi 1 revision 1 version of pin 3 or GPIO 0
RPI_V2_GPIO_P1_03 which is the Pi 1 revision 2 version of pin 3 or GPIO 2
RPI_BPLUS_GPIO_J8_03 for all models after the B+

You can see that this can be confusing but the change in the pinouts is also confusing. If you are using the Pi Compute module then don't worry about the enumeration, simply use the GPIO number.

In general choose enumeration values that start with one of:

- RPI_GPIO for Pi 1 revision 1
- RPI_V2_GPIO for Pi 1 revision 2
- RPI_BPLUS_GPIO for all modern Pis from the B+ on.

Drive Electrical Characteristics

The characteristics of the Pi's I/O lines are quite complicated and best tackled in stages.

All of the GPIO lines can either be used as general purpose GPIO lines or a dedicated alternative purpose such as implementing a serial interface etc. In this and closely following chapters the subject is the general purpose GPIO lines. Later chapters deal with alternate uses. What we are concerned with in this chapter is just the basic configuration of a GPIO line.

The key feature is that, as an input, the GPIO line is high impedance you can effectively ignore it when you connect to another circuit because it draws very little current. In output mode a single GPIO line can source and sink 16mA – but the situation is a little more complicated than this suggests.

Unfortunately the Pi power supply can only supply enough power for all of the GPIO lines working at 3mA each. If you use too much current drive then the 3.3V supply will fail. For a Pi 1 the limit is around 50mA in total and for a Pi 2 and later then you can draw 100mA. However, when you get close to these limits you might find that current spikes cause strange behavior.

In practice if you are planing to use more than 3mA from multiple GPIO lines consider using a transistor. If your circuits draw more than 50 or 100mA from the 3.3V supply rail consider a separate power supply. You can use the 5V supply with a regulator if you need even more 3.3V supply current.

Notice that there is a subtle distinction here between current supplied by a GPIO line, which should always be less than 16mA, and the current taken from the 3.3V power supply, which should be less than 100mA. The situation is complicated because the amount of power the Pi takes from the 3.3V supply depends on what peripherals it is using. Notice that the 16mA limit means that you cannot safely drive a standard 20mA red LED without restricting the current to below 16mA. A better solution is to use a low power 2mA LED.

Finally it is worth mentioning that the GPIO line can be configured to use push-pull, pull up or pull down drive. In addition you can set the strength of the drive, a topic covered in Chapter 6.

Output

The bcm2835 functions that you need to make use of a pin in output mode are very simple. The basic configuration function is:

```
void bcm2835_gpio_fsel (uint8_t pin, uint8_t mode)
```

This will set a pin specified by GPIO number to a given mode. The two most commonly use modes are:

```
BCM2835_GPIO_FSEL_INPT
BCM2835_GPIO_FSEL_OUTP
```

These set the GPIO line to either input or output.

So to set the GPIO line connected to pin 7 on a Pi B+ or later you would use:

```
bcm2835_gpio_fsel(RPI_BPLUS_GPIO_J8_07, BCM2835_GPIO_FSEL_OUTP);
```

Once you have set the line to output there are a range of ways to set its state to high or low voltage output. The number of possibilities is initially confusing but they each have their particular use.

The simplest and most often used is:

```
void bcm2835_gpio_write (uint8_t pin, uint8_t on)
```

As always you specify the GPIO number or use one of the Physical pin enumeration values. The on parameter can be either HIGH or LOW. So to set the GPIO line on pin 7 to high you would use:

```
bcm2835_gpio_write(RPI_BPLUS_GPIO_J8_07, HIGH);
```

and to set it low:

```
bcm2835_gpio_write(RPI_BPLUS_GPIO_J8_07, LOW);
```

As HIGH is defined to be 1 and LOW 0 you can also write

```
bcm2835_gpio_write(RPI_BPLUS_GPIO_J8_07, 1);
```

and use a variable if you want to:

```
int state=1;
bcm2835_gpio_write(RPI_BPLUS_GPIO_J8_07, state);
```

When you want to call a single function and set the state of the line, **write** is useful. However, there are times when you always want to set a line high or low. In this case you can use one of:

```
void bcm2835_gpio_set (uint8_t pin)
void bcm2835_gpio_clr (uint8_t pin)
```

As you can guess **set** sets the line to high and **clr** sets the line low. For example, to set pin 7 high:

```
void bcm2835_gpio_set (RPI_BPLUS_GPIO_J8_07);
```

Multi Functions

So far the functions have allowed us to change one line at at time. If you want to change more than one line then there are **multi** equivalents of the write, set and clr functions:

```
void bcm2835_gpio_write_multi (uint32_t mask, uint8_t on)
void bcm2835_gpio_set_multi (uint32_t mask)
void bcm2835_gpio_clr_multi (uint32_t mask)
```

In this case you have to supply a "mask" to indicate which GPIO lines are to be altered. The mask is very simple; each of the 32 bits in the mask represents a GPIO line - bit zero is for GPIO 0, bit one is for GPIO 1 and so on. Of course the problem here is that you can select GPIO lines that aren't brought out on the Pi's connector and which GPIO corresponds to which pin? Fortunately it is very easy to automatically make up a mask that corresponds to any set of GPIO lines specified by pin number. Suppose you want a mask for pin 3 then this means you need to set the third bit in the mask. This can be done using $1<<3$, i.e. 1 shifted three places to the left.

This is the mask you require and it has been found by a general algorithm. If you want a mask for pin n all you have to do is:

```
1<<n
```

Now suppose you want a mask for pin n and pin m. All you have to do is OR | the masks for each pin together so the complete mask is:

(1<<n) | (1<m)

Of course, you can use the pin enumeration in place of pin numbers. So, to create a mask for pin 3 and pin 5, you would use:

```
uint32_t mask=(1 << RPI_GPIO_P1_03) | (1 << RPI_GPIO_P1_05);
```

Once you have the mask you can use it in any of the multi functions.

For example:

```
        bcm2835_gpio_set_multi (mask);
```

sets both pin 3 and pin 5 to high in a single operation.

There is another mask function which can be used to set multiple GPIO lines to different values:

```
        void bcm2835_gpio_write_mask (uint32_t value, uint32_t mask)
```

In this case the **mask** parameter works in the same way and specifies which GPIO lines are to be involved. The difference is that the **value** parameter determines what each of the lines is to be set to. So, for example, if bit 6 of the mask is a 1 then GPIO line 6 will be set to whatever bit 6 of the value parameter is. This allows you to set multiple GPIO lines to different states.

For example:

```
        uint32_t mask=(1 << RPI_GPIO_P1_03) | (1 << RPI_GPIO_P1_05);
        uint32_t value=1<< RPI_GPIO_P1_05);
        bcm2835_gpio_write_mask (value, mask);
```

will set pin 3 to low and pin 5 to high because the mask specifies these pins and in value the bit corresponding to pin 3 is low and the bit corresponding to pin 5 is high. Notice the state of bits in value that do not correspond to bits set to 1 in mask have no effect.

The mask function are very useful when you want coordinated changes across a number of GPIO lines.

Setting Drive Type

The GPIO output can be configured into one of a number of modes but the most important is pull-up/down. Before we get to the code to do the job it is worth spending a moment explaining the three basic output modes, pushpull, pullup and pulldown.

Pushpull Mode

In pushpull mode two transistors of opposite polarity are used:

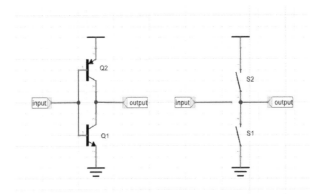

The circuit behaves like the two-switch equivalent shown on the right. Only one of the transistors, or switches is "closed" at any time. If the input is high then Q1 is saturated and the output is connected to ground - exactly as if S1 was closed. If the input is low then Q2 is saturated and it is as if S2 was closed and the output is connected to 1.8V.

You can see that this pushes the output line high with the same "force" as it pulls it low. This is the standard configuration for a GPIO output.

Pullup Mode

In pullup mode one of the transistors is replaced by a resistor:

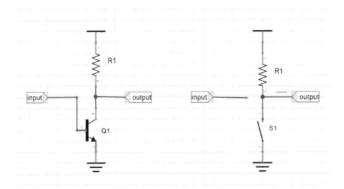

In this case the circuit is equivalent to having a single switch. When the switch is closed the output line is connected to ground and hence driven low. When the switch is open the output line is pulled high by the resistor.

You can see that in this case the degree of pulldown is greater than the pullup, where the current is limited by the resistor. The advantage of this mode is that it can be used in an AND configuration. If multiple GPIO or other lines are connected to the output, then any one of them being low will pull the output line low. Only when all of them are off does the resistor succeed in pulling the line high. This is used, for example, in a serial bus configuration like the I2C bus.

Pullup Mode

Finally the pulldown mode, which is the best mode for driving general loads, motors, LEDs, etc, is exactly the same as the pullup only now the resistor is used to pull the output line low.

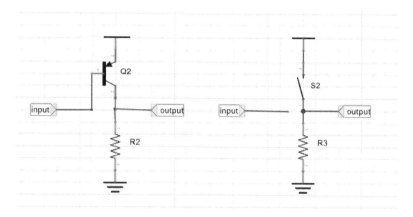

The line is held high by the transistor but pulled low by the resistor only when all the switches are open. Putting this the other way round - the line is high if any one switch is closed.

Setting Output Mode

To set the mode for a GPIO line the simplest function to use is:

```
bcm2835_gpio_set_pud (uint8_t pin, uint8_t pud)
```

where the **pin** is specified in the usual way and **pud** can be any of:

```
BCM2835_GPIO_PUD_OFF
BCM2835_GPIO_PUD_DOWN
BCM2835_GPIO_PUD_UP
```

Off is the default and you have to explicitly set down and up if required.

The internal pullup/down resistors are in the range 50K to 65K Ohms. There are also external 1.8K Ohm pullups on pins 3 and 5. The only way to remove these pullups is to unsolder the resistors from the board.

How Fast?

A fundamental question that you have to answer for any processor intended for use in embedded or IoT projects is, how fast can the GPIO lines work?

Sometimes the answer isn't of too much concern because what you want to do only works relatively slowly. Any application that is happy with response times in the tens of millisecond region will generally work with almost any processor. However, if you want to implement custom protocols or anything that needs microsecond responses the question is much more important.

It is fairly easy to find out how fast a single GPIO line can be used if you have a logic analyzer or oscilloscope. All you have to do is run the program:

```
bcm2835_gpio_fsel(RPI_BPLUS_GPIO_J8_07, BCM2835_GPIO_FSEL_OUTP);
for(;;) {
 bcm2835_gpio_write(RPI_BPLUS_GPIO_J8_07, HIGH);
 bcm2835_gpio_write(RPI_BPLUS_GPIO_J8_07, LOW);
}
```

What you will see depends on which version of the Pi you are working with and the quality of the instrument you are using. For the Pi 2 and Zero pulses are in the range 60 to 100 nanoseconds and not very even. For the Pi 3 you will see the same pattern but the pulses are around 43 nanoseconds. Using an oscilloscope reveals the pulses are very rough and irregular. A logic analyzer will often read two pulses as one because of the irregularity and lack of sampling rate.

You will also see a regular interruption to the pulse train every 0.125ms and few much bigger interruptions every few milliseconds depending on the loading of the processor. We'll return to the topic of how CPU loading effects program in Chapter 7: Near Real Time Linux.

It doesn't make any difference if you use set and clr or any of the other functions. You can also use a while(1) loop in place of the for loop - it makes no difference to the overall timing.

So you can generate nano-second pulses using the Pi but not very accurately. For accuracy you have to move to the microsecond range, which is usually sufficient for most applications.

usleep

To generate pulses of a known duration we need to pause the program between state changes. The simplest way of pausing a thread for a number of microseconds is to use usleep - which is still in common use even if it is deprecated in Posix.

To try this, include a call to usleep(10) to delay the pulse:

```
for(;;)
{
 bcm2835_gpio_set(RPI_BPLUS_GPIO_J8_07);
 usleep(10);
 bcm2835_gpio_clr(RPI_BPLUS_GPIO_J8_07);
 usleep(10);
}
```

You will discover that adding usleep(10) doesn't increase the pulse length by 10 microseconds but by around 80 microseconds. You will also discover that longer glitches have gone.

What seems to be happening is that calling usleep yields the thread to the operating system and this incurs an additional 74 microsecond penalty due to calling the scheduler. There are also losses that are dependent on the time you set to wait - usleep only promises that your thread will not restart for **at least** the specified time.

If you look at how the delay time relates to the average pulse length things seem fairly simple:

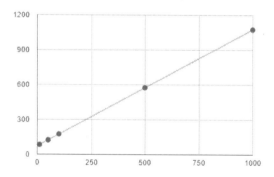

The equation of the line is approximately

```
pulse length = delay + 74
```

What this means is that if you want to set a delay less than 74 microseconds don't use usleep.

For the Pi 3 the equation is slightly different:

```
pulse length = delay + 56
```

The same isn't true of the delayMicroseconds function

```
void bcm2835_delayMicroseconds(time)
```

This uses a busy wait loop for times shorter than 450 microseconds and a system delay like usleep for longer periods. We first need to look at how a busy wait works.

Busy Wait

For pulses of less than about 100 microseconds it is better to use a busy wait, i.e. a loop that does nothing. You have to be a little careful about how you insert a loop that does nothing because optimizing compilers have a tendency to take a null loop out in an effort to make your program run faster. To stop an optimizing from removing busy wait loops make sure you always declare loop variables as volatile.

To generate a pulse of a given length you can use:

```
volatile int i;
for(;;)
{
    for(i=0;i<n;i++){};
    bcm2835_gpio_write(RPI_BPLUS_GPIO_J8_07, HIGH);
    for(i=0;i<n;i++){};
    bcm2835_gpio_write(RPI_BPLUS_GPIO_J8_07, LOW);
}
```

where n is set to a value that depends on the machine it is running on. For the Pi 2 or Pi Zero, for t greater than or equal to 0.5 microseconds you can work out n using

```
n = 100 * t
```

with t in microseconds.

For a Pi 3 we have:

```
n= 170 * t - 8
```

For values of n that give t<0.5 microseconds the pulse quality is usually so low that it can be difficult to measure the pulse width.

For example, if you want 1 microsecond pulses on a Pi Zero then n=100 and the result can be seen below:

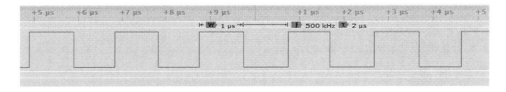

Notice that the pulses vary from about 0.93 to 1 microsecond. but this is accurate enough for most applications.

Automatic Busy Wait Calibration

It is usually said that the big problem with using busy waits is that they depend on how fast the CPU is working. The other big problem with them is

46

that they lock up the CPU and stop it from doing anything else, but this is a minor problem with a multicore processor.

You can set constants at the start of a program to allow it to work with different versions of the Pi but it is also fairly simple to add a calibration routine. All you have to do is time how long a set number of loops take and then work out how many loops you need for a busy wait of 1 microsecond and use this to derive all other delay times.

For example:

```
#include <stdio.h>
#include <stdlib.h>
#include <bcm2835.h>
#include <time.h>

#define BILLION 1000000000L

int main(int argc, char** argv) {
    struct timespec btime, etime;

    volatile int i;
    clock_gettime(CLOCK_REALTIME, &btime);
    for (i = 0; i < 10000000; i++) {
    };
    clock_gettime(CLOCK_REALTIME, &etime);
    double nseconds =
            (double) ((etime.tv_sec - btime.tv_sec)* BILLION)+
            (double) (etime.tv_nsec - btime.tv_nsec);
    int n = (int) 10 / nseconds * BILLION + 0.5;
    printf("time = %f (s)  \n \r", nseconds / BILLION);
    printf("n= %d \n\r", n);
    return (EXIT_SUCCESS);
}
```

If you run this on a Pi Zero you will see that n=100, i.e. you need 100 busy wait loops to delay for one microsecond and on a Pi 3 n=150.

You can also create a function that does the same job:

```
int busyWaitCalibrate() {
    struct timespec btime, etime;
    volatile int i;
    clock_gettime(CLOCK_REALTIME, &btime);
    for (i = 0; i < 10000000; i++) {};
    clock_gettime(CLOCK_REALTIME, &etime);
    double nseconds = (double) ((etime.tv_sec - btime.tv_sec)
     * 1000000000L)+(double) (etime.tv_nsec - btime.tv_nsec);
    int n = (int) 10 / nseconds * 1000000000L + 0.5;
    return n;
}
```

Note you need to include time.h to use the function:

```
#include <time.h>
```

Also notice that clock_gettime isn't part of the C standard and you have to select program type C in NetBeans to make it work.

If you are going to use busyWaitCalibrate it is a good idea to take a few samples and average them to make sure you get a sensible value for n.

delayMicroseconds

For delays of 1 microsecond up you can avoid all of the problems of calibrating your own busy wait and simply use delayMicroseconds.

For delays of 1 to 450 microseconds this uses a busy wait with an automatic calibration. It simply sits in a loop reading the system clock until the required number of microseconds has gone by. Of course this isn't particularly accurate for a short wait and a hand constructed busy wait for loop can be set to create the time delay you want more accurately.

For example on a Pi Zero or 2:

```
for(;;)
{
 bcm2835_gpio_set(RPI_BPLUS_GPIO_J8_07);
 for(i=0;i<102;i++){};
 bcm2835_gpio_clr(RPI_BPLUS_GPIO_J8_07);
 for(i=0;i<102;i++){};
}
```

produces pulses that are measured as 0.95 to 1 microsecond.

The equivalent program using delayMicroseconds is:

```
for(;;)
{
 bcm2835_gpio_set(RPI_BPLUS_GPIO_J8_07);
 bcm2835_delayMicroseconds(1);
 bcm2835_gpio_clr(RPI_BPLUS_GPIO_J8_07);
 bcm2835_delayMicroseconds(1);
}
```

produces pulses that are measured as 0.875 to 1.25.

As you can see the simple busy wait is more accurate and more consistent than delayMicroseconds. However as the delay increases, the errors in delayMicroseconds become less important. In practice you can generally use delayMicroseconds unless you are generating pulses less than 10 microseconds and need the accuracy.

Phased Pulses

As a simple example of using the bcm2835 output functions lets try to write a short program that pulses two lines - one high and one low and then one low and one high i.e. two pulse trains out of phase by 180 degrees.

The simplest program to do this job is:

```
#include "bcm2835.h"
#include <stdio.h>
#include <unistd.h>
int main()
{
 bcm2835_init();
 bcm2835_gpio_context pin15 = bcm2835_gpio_init(15);
 bcm2835_gpio_dir(pin15, bcm2835_GPIO_OUT_HIGH);
 bcm2835_gpio_context pin31 = bcm2835_gpio_init(31);
 bcm2835_gpio_dir(pin31, bcm2835_GPIO_OUT_LOW);
 for (;;) {
  bcm2835_gpio_write(pin15, 0);
  bcm2835_gpio_write(pin31, 1);
  bcm2835_gpio_write(pin15, 1);
  bcm2835_gpio_write(pin31, 0);
 }
 return bcm2835_SUCCESS;
 }
}
```

Notice that there is no delay in the loop so the pulses are produced at the fastest possible speed.

Using a logic analyzer reveals that the result isn't what you might expect:

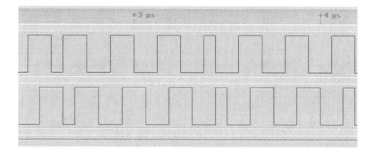

At this high speed the pulses aren't perfectly regular and come in two sizes, but you can also see that the pulse trains are not 180 degrees out of phase. The top train switches on and the bottom train takes about half a pulse before it switches on although the intent is for both actions to occur at the same time. The point is that it does take quite a long time to access and change the state of an output line.

Of course if we include a delay to increase the pulse width then the delay caused by accessing the GPIO lines in two separate actions isn't so obvious:

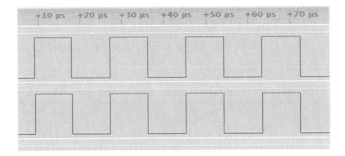

In this case n=1000 busy wait loops:

```
volatile int i;
for(;;){
 bcm2835_gpio_write(RPI_BPLUS_GPIO_J8_07, HIGH);
 bcm2835_gpio_write(RPI_BPLUS_GPIO_J8_11, HIGH);
 for(i=0;i<1000;i++){};
 bcm2835_gpio_write(RPI_BPLUS_GPIO_J8_07, LOW);
 bcm2835_gpio_write(RPI_BPLUS_GPIO_J8_11, LOW);
 for(i=0;i<1000;i++){};
}
```

You will notice that the pulses are now roughly 10 microseconds wide and they are changing at what looks like nearer to being the same time - of course they aren't. There is still a lag, but in many applications it might not be important. In other applications it could be crucial. For example, if the two pulse trains were driving different halves of a motor controller bridge there would be a significant time when both were high - so shorting the power supply. It might only be for 10 microseconds, but over time it could well damage the power supply. Of course, any sensible, cautious, engineer wouldn't feed a motor control bridge from two independently generated pulse trains unless they were guaranteed not to switch both sides of the bridge on at the same time.

A better way to generate pulses that are in phase is to use a multi function and a mask. For example if you change the first program to:

```
bcm2835_gpio_fsel(RPI_BPLUS_GPIO_J8_07,
BCM2835_GPIO_FSEL_OUTP);
bcm2835_gpio_fsel(RPI_BPLUS_GPIO_J8_11,
BCM2835_GPIO_FSEL_OUTP);
uint32_t mask=(1 << RPI_GPIO_P1_07) | (1 <<RPI_GPIO_P1_11);
for(;;)
{
 bcm2835_gpio_set_multi (mask);
 bcm2835_gpio_clr_multi (mask);
}
```

the two GPIO lines do change at the same time even at the highest speed:

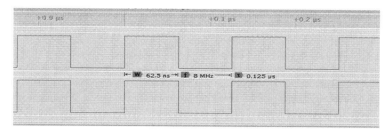

It is clear that if you want to synchronize the changing of GPIO lines you should use the multi functions and a mask.

Can We Do Better?

If by better you mean faster - probably not enough to make it worth the effort. There is some overhead in calling a function, but this is tiny. How to directly address the GPIO without the use of a library is covered in chapter 6, but more for educational reasons than to increase the speed of operation.

A more interesting question is whether it is possible to increase the accuracy of the pulses. This might be possible by turning off interrupts and using internal timers but it would interfere with the normal operation of Linux and again probably isn't going to be worth it.

Chapter 4

SYSFS The Linux Way To GPIO

There is a Linux-based approach to working with GPIO lines and serial buses that is worth knowing about because it provides an alternative to using the bcm2835 library. Sometimes you need this because you are working in a language for which direct access to memory isn't available. It is also the only way to make interrupts available in a C program.

Having Linux on a system that is being used for real time control is quite different to the situation with most microcontrollers where nothing gets between your code and the hardware. The sophistication of Linux is a great advantage when it comes to interfacing with complex hardware such as WiFi, but it is a distinct disadvantage when it comes to interfacing with simple fast hardware like the GPIO. Put simply, you have to learn to do things in a way that Linux finds natural even if this seems strange and convoluted to you as a microcontroller programmer.

Take, for example, GPIO access - how can this be made available to the general programmer in a way that is natural to Linux? You can't simply allow direct memory access to the hardware because this cuts across Linux's control of memory allocation and security. You have to find something that Linux already supports in a general way to map the GPIO access on to.

A key principle of Linux is that everything is a file or a folder. As far as possible, Linux deals with external hardware by treating it as if it was a file system. This is reasonable because external hardware either wants to receive data as commands or something to store or display, or it want to send data as responses or user input. So most hardware interacts with Linux as a source or a sink of data and this is exactly what a file is all about.

This "everything is a file" approach only really fails when issues of performance enter the picture. Accessing a piece of hardware as if it was a file when it isn't can be slow. In normal use direct memory access is much faster and it is what the bcm2835 library is all about. We look at how this works in more detail in Chapter 6.

So file-based access to the hardware can be slow, but it has the huge advantage that it is language-independent. Every language has the facilities needed to open, read/write and close a file and so has the facilities needed to work with hardware via the file system.

It also has the advantage that it works with Linux rather than just ignoring it. The system knows about files and understands how to work with them. This allows it to offer advanced features like interrupts to GPIO users that fit in with the way other Linux interrupts work, more of this in the next chapter.

It may seem crazy, especially if you know how the underlying hardware works, to treat a single GPIO line as it if was a file but it works. Files are a fundamental data type in Linux and a GPIO line is something you read from or write too just like a file. From the Linux point of view it makes perfect sense. The big problem is that the details of how hardware is represented as a file system is poorly documented and you have to find out about it by guessing, trial and error, reverse engineering, or by reading code the makes use of it.

Working with Sysfs

Sysfs is a virtual file system that provides all sorts of access to hardware and the operation of the Linux kernel. You can spend a lot of time exploring sysfs, but the only part we are particularly interested in is the **gpio** folder. Sysfs is usually mounted in the **sys** folder and the folder that corresponds to the gpio device is usually:

/sys/class/gpio

To see what is in the folder, simply list it:

ls /sys/class/gpio

```
pi@raspberrypi:    ls /sys/class/gpio
export  gpio4  gpiochip0  unexport
pi@raspberrypi:    ▮
```

The list includes the GPIO lines that are already in use by some process or other. Notice that the gpio numbers are not external pin numbers, but internal GPIO numbers. So for example to use the GPIO line that is on physical pin 7 on the connector you need to refer to GPIO 4.

The steps in using a line are always the same:

- Reserve or "export" the GPIO line so that no other process can use it
- Set its direction and read or write it
- Unreserve it or unexport it

You can do these steps from any language that supports file operations including the shell.

You might ask why you have to "export" or reserve a GPIO line rather than just use it? The answer is that the export operation will only work if the OS, or some other process, hasn't claimed the GPIO line for its own use. You can think of the export/unexport process as making sure that you don't misuse GPIO lines and that you don't share them with other processes.

54

To reserve a GPIO line you have to write its number to the export folder and you can do this using the shell command. For example, assuming we want to work with GPIO 4:

```
echo 4 > /sys/class/gpio/export
```

You can of course change 4 to any valid gpio number.

You can do the same job in C:

```c
#include <stdio.h>
#include <string.h>
 int main(int argc, char** argv) {
    int gpio = 4;
    FILE* fd = fopen("/sys/class/gpio/export", "w");
    fprintf(fd, "%d", gpio);
    fclose(fd);
    return 0;
}
```

If you are not familiar with C file operations, the **fopen** function opens export for write, the **fprintf** string prints the number of the gpio line and then the file is closed with **fclose**.

Once you have the pin reserved, you will see a gpio4 folder corresponding to it in /sys/class/gpio. Now that you have it reserved, you can set its direction and read/write it. To do this you have to read from or write to the appropriate sub folder of the gpio folder just created.

If you list all of the folders in gpio4 you will see:

```
pi@raspberrypi:    ls /sys/class/gpio/gpio4
active_low  device  direction  edge        subsystem  uevent  value
pi@raspberrypi:    ▉
```

Each of these folders controls some aspect of the GPIO line's functioning. The most important are **direction** in which the line can be set to **in** or **out**; and **value** in which can be set to 0 or 1 for output and read 0 or 1 for input. There is also **active_low** which determines which way the logic operates. It determines if the line low corresponds to a 1 or a 0.

For example, to read GPIO 4 from the command line use:

```
echo "in" > /sys/class/gpio/gpio4/direction
cat /sys/class/gpio/gpio4/value
```

and to set it as output and then high and low use:

```
echo "out" > /sys/class/gpio/gpio4/direction
echo 1 > /sys/class/gpio/gpio4/value
echo 0 > /sys/class/gpio/gpio4/value
```

You can do the same using C, but it is slightly more verbose due to the need to open and close files and build the appropriate strings.

Toggling a Line

As an example consider the following C program which sets GPIO 4 to output and then toggles it high and low as fast as possible:

```
#include <stdio.h>
#include <string.h>

int main(int argc, char** argv) {
    int gpio = 4;
    char buf[100];

    FILE* fd = fopen("/sys/class/gpio/export", "w");
    fprintf(fd, "%d", gpio);
    fclose(fd);

    sprintf(buf, "/sys/class/gpio/gpio%d/direction", gpio);
    fd = fopen(buf, "w");
    fprintf(fd, "out");
    fclose(fd);

    sprintf(buf, "/sys/class/gpio/gpio%d/value", gpio);
    fd = fopen(buf, "w");

    for (;;) {
        fd = fopen(buf, "w");
        fprintf(fd, "1");
        fclose(fd);
        fd = fopen(buf, "w");
        fprintf(fd, "0");
        fclose(fd);
    }
    return 0;
}
```

The program first exports gpio4 and then writes "out" to its direction folder to set the line to output. After this the value file is open for writing and "1" and "0" are written to the file repeatedly. Notice the use of **sprintf** to create strings which incorporate the number of the gpio line you are using so that you can open the correct folder.

You might be puzzled by the loop that opens the file, writes a value and then closes it. Why not just keep the file open? The reason is that the file buffer isn't flushed unless the file is closed. This is the usual way of dealing with the problem, but it is not very fast and it is part of the reason that SYSFS has a bad reputation.

If you try out the program you will discover that the pulse train has a frequency of around 2KHz on a Pi 2/Zero and a pulse width of 200 microseconds:

We can, however, do much better by not closing the file every time we write to it. Instead we can use **fflush** to flush the file buffer:

If you change the for loop to:

```
for (;;) {
        fprintf(fd, "1");
        fflush(fd);
        fprintf(fd, "0");
        fflush(fd);
    }
```

the difference is quite amazing.

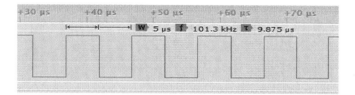

Now the frequency is 100kHz and the pulse width is 5 microseconds. which is still about 10 time slower than using the library and direct memory access.

The point is that opening and closing files is expensive in terms of overhead, but reading and writing isn't. If you are using sysfs then it is worth keeping files open, which is not what most of the example sysfs programs do. They tend to provide a function that writes to the GPIO line by first opening the file, writing to it and then closing it. Of course when you use a function to write to the GPIO line you generally don't notice the repeated opening and closing of the file.

It is tempting to try to write a general purpose sysfs GPIO access library, but in practice it is quite difficult to organize things so that files are opened and closed at reasonable times without making the whole thing inefficient. You can either opt to keep track of what files are open, and hence avoid reopening them, or you can test to see it files are open before working with them. The first is efficient and complicated, the second is slow but simple.

A Simple Fast Sysfs System

It is possible to create a simple fast sysfs GPIO system by abandoning the need to follow the underlying structure - don't create export, direction, value file handling functions, but concentrate on the GPIO lines. All you really need is an **openGPIO** function that gets a single GPIO line ready for use either as an input or an output. The trick to keeping things fast is to open the value file and keep it open until another call to openGPIO causes it to change direction.

To do this for all the GPIO lines we need to keep track of the files that are open using an array of file descriptors:

```
FILE fd[32] = {};
```

Now we have one file descriptor per GPIO line. The open function only needs the gpio number and the direction in which we want to open it:

```
int openGPIO(int gpio, int direction) {
    if (gpio < 0 || gpio > 31) return -1;
    if (direction < 0 || direction > 1)return -2;
```

Next we have to check to see if the file descriptor is non-null. If it is the GPIO line is already in use and we have to close the file and unexport it:

```
int len;
char buf[BUFFER_MAX];
 if (fd[gpio] != NULL) {
    close(fd[gpio]);
    fd[gpio] = open("/sys/class/gpio/unexport", O_WRONLY);
    len = snprintf(buf, BUFFER_MAX, "%d", gpio);
    write(fd[gpio], buf, len);
    close(fd[gpio]);
}
```

We can now export the GPIO line and set the direction specified and finally open the value file:

```
fd[gpio] = open("/sys/class/gpio/export", O_WRONLY);
len = snprintf(buf, BUFFER_MAX, "%d", gpio);
write(fd[gpio], buf, len);
close(fd[gpio]);

len = snprintf(buf, BUFFER_MAX,
        "/sys/class/gpio/gpio%d/direction", gpio);
fd[gpio] = open(buf, O_WRONLY);
if (direction == 1) {
    write(fd[gpio], "out", 4);
    close(fd[gpio]);
    len = snprintf(buf, BUFFER_MAX,
        "/sys/class/gpio/gpio%d/value", gpio);
    fd[gpio] = open(buf, O_WRONLY);

} else {
```

```
            write(fd[gpio], "in", 3);
            close(fd[gpio]);
            len = snprintf(buf, BUFFER_MAX,
                  "/sys/class/gpio/gpio%d/value", gpio);
            fd[gpio] = open(buf, O_RDONLY);
    }
    return 0;
}
```

If you are planning to use this in production you would need to add error handling to the file opens and writes.

At the end of the openGPIO function the line's file descriptor is set to the value file ready to read or write so a write function is simply:

```
int writeGPIO(int gpio, int b) {
    if (b == 0) {
        write(fd[gpio], "0", 1);
    } else {
        write(fd[gpio], "1", 1);
    }
    lseek(fd[gpio], 0, SEEK_SET);
    return 0;
}
```

Notice that there are no error checks in this function to keep it fast. It is up to the user to make sure that the GPIO line has been opened and in the correct direction. If you want to add checks they are easy enough but they do slow things down.

Create a main program something like:

```
#include <stdio.h>
#include <string.h>
#include <fcntl.h>
#include <unistd.h>

#define BUFFER_MAX 50
FILE *fd[32] = {};

int openGPIO(int pin, int direction);
int writeGPIO(int gpio, char value);

int main(int argc, char** argv) {
    openGPIO(4, 1);
    for (;;) {
        writeGPIO(4, 1);
        writeGPIO(4, 0);
    }
    return 0;
}
```

The speed is almost the same as the raw write loop at around 3.5 microsecond pulses.

A read function is just as easy and simple:

```
int readGPIO(int gpio) {
    char value_str[3];
    int c = read(fd[gpio], value_str, 3);
    lseek(fd[gpio], 0, SEEK_SET);

    if (value_str[0] == '0') {
        return 0;
    } else {
        return 1;
    }

}
```

This function is used in an example in the next chapter.

The Value of Sysfs

So having seen it in action, is sysfs worth it?

From C probably not for general use. You have all the GPIO control you need using the bcm2865 library. What is more there are missing features from the sysfs facilities. For example there seems to be no way to control the pin modes – pullup/pulldown - and no way to select drive strength. However it is worth noting that sysfs isn't as slow as it is usually painted and it can be useful in languages that don't have direct access to the GPIO registers.

Finally there is one important area where sysfs does become important even if you are working with C. Linux does not support interrupts in user mode - only in kernel mode. What this means is that you cannot work with GPIO interrupts using C. However, there is a mechanism in Linux for allowing user mode programs to react to file events and this can be used to implement a sort of GPIO interrupt facility. More of this in the next chapter.

Chapter 5
Input and Interrupts

There is no doubt that input is more difficult than output. When you need to drive a line high or low you are in command of when it happens, but input is in the hands of the outside world. If your program isn't ready to read the input, or if it reads it at the wrong time, then things just don't work. What is worse, you have no idea what your program was doing relative to the event you are trying to capture. Welcome to the world of input.

GPIO Input

GPIO input is a much more difficult problem than output from the point of view of measurement and verification. For output at least you can see the change in the signal on a logic analyzer and know the exact time that it occurred. This makes if possible to track down timing problems and fine tune things with good accuracy.

Input on the other hand is "silent" and unobservable. When did you read in the status of the line? Usually the timing of the read is with respect to some other action that the device has taken. For example, you read the input line 20 microseconds after setting the output line high.

In some applications the times are long and/or unimportant but in some they are critical and so we need some strategies for monitoring and controlling read events.

The usual rule of thumb is to assume that it takes as long to read a GPIO line as it does to set it. This means we can use the delay mechanisms that we looked at with output in mind for input.

One common and very useful trick when you are trying to get the timing of input correct is to substitute an output command to a spare GPIO line and monitor it with a logic analyzer. Place the output instruction just before the input instruction and where you see the line change on the logic analyzer should be close to the time that the input would be read in the unmodified program. You can use this to debug and fine tune and then remove the output statement.

Basic Input Functions

We have already met the function that sets a GPIO line to input or output:

```
void bcm2835_gpio_fsel(uint8_t pin,uint8_t mode)
```

To set the GPIO line of your choice to input simply use

```
BCM2835_GPIO_FSEL_INPT
```

for the mode.

Once set to input, the GPIO line is high impedance, it won't take very much current no matter what you connect it to, and you can read its input state using:

```
uint8_t bcm2835_gpio_lev(uint8_t pin)
```

This is all there is to using GPIO line as an input, apart from the details of the electronics and the small matter of interrupts.

Basic Input Circuit - The Switch

One of the most common input circuits is the switch or button. If you want another external button you can use any GPIO line and the following circuit:

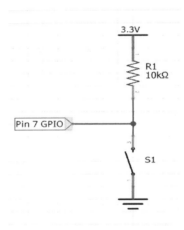

The 10K resistor isn't critical in value. It simply pulls the GPIO line high when the switch isn't pressed. When it is pressed a current of a little more than 0.3mA flows in the resistor. If this is too much increase the resistance to 100K or even more - but notice that the higher the resistor value the noisier the input to the GPIO and the more it is susceptible to RF interference.

If you want a switch that pulls the line high instead of low, to reverse the logic just swap the positions of the resistor and the switch in the diagram.

Although the switch is the simplest input device, it is very difficult to get right. When a user clicks a switch of any sort the action isn't clean - the switch bounces. What this means is that the logic level on the GPIO line goes high then low and high again and bounces between the two until it settles down. There are electronic ways of debouncing switches, but software does the job much better. All you have to do is insert a delay of a millisecond or so after detecting a switch press and read the line again - if it is still low then record a switch press. Similarly, when the switch is released, read the state twice with a delay. You can vary the delay to modify the perceived characteristics of the switch.

A more sophisticated algorithm is based on the idea of integration to debounce a switch. All you have to do is read the state multiple times, every few milliseconds say, and keep a running sum of values. If you sum ten values each time then a total of between 6 and 10 can be taken as an indication that the switch is high. A total less than this indicates that the switch is low.

The Potential Divider

If you have an input that is outside of the range of 0 to 3.3V then you can reduce it using a simple potential divider. In the diagram V is the input from the external logic and Vout is the connection to the GPIO input line:

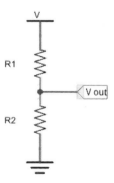

You can spend a lot of time on working out good values of R1 and R2. For loads that take a lot of current you need R1+R2 to be small and divided in the same ratio as the voltages.

For example, for a 5V device R1=18K and R2=33K work well to drop the voltage to 3.3V.

The problem with a resistive divider is that it can round off fast pulses due to the small capacitive effects. This usually isn't a problem, but if it is then the solution is to use an FET again as an active buffer.

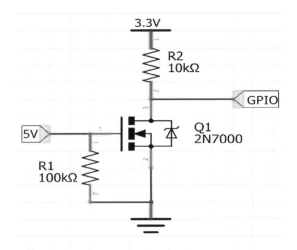

Notice that this is an inverting buffer, but you can usually ignore this and simply correct in software, i.e. read a 1 as a low and a 0 as a high state.
The role of R1 is to make sure the FET is off when the 5V signal is absent and R2 limits the current in the FET to about 0.3mA.

In most case you should try the simple voltage divider and only move to an active buffer if it doesn't work.

How Fast Can We Measure?

The simplest way to find out how quickly we can take a measurement is to perform a pulse width measurement using a busy wait. Apply in square wave to GPIO 4 i.e. pin 7 we can measure the time that the pulse is high using:

```
#include <stdio.h>
#include <stdlib.h>
#include <bcm2835.h>
#include <sched.h>
#include <sys/mman.h>

int main(int argc, char** argv) {
    const struct sched_param priority = {1};
    sched_setscheduler(0, SCHED_FIFO, &priority);
    mlockall(MCL_CURRENT | MCL_FUTURE);
if (!bcm2835_init()) return 1;
```

```
    bcm2835_gpio_fsel(RPI_GPIO_P1_07,BCM2835_GPIO_FSEL_INPT);

    volatile int i;
    while (1) {
      while (1 == bcm2835_gpio_lev(RPI_GPIO_P1_07));
            while (0 == bcm2835_gpio_lev(RPI_GPIO_P1_07));
            for (i = 0; i < 5000; i++) {
                if (0 == bcm2835_gpio_lev(RPI_GPIO_P1_07)) break;
            }
            printf("%d\n\r", i); fflush(stdout);
      }

      return (EXIT_SUCCESS);
}
```

This might look a little strange at first.

The inner while loops are responsible for getting us to the right point in the waveform. First we loop until the line goes low, then we loop until it goes high again and finally measure how long before it goes low. You might think that we simply have to wait for it to go high and then measure how long till it goes low, but this misses the possibility that the signal might be part way through a high period when we first measure it.

If you run this program with different pulse widths on a Pi Zero/2 the result are very regular:

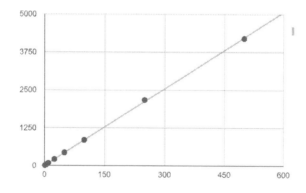

(y axis loop count; x axis pulse time in microseconds)

The equation relating time t and loop count n for a Pi Zero/2 is:

```
t=0.12 n + 0.002 microseconds
```

For a Pi 3 the equation is:

```
t=0.2 n + 1.6 microseconds
```

This works down to about 1 microsecond or slightly less.

If you want to record the time in microseconds rather than using a loop count then you could use:

```
uint64_t t;
volatile int i;
while (1) {
    while (1 == bcm2835_gpio_lev(RPI_GPIO_P1_07));
    while (0 == bcm2835_gpio_lev(RPI_GPIO_P1_07));
    t= bcm2835_st_read();
    for (i = 0; i < 5000; i++) {
        if (0 == bcm2835_gpio_lev(RPI_GPIO_P1_07)) break;
    }
    t= bcm2835_st_read()-t;
    printf("%d,%ld\n\r",i,t);
    fflush(stdout);
}
```

This can be measured down to around 1 microsecond with an accuracy of 0.5 microseconds:

Pulse width	System Time
1	5
2.5	18.2
5	40
10	84
25	214
50	440

Notice that in either case if you try measuring pulse widths much shorter than the lower limit that works you will get results that look like longer pulses are being applied. The reason is simply that the Pi will miss the first transition to zero but will detect a second or third or later transition. This is the digital equivalent of the aliasing effect found in the Fourier Transform or general signal processing.

Interrupts Considered Harmful?

There is a general feeling that real-time programming and interrupts go together and if you are not using an interrupt you are probably doing something wrong. In fact the truth is that if you are using an interrupt you are probably doing something wrong. Some organizations are so convinced that interrupts are dangerous that they are banned from being used at all.

Interrupts are only really useful when you have a low frequency condition that needs to be dealt with on a high priority basis. Their use can simplify the logic of your program, but rarely does using an interrupt speed things up because the overhead involved in interrupt handling is usually quite high.

For example, suppose you want to react to a doorbell push button. You could write a polling loop that simply checks the button status repeatedly and forever or you could write an interrupt service routine (ISR) to respond to the doorbell. The processor would be free to get on with other things until the doorbell was pushed when it would then stop what it was doing and transfer its attention to the ISR.

How good a design this is depends on how much the doorbell press has to interact with the rest of the program and how many doorbell pushes you are expecting. It takes time to respond to the doorbell push and then the ISR has to run to completion - what is going to happen if another doorbell push happens while the first push is still being processed? Some processors have provision for forming a queue of interrupts, but it doesn't help with the fact that the process can only handle one interrupt at a time. Of course, the same is true of a polling loop, but if you can't handle the throughput of events with a polling loop you can't handle it using an interrupt either because interrupts add the time to transfer to the ISR and back again.

Finally, before you dismiss the idea of having a processor do nothing but ask repeatedly "is the doorbell pressed", consider what else it has to do. If the answer is "not much" then a polling loop might well be your simplest option. Also, if the processor has multiple cores, then the fastest way of dealing with any external event is to use one of the cores in a polling loop.

Despite their attraction, interrupts are usually a poor choice.

Interrupts and the bcm2835 Library

The bcm2835 library doesn't support interrupts and for all the reasons given. The reason is that Linux doesn't support user mode interrupts. However, it is possible to make interrupts work in user mode and this is something explained at the end of this chapter, but it involves using sysfs.

The bcm2835 GPIO hardware has a very sophisticated and impressive list of conditions that you can set to trigger an event. These are all made available via the bcm2835 library as a set of set and clear functions.

There are four groups of functions that work with any of high, low, rising edge or falling edge detection:

High Detect

```
void bcm2835_gpio_hen(uint8_t pin)
void bcm2835_gpio_clr_hen(uint8_t pin)
```

Low Detect

```
void bcm2835_gpio_len(uint8_t pin)
void bcm2835_gpio_clr_len(uint8_t pin)
```

Falling Edge Detect

```
void bcm2835_gpio_fen(uint8_t pin)
void bcm2835_gpio_clr_fen(uint8_t pin)
```

Rising Edge Detect

```
void bcm2835_gpio_ren(uint8_t pin)
void bcm2835_gpio_clr_ren(uint8_t pin)
```

It is obvious that the rising and falling events occur when the input changes from low to high and high to low respectively, but when do the high and low level events occur? The answer is that the high or low level event is triggered as soon as the line is high or low and the event is enabled. This means that you could trigger the event as soon as you enable it if the line is already high or low. The event also stays set as long as the high or low status persists and trying to reset it has no effect. In practice edge detection is usually the most useful.

There are also two groups that work with asynchronous version of rising and falling edge detection. These are simply faster versions of the previous two:

Asynchronous Falling Edge Detect

```
void bcm2835_gpio_afen(uint8_t pin)
void bcm2835_gpio_clr_afen(uint8_t pin)
```

Asynchronous Rising Edge Detect

```
void bcm2835_gpio_aren(uint8_t pin)
void bcm2835_gpio_clr_aren(uint8_t pin)
```

It is worth explaining that the asynchronous versions may be faster but they are not "debounced".

Each of these events, if set and if triggered set bits in an event detection register. The setting of these status bits can also be set to cause an interrupt but there is no way of directly handling such an interrupt in user mode. The functions that let you test the status bits are:

Return or clear a specific bit

```
uint8_t bcm2835_gpio_eds(uint8_t pin)
void bcm2835_gpio_set_eds(uint8_t pin)
```

Return or clear a set of bits using a mask

```
uint32_t bcm2835_gpio_eds_multi(uint32_t mask)
void bcm2835_gpio_set_eds_multi(uint32_t mask)
```

Notice that after an event has been detected you have to clear the status bit for the event to be detected again. As already mentioned, clearing bits for high or low events only works if the level isn't currently high or low respectively.

Measuring Pulses With Events

Now we have all of the functions we need to implement a pulse measurement program using events. In this case we can measure the width of any pulse as the distance between a rising and a falling edge or a falling and a rising edge.

To do this we need to set the rising and falling edge detection for the pin:

```
bcm2835_gpio_fsel(RPI_GPIO_P1_07, BCM2835_GPIO_FSEL_INPT);
bcm2835_gpio_fen(RPI_GPIO_P1_07);
bcm2835_gpio_ren(RPI_GPIO_P1_07);
```

Now Pin 7 will trigger an edge event if it goes from low to high or high to low. So now all we have to do is test the status register for the event and clear it after it has been detected

```
volatile int i;
while (1) {
    bcm2835_gpio_set_eds(RPI_GPIO_P1_07);
    while (0 ==bcm2835_gpio_eds(RPI_GPIO_P1_07));
    bcm2835_gpio_set_eds(RPI_GPIO_P1_07);
    for (i = 0; i < 5000; i++) {
        if (1 == bcm2835_gpio_eds(RPI_GPIO_P1_07)) break;
    }
    printf("%d\n\r", i);
    fflush(stdout);
}
```

Notice that we clear the edge event and then wait for another and use the number of loops as a measure of the pulse time.

This program produces very similar results as the previous program that simply read the inputs on the GPIO line.

In this case there is no real advantage in using the events approach to polling. However if you had multiple GPIO lines and perhaps multiple conditions to test you could set all the events you were interested in and then check to see if any of them had happened with a single bcm2835_gpio_eds_multi function call. Of course you would then probably have to work out what had triggered the event, but it does have a potential advantage to implement things this way.

Interrupts

Linux does provide a way for system interrupts to communicate with user mode programs but, if you know how interrupts work, you might not think it a good implementation. However, if you accept the basic premise of restricting the situations in which interrupts are used, you have to agree that it isn't a bad way of doing things.

The basic idea is that a user mode program can wait for a file operation to complete. Linux will suspend the thread concerned and restart it only when the file operation is complete. This is a completely general mechanism and you can use it to wait for any file based operation to complete including file operations in sysfs.

Any GPIO line that is capable of generating an interrupt has an edge directory in sysfs. This can be set to none, rising, falling or both to set the corresponding edge interrupt. So the first thing we need is an extension to the sysfs functions introduced in the previous chapter.

int setEdgeGPIO(int gpio, char *edge) {

```
        char buf[BUFFER_MAX];
        int len = snprintf(buf, BUFFER_MAX,
                    "/sys/class/gpio/gpio%d/edge", gpio);
        int fd = open(buf, O_WRONLY);
        write(fd, edge, strlen(edge) + 1);
        close(fd);
        return 0;
    }
```

This simply writes whatever edge is to the edge directory. Notice that for simplicity no checks are included for the GPIO pin being exported and set to input.

So now we can set the interrupt we want to use but how do we wait for it to happen?

The solution is the standard Linux function poll:

```
        #include <poll.h>
        int poll(fdset[],n,timeout)
```

where fdset is a struct that specifies the file descriptor and the event you want to wait for, n is the size of the array and timeout is the timeout in milliseconds.

If you call poll then it will wait for the specified event on the file descriptors until the timeout is up when it returns. In fact what actually happens is a little more complicated. The thread that called poll is suspended until the event occurs and then the system restarts it. This is not really an interrupt as in a true interrupt the thread would continue to execute until the interrupt occurred when it would run the ISR specified. This may not be an interrupt proper, but with a little more work it can provide more or less the same behavior.

First let's construct the simplest possible example using poll to wait for a raising edge on GPIO 4 (pin 7).

First we need to open GPIO 4 and set edge to rising:

```
openGPIO(4, 0);
setEdgeGPIO(4, "rising");
```

Note that you don't have to use the sysfs functions given you can do the job any way that works but you must use sysfs because you need a file descriptor to pass to the poll function in the fdset struct:

```
struct pollfd fdset[1];
    for (;;) {
        fdset[0].fd = fd[4];
        fdset[0].events = POLLPRI;
        fdset[0].revents = 0;
```

In this case we are only polling on a single file descriptor and this is stored in the **fd** field - recall that the openGPIO function stores the file descriptor for the value folder in fd[gpip number]. The events field is a bit mask, set in this case to POLLPRI, which is defined as "there is urgent data to read". Other event types are documented in the Linux man pages.

The revents field is a bit mask with the same format as events filled in by the poll function when it returns to indicate the event that occurred.

Now everything is in place to call poll to wait for the event, which might already have happened:

```
int rc = poll(fdset, 1, 5000);
```

The timeout is set to five seconds. You can specify a negative timeout if you want to wait indefinitely or a zero timeout if you don't want to wait at all.

The **rc** return value is either 0 for a timeout, a positive value giving the file descriptor that fired the interrupt, or a negative error value.

```
    if (rc < 0) {
        printf("\npoll() failed!\n");
        return -1;
    }
    if (rc == 0) {
        printf(".");
    }
    if (fdset[0].revents & POLLPRI) {
        lseek(fd[4], 0, SEEK_SET);
        int val=readGPIO(4);
        printf("\npoll() GPIO 4 interrupt occurred %d\n\r",val);

    }
    fflush(stdout);
}
```

If the event has occurred on the file descriptor we set, then to clear the interrupt we seek to the start of the file. You can also read the current value of the GPIO line.

If you try this out you will discover that when pin 7 is toggled from low to high you get an interrupt.

Complete Listing

```c
#include <stdio.h>
#include <string.h>
#include <bcm2835.h>
#include <fcntl.h>
#include <unistd.h>
#include <poll.h>

#define BUFFER_MAX 50
int fd[32] = {0};

int openGPIO(int pin, int direction);
int writeGPIO(int gpio, int value);
int readGPIO(int gpio);
int setEdgeGPIO(int gpio, char *edge);


int main(int argc, char** argv) {
    if (!bcm2835_init())
        return 1;

    openGPIO(4, 0);
    setEdgeGPIO(4, "rising");
    struct pollfd fdset[1];
    for (;;) {

        fdset[0].fd = fd[4];
        fdset[0].events = POLLPRI;
        fdset[0].revents = 0;

        int rc = poll(fdset, 1, 5000);
        if (rc < 0) {
            printf("\npoll() failed!\n");
            return -1;
        }
        if (rc == 0) {
            printf(".");
        }
        if (fdset[0].revents & POLLPRI) {
            lseek(fd[4], 0, SEEK_SET);
            int val=readGPIO(4);
            printf("\npoll() GPIO 4 interrupt occurred %d\n\r",val);

        }
        fflush(stdout);
    }
    return 0;
}
```

```c
int openGPIO(int gpio, int direction) {
    if (gpio < 0 || gpio > 31) return -1;
    if (direction < 0 || direction > 1)return -2;
    int len;
    char buf[BUFFER_MAX];
    if (fd[gpio] != 0) {
        close(fd[gpio]);
        fd[gpio] = open("/sys/class/gpio/unexport", O_WRONLY);
        len = snprintf(buf, BUFFER_MAX, "%d", gpio);
        write(fd[gpio], buf, len);
        close(fd[gpio]);
        fd[gpio] = 0;
    }

    fd[gpio] = open("/sys/class/gpio/export", O_WRONLY);
    len = snprintf(buf, BUFFER_MAX, "%d", gpio);
    write(fd[gpio], buf, len);
    close(fd[gpio]);
    len = snprintf(buf, BUFFER_MAX,
               "/sys/class/gpio/gpio%d/direction", gpio);
    fd[gpio] = open(buf, O_WRONLY);
    if (direction == 1) {
        write(fd[gpio], "out", 4);
        close(fd[gpio]);
        len = snprintf(buf, BUFFER_MAX,
            "/sys/class/gpio/gpio%d/value", gpio);
        fd[gpio] = open(buf, O_WRONLY);

    } else {
        write(fd[gpio], "in", 3);
        close(fd[gpio]);
        len = snprintf(buf, BUFFER_MAX,
                "/sys/class/gpio/gpio%d/value", gpio);
        fd[gpio] = open(buf, O_RDONLY);
    }
    return 0;
}

int writeGPIO(int gpio, int b) {
    if (b == 0) {
        write(fd[gpio], "0", 1);
    } else {
        write(fd[gpio], "1", 1);
    }

    lseek(fd[gpio], 0, SEEK_SET);
    return 0;
}
```

```
int readGPIO(int gpio) {
    char value_str[3];
    int c = read(fd[gpio], value_str, 3);
    lseek(fd[gpio], 0, SEEK_SET);

    if (value_str[0] == '0') {
        return 0;
    } else {
        return 1;
    }

}

int setEdgeGPIO(int gpio, char *edge) {
    char buf[BUFFER_MAX];
    int len = snprintf(buf, BUFFER_MAX,
                    "/sys/class/gpio/gpio%d/edge", gpio);
    int fd = open(buf, O_WRONLY);
    write(fd, edge, strlen(edge) + 1);
    close(fd);
    return 0;
}
```

An Interrupt Function

Advanced: Skip unless you need to use it

The poll function gets you as close to an interrupt handler as you can get in user mode, but there is one thing missing - the thread is suspended while waiting for the interrupt. This is generally not what you want to happen.

You can create a better approximation to a true interrupt by running the poll function on another thread. That is, if the main program wants to work with an interrupt you have to define an interrupt handling function that will be called when the interrupt occurs. Next you have to create a new thread that sets everything up and then calls poll on the file descriptor. This causes your new thread to be suspended, but you don't care because its only purpose is to wait for the interrupt and meanwhile your program's main thread continues to run and do useful work. When the interrupt occurs, the new thread is restarted and it checks that the interrupt was correct and then calls your interrupt handler. When the interrupt handler completes, the thread cleans up and calls poll again to wait for another interrupt.

This is all very straightforward conceptually, but it does mean using threads, which is an advanced technique that tends to make programs more difficult to debug and prone to esoteric errors. This is in the nature of using interrupts, however.

In the following program the basic skeleton of an interrupt handling framework is developed, without error checking or error recovery. If you are going to use this sort of approach in the real world you would have to add code that handles what happens when something goes wrong, whereas this code works when everything goes right.

First we need to include the pthreads library and this isn't just a matter of adding the include:

```
#include <pthread.h>
```

You also have to specify the name of the library that you want the linker to add to your program. To do this right click on the project and select properties. Select Build,Linker in the dialog box that appears, click the three dots in the Libraries section, click Add Library and specify pthread. Don't make the mistake of trying to add a Library File.

To make the idea work we need two new functions, one to create a new thread and run the second, which sets up the interrupt and waits using poll.

The first is called attachGPIO because it attaches a specified GPIO line, edge event and interrupt handler:

```
int attachGPIO(int gpio, char *edge, eventHandler func) {
    openGPIO(gpio, 0);
    setEdgeGPIO(gpio, edge);
    readGPIO(gpio);
    intData.fd = fd[gpio];
    intData.gpio=gpio;
    intData.func = func;
    pthread_t intThread;
    if (pthread_create(&intThread,
            NULL, waitInterrupt, (void*) &intData)) {
        fprintf(stderr, "Error creating thread\n");
        return 1;
    }
    return 0;
}
```

The first part of the function sets up the specified GPIO as an input and sets the edge event you want to respond to. It then does a read to clear any interrupts. Then it creates a new thread using the second function waitInterrupt, which waits for the interrupt and calls the interrupt function passed as the third parameter as a function pointer.

To make this work we need to define the eventHander type:

```
typedef void (*eventHandler)();
```

which simply defines the function used for the event handler as having no result and no input parameters. We also need to pass some data to the waitInterrupt function. The pthread_create function lets you do this, but only by passing a single pointer to void, i.e. any data type.

We need to pass the file descriptor and the interrupt function to call to waitInterrupt so we have to pack them into a struct. What is more this struct has to be available after the attachGPIO function has terminated since the new thread keeps waitInterrupt running long after attachGPIO has completed.

The correct solution is to get the function to create the struct on the heap, but a simpler and workable solution is to create it as a global variable which lives for the entire life of the program:

```
typedef struct {
    int fd;
    int gpio;
    eventHandler func;
} intVec;

intVec intData;
```

It is this structure that is passed to waitInterrupt with the file descriptor and function pointer.

Next we have to write waitInterrupt:

```
void *waitInterrupt(void *arg) {

    intVec *intData = (intVec*) arg;
    int gpio=intData->gpio;
    struct pollfd fdset[1];
    fdset[0].fd = intData->fd;
    fdset[0].events = POLLPRI;
    fdset[0].revents = 0;
    for (;;) {
        int rc = poll(fdset, 1, -1);
        if (fdset[0].revents & POLLPRI) {
            intData->func();
            lseek(fdset[0].fd, 0, SEEK_SET);
            readGPIO(gpio);
        }
    }
    pthread_exit(0);
}
```

This unpacks the data passed to it using the **arg** pointer into a **pollfd** struct as before. Then it repeatedly calls poll which suspends the thread until the interrupt occurs. Then it wakes up and checks that it was the correct interrupt and if so it calls the interrupt routine and when this has finished resets the interrupt.

To try this out we need a main program and an interrupt function. The interrupt function simply counts the number of times it has been called:

```
static int count;
void myIntHandler() {
    count++;
};
```

The main program to test this is something like:

```
int main(int argc, char** argv) {
    attachGPIO(4, "both", myIntHandler);
    for (;;) {
      printf("Interrupt %d\n\r",count);
      fflush(stdout);
    };
    return 0;
}
```

It simply attaches the handler to the GPIO line and then prints the count variable in an infinite loop.

When you run the program you will see count increment every time there is an interrupt. Notice the count is incremented while the main program repeatedly prints the count; the use of a second thread really does let the main program get on with other work.

It is often argued that this approach to interrupts is second class, but if you think about how this threaded use of poll works, you have to conclude that it provides all of the features of an interrupt. The interrupt routine is idle and not consuming resources until the interrupt happens when it is activated and starts running. This is how a traditional interrupt routine behaves. There might even be advantages in a multicore system, as the interrupt thread could be scheduled on a different core from the main program and hence run concurrently. This might, however, be a disadvantage if you are not happy about making sure that the result is a well behaved system.

There are some other disadvantages of this approach. The main one is that the interrupt routine is run on a different thread and this can cause problems with code that isn't thread-safe - UI components, for example. It also more difficult to organize interrupts on multiple GPIO lines. It is generally said that you need one thread per GPIO line, but in practice a single thread can wait on any number of file descriptors and hence GPIO lines. A full general implementation as part of the bcm2835 library, say, would need functions to add and remove GPIO lines and interrupt handlers as well as the routine that just adds an interrupt handler.

Finally the big problem with this approach to interrupts is speed. Let's find out how much overhead is inherent in using this approach to interrupts by repeating the pulse width measurement. This time we can't simply print the results as this would stop the interrupt handling. As a compromise we save 20 readings in an array and then print them. It is also important to keep the interrupt handling routines short as how long they take to complete governs how fast the next interrupt can be handled. If the interrupt handling routine takes longer, the pulse width that can be measured is longer.

```c
uint64_t t[20];
static volatile int count = 0;
void myIntHandler() {
        t[count++]=bcm2835_st_read();
 };

int main(int argc, char** argv) {
    if (!bcm2835_init())
        return 1;
    attachGPIO(4, "both", myIntHandler);
    for (;;) {
        if (count >= 20)break;
    };
    int i;
    for (i = 1; i < 19; i++) {
        printf("%llo\n\r", (t[i + 1] - t[i])/1000);
    }
    fflush(stdout);
    return 0;
}
```

Notice we have interrupt handler called when there is a rising edge and a falling edge. It records reasonably accurate times for pulses longer than 100 milliseconds on both the Pi Zero/2. This makes this approach to interrupts suitable for infrequent non-urgent events and unsuitable for fast protocols or high priority tasks. The very slow timing is most probably due to the time to stop and restart the thread coupled with a slow processing of the hardware interrupt. Even so, 100 milliseconds is very slow and there might be a scheduling or some other tweak that would make it faster. Using FIFO scheduling doesn't seem to help, see Chapter 7.

At the moment polling - real polling - is faster. In fact, it would be faster to use the second thread to poll the GPIO state and run the interrupt handler directly without the help of sysfs and its interrupt facilities. For a multicore Pi this would be very similar to an interrupt handler.

Now that we have explored many of the ideas in using the GPIO lines for output and input the next question is whether we can do better by accessing the hardware directly.

Chapter 6

Memory Mapped GPIO

The bcm2835 library uses direct memory access to the GPIO and other peripherals. In this chapter we look at how this works. You don't need to know this, but if you need to modify the library or access features that the library doesn't expose this is the way to go.

Accessing the hardware directly isn't something that everyone wants or needs to do, but knowing how it all works gives you a different perspective. It means you can think about what you are doing, even if is only using the bcm2835 library in a broader and deeper way. In this chapter we look in more detail at the GPIO, its hardware and how it is controlled by the software. In particular, we look as the ingenious method that Linux uses to allow you to access peripherals or any memory you want to.

This is useful in a wider context because you can use the same techniques to map any file into memory. The same techniques can be used to work with other hardware in the bcm2835 that perhaps the library doesn't cater for.

All of the peripherals that are directly connected to the processor are memory mapped. What this means is that there are a set of addresses that correspond to "registers" that control and give the devices status. Using these is just a matter of knowing what addresses to use and what the format of the registers is and how to directly use memory under Linux.

Easy to say, slightly more difficult to get right. However, after you have got it right you can't understand what the fuss was about. The best way to understand how all of this works is to find out about a particular peripheral - the GPIO.

The GPIO Registers

If you look at the manual for the BCM2835 processor you will find a long section on the registers that are connected to the GPIO lines. This looks very complicated but in fact it comes down to a very simple pattern.

There are 54 GPIO lines arranged as two banks, not all usable on the Pi.

For each GPIO line there is a three bit configuration code that sets it to input or output or one of the alternate functions:

```
000 = GPIO Pin is an input
001 = GPIO Pin is an output
100 = GPIO Pin takes alternate function 0
101 = GPIO Pin takes alternate function 1
110 = GPIO Pin takes alternate function 2
111 = GPIO Pin takes alternate function 3
011 = GPIO Pin takes alternate function 4
010 = GPIO Pin takes alternate function 5
```

These three bits are packed into five 32-bit function select or configuration registers. The first function select register holds the configuration bits for GPIO 0 to 9, i.e. 10 GPIO lines with GPIO 0 as the first three low order bits, and GPIO 9 as the bits 27, 28 and 29. Bits 30 and 31 are unused in each of the registers.

The first register is:

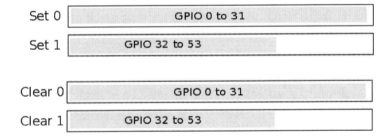

Basically the three configuration bits are packed into the 32-bit registers as best they can be. This arrangement continues for the next four registers, which control ten GPIO lines each, but the fifth register only holds the configuration bits for GPIO 50 to 53 and bits 12 to 31 are unused. Packing 54 GPIO lines into multiples of 32 bits is always going to leave some bits over.

Once the GPIO lines are configured into either input or output you can use the set and clear registers to set them high or low and the Level registers to read the state of inputs.

There are two Set and two Clear registers. The first register of each pair controls GPIO lines 0 to 31 and the second pair controls GPIO lines 32 to 53. One bit is assigned per line and the second register of each pair has bits 22 to 31 unused. That is, bit zero in Set 0 or Clear 0 controls GPIO 0 etc.

If you write to either register then the lines that correspond to 1 bits are set or cleared according to which register you write to. There is no simple Out register that you can write to simultaneously set and clear bits. The reason is that you can use Set and Clear to set or clear any GPIO lines without changing the state of the others.

For example, suppose you want to set GPIO 0 to a 1 then you would write 0x01 to the Set 0 register. In this case the 0 bits have no effect. A general Out register would also set all of the other lines it controlled to low in response to the zeros. This means controlling GPIO lines with a general Out register usually involves a read to establish the current state of all of the GPIO lines, then a logical operation to set or clear a particular line followed by a write. Having Set and Clear registers means you can set any group of lines to high or low in one write operation. However what you cannot do is set lines high and low at the same time.

To summarize, the main registers controlling the GPIO lines are:

FSEL0-FSEL5	Configuration registers three bits for each GPIO line
SET0 SET1	Set any group of GPIO lines high
CLR0 CLR1	Set any group of GPIO lines low
LEV0 LEV1	Read the state of all GPIO lines

There are also pairs of registers that control the event detection and interrupts which follow the description on of the functions in the interrupt section of the previous chapter. These are:

EDS0 EDS1	Event detect status
REN0 REN1	Rising edge detect enable
FEN0 FEN1	Falling edge detect enable
HEN0 HEN1	High detect enable
LEN0 LEN1	Low detect enable

There are two async version of the edge detection enables:

AREN0   Async rising edge detect enable
AREN1

AFEN0   Async falling edge detect enable
AFEN1

There are also three registers that let you set the pullup/pulldown behavior of any GPIO line:

UD   Pull up/down enable
UDCLK0   Enable clock
UDCLK1

You will notice that, unlike the other enable registers, there is only a single 32-bit Pull up/down register to control 53 GPIO lines. In fact only the first two low bits control anything.

b1	b0	
0	0	Pushpull
0	1	Pulldown
1	0	Pullup
1	1	Reserved

To set which GPIO line the new state refers to, you have to use the UDCKL pair of registers. The procedure is surprisingly complicated:

1. Set the state required in the UD register

2. Wait 150 clock cycles for the hardware to settle

3. Write a 1 to each bit position in UDCKL0/1 to determine which GPIO lines the new state will apply to

4. Wait 150 clock cycles for the hardware to settle

5. Write all zeros to UD and UDCKL0/1 to clear the set state

The bcm2835 library provides functions that expose this clocking procedure and a function that hides it from you:

```
bcm2835_gpio_set_pud (uint8_t pin, uint8_t pud)
```

simply sets the pin you select to the specified pullup/down.

There is one more set of registers to consider that it not listed in the standard documentation for reasons that are not clear. There are three PAD registers that set the fine details of the GPIO drive. You can consider the PAD registers as additional to the PUD registers.

The three registers control groups of GPIO lines:

> PAD0 GPIO 0 -27
> PAD1 GPIO 28-45
> PAD2 GPIO 46-53

The configuration is set in bits 0 to 5:

bits 2,1 0	Drive Strength
	000 = 2mA
	001 = 4mA
	n = (n+1)*2mA
bit 3 controls hysteresis	0 = disabled
	1= enabled
bit 4 controls slew rate	0=slew rate limited
	1 = slew rate not limited

The top 8 bits of the PAD registers have to be set to 0x5A to allow the PAD register to be written to. This is misleadingly called a PASSWRD.

There isn't much documentation on hysteresis and slew rate but broadly speaking hysteresis makes the input a Schmitt trigger and slew rate puts a small capacitive load on the input.

The Drive Strength setting deserves explanation. This isn't the amount of current that the pin can supply. It is the effective output resistance. Each time the drive current is increased by 2mA another transistor is used in the drive, so lowering the output resistance. This has the effect of increasing or decreasing the voltage.

This is a subtle idea and is related to how much current is needed to make the output 3.3V or 0V. For example, if you have a 2mA drive current then a load that draws 2mA will have a voltage across it within the tolerances for 3.3V logic for a 0 and a 1. If the load draws more than 2mA then the output voltages will not meet the tolerances of 0.8V for 0 and 1.3V for 1. For example, if the line is being driven low then sinking more than 2mA will make the output voltage greater than 0.8V and the output will not be read as a 0.

The drive current is not a maximum current that can be supplied and it is certainly not a current limiting value. If you short an output to 0V or 3.3V then it will supply as much current as it can before overheating and failing. The power up defaults for PAD registers are Slew rate unlimited, hysteresis enabled and drive current of 8mA.

Where Are The Registers?

The only question we have to answer now is where are the registers?This turns out to be a difficult question to answer because the processor implements memory mapping, which essentially means that any physical address can appear almost anywhere in the memory map of a running program.

According to the Pi documentation, all of the peripheral registers, including the GPIO registers we have been describing, are in a block of memory 0x2000 0000 to 0x20FF FFFF but this has been changed to start at 0x3F00 0000 for the Pi Zero/2 and 3, which is a source of much confusion.

So in the Pi 1 the peripheral registers start at 0x2000 0000. For a Pi Zero/2 and 3, the register's start is indicated by the contents of a file setup by the Linux Device Tree. This use of a file to record where the registers start means that any changes in the future are taken care of automatically.

To find out where the registers are you have to read:

```
/proc/device-tree/soc/ranges
```

which contains three 4-byte values: the address of the start of the memory; the second byte and its size; and the third byte. In practice reading the file returns 0x3F00 0000 for a Pi 2/3, but this could change in the future.

The best way to discover where the peripheral registers are located is to try to read the file and use the default 0x2000 0000 if it isn't present.

For example:

```
bcm2835_peripherals_base=  0x20000000;
int fp;
if ((fp = fopen("/proc/device-tree/soc/ranges" , "rb")))
{
  unsigned char buf[8];
 if (fread(buf, 1, sizeof(buf), fp) == sizeof(buf))
    bcm2835_peripherals_base =
            (uint32_t *)(buf[4] << 24 |
            buf[5] << 16 |
            buf[6] << 8  |
            buf[7] << 0);
    fclose(fp);
    }
```

In practice it is easier to rely on the bcm2835 library and the variable:

```
bcm2835_peripherals_base
```

which is set to the start of the peripherals area when you initialize the library and is therefore set correctly for all Pis.

Register addresses can be specified as offsets from bcm2835_peripherals_base but it is easier to take the offsets from where the first register belonging to the device is. So for the GPIO the first GPIO register is at 0x20 0000, which is

```
BCM2835_GPIO_BASE
```

in the bcm2835 library. That is, the starting address of the GPIO registers is given by:

```
gpio address  = bcm2835_peripherals_base + BCM2835_GPIO_BASE
```

The offsets for each of the registers from this address is:

0x0000	GPFSEL0 GPIO Function Select 0
0x0004	GPFSEL1 GPIO Function Select 1
0x0008	GPFSEL2 GPIO Function Select 2
0x000C	GPFSEL3 GPIO Function Select 3
0x0010	GPFSEL4 GPIO Function Select 4
0x0014	GPFSEL5 GPIO Function Select 5
0x001C	GPSET0 GPIO Pin Output Set 0
0x0020	GPSET1 GPIO Pin Output Set 1
0x0028	GPCLR0 GPIO Pin Output Clear 0
0x002C	GPCLR1 GPIO Pin Output Clear 1 32 W
0x0034	GPLEV0 GPIO Pin Level 0
0x0038	GPLEV1 GPIO Pin Level 1
0x0040	GPEDS0 GPIO Pin Event Detect Status 0
0x0044	GPEDS1 GPIO Pin Event Detect Status 1
0x004C	GPREN0 GPIO Pin Rising Edge Detect Enable 0
0x0050	GPREN1 GPIO Pin Rising Edge Detect Enable 1
0x0058	GPFEN0 GPIO Pin Falling Edge Detect Enable 0
0x005C	GPFEN1 GPIO Pin Falling Edge Detect Enable 1
0x0064	GPHEN0 GPIO Pin High Detect Enable 0
0x0068	GPHEN1 GPIO Pin High Detect Enable 1
0x0070	GPLEN0 GPIO Pin Low Detect Enable 0
0x0074	GPLEN1 GPIO Pin Low Detect Enable 1
0x007C	GPAREN0 GPIO Pin Async. Rising Edge Detect
0x0080	GPAREN1 GPIO Pin Async. Rising Edge Detect 1
0x0088	GPAFEN0 GPIO Pin Async. Falling Edge Detect 0
0x008C	GPAFEN1 GPIO Pin Async. Falling Edge Detect 1
0x0094	GPPUD GPIO Pin Pull-up/down Enable
0x0098	GPPUDCLK0 GPIO Pin Pull-up/down Enable Clock
0x009C	GPPUDCLK1 GPIO Pin Pull-up/down Enable Clock

The only registers missing from this list are the PAD control registers and these are located in a different area of memory at:

```
BCM2835_GPIO_PADS=bcm2835_peripherals_base+BCM2835_GPIO_PADS
                =0x20100000 or
                =0x3F100000 for Pi2
```

and the offsets are:

```
        0x002c PADS0 (GPIO 0-27)
        0x0030 PADS1 (GPIO 28-45)
        0x0034 PADS2 (GPIO 46-53)
```

You can work out the address of any register listed in the documentation by finding the base address for the registers and adding its offset.

It is worth knowing that you can use:

```
        cat /proc/iomem
```

to discover where devices are in memory. On a Pi 2 or 3 you will see:

```
        00000000-3affffff : System RAM
        00008000-007e641f : Kernel code
        0085e000-0098c1ab : Kernel data
        3f006000-3f006fff : dwc_otg
        3f007000-3f007eff : /soc/dma@7e007000
        3f00b840-3f00b84e : /soc/vchiq
        3f00b880-3f00b8bf : /soc/mailbox@7e00b800
        3f200000-3f2000b3 : /soc/gpio@7e200000
        3f201000-3f201fff : /soc/uart@7e201000
        3f201000-3f201fff : /soc/uart@7e201000
        3f202000-3f2020ff : /soc/sdhost@7e202000
        3f980000-3f98ffff : dwc_otg
```

Linux Memory Access /dev/mem

If you recall the discussion in Chapter 4 on sysfs, Linux likes to have every I/O device look as much like a file as possible. This is a basic principle of Unix that Linux has taken to heart and in the main it sort of works. However sometimes you have to think that we are going the long way round to get a job done.

For example, how do you think Linux gives your user mode program access to raw memory?

Yes, that is correct. It represents the memory as a single binary file /dev/mem.

This is character device file that is an image of user mode memory. And when you read or write byte n this is the same as reading and writing the memory location at byte address n. You can move the pointer to any memory location using lseek and read and write blocks of bytes using fread and fwrite.

It is simple but it takes some time to get used to the idea.

For example to open the file to read and write it you might use:

```
int memfd = open("/dev/mem", O_RDWR | O_SYNC);
```

The O_RDWR opens the file for read and write and the O_SYNC flag makes the call blocking.

After this you can lseek to the memory location you want to work with. For example to go to the start of the GPIO registers you would use:

```
uint32_t p = lseek(memfd, (off_t) 0x3f200000, SEEK_SET);
```

for the Pi 3 or

```
uint32_t p = lseek(memfd, (off_t) 0x20200000, SEEK_SET);
```

for the Pi 1. Notice that these are the base address plus 0x20 000

Next you could read the 32 bits starting at that location i.e. the FSEl0 register:

```
int n = read(memfd, buffer, 4);
```

Unfortunately at the moment if you try this then you will find that it doesn't work and you get a bad address error. You can read and write other memory locations but the peripheral registers don't seem to work. If they did this would be a perfectly good way to read and write the registers.

As this doesn't work we need to move on to what does.

Memory Mapping Files

The Linux approach to I/O places the emphasis on files but there are times when reading and writing a file to an external device like a disk drive is too slow. To solve this problem Linux has a memory mapping function which will read any portion of a file into user memory so that you can work with is directly using pointers. This in principle is a very fast way to access any file - including /dev/mem.

This seems like a crazy round about route to get at memory. First implement memory access as a file you can read and then map that file into memory so that you can read it as if it was memory - which it is. However if you follow the story it is logical. What is more it solves a slightly different problem very elegantly. It allows the fixed physical addresses of the peripherals into the user space virtual addresses. In other words when you memory map the /dev/mem file into user memory it can be located anywhere and the address of the start of the register area will be within your programs allocated address space. This means that all of the addresses we have been listing will change. Of course as long as we work with offsets from the start of memory this is no problem - we update the staring value and use the same offsets.

Lets see how this works in practice.

The key function is mmap

```
void *mmap(
 void *addr,
 size_t length,
 int prot,
 int  flags,
 int fd,
 off_t offset
);
```

The function memory maps the file corresponding to the file descriptor fd into memory and returns its start address. The offset and length parameters control the portion of the file mapped i.e. the mapped portions starts at the byte given by offset and continues for length bytes.

There is a small complication in that for efficiency reasons the file is always mapped in units of the page size of the machine. So if you ask for a 1Kbyte file to be loaded into memory then, on the Pi with a 4Kbyte page size, 4Kbytes of memory will be allocated. The file will occupy the first 1Kbytes and the rest will be zeroed.

You can also specify the address that you would like the file loaded to in your programs address space but the system doesn't have to honor this request - it just uses it as a hint. Some programmers reserve and area of memory using malloc say and then ask the system to load the file into it - as this might not happen it seems simpler to let the system allocate the memory and pass NULL as the starting address.

Prot and flags specify various ways the file can be memory mapped and there are a lot of options - see the man page for details.

Notice that this is a completely general mechanism and you can use it to map any file into memory. For example if you have graphics file - image.gif - then you could load it into memory to make working with it faster. Many databases use this technique to speed up their processing.

Now all we have to do is map /dev/mem into memory.

First we need to open the /dev/mem device as usual:

```
uint32_t memfd = open("/dev/mem", O_RDWR | O_SYNC);
```

As long as this works we can map the file into memory.

We want to map the file starting at either 0x2020 0000 for the Pi 1 or starting at 0x3F20 0000 for the Pi 2 or later. If we only want to work with the GPIO registers then we only need offsets of 0000 to 00B0 i.e. 176 bytes but as we get the a complete 4K page we might as well map 4KBytes worth of address space:

```
uint32_t * map = (uint32_t *)mmap(
                NULL,
                4*1024,
                (PROT_READ | PROT_WRITE),
                MAP_SHARED,
                memfd,
                0x3f200000);
```

If you try this remember to change the offset to be correct for the Pi you are using or better us bcm2835_peripherals_base to specify the address.

Notice also that we haven't set an address for the file to be loaded into - the system will take care of it and return the address in map. We also have asked for read/write permission and allowed other processes to share the map. This makes map a very important variable because now it gives the location of the start of the GPIO register area but in user space. The bcm2835 has a standard variable for this:

`bcm2835_peripherals`

Now we can read and write a 3KByte block of addresses starting at the first GPIO register i.e. FSEL0.

For example to read FSEL0 we would use:

`printf("fsel0 %X \n\r",*map);`

To access the other registers we need to add their offset but there is one subtle detail. The pointer to the start of the memory has been caste to a uint32_t because we want to read and write 32 bit registers. However by the rules of pointer arithmetic when you add one to a pointer you actually add the size of the date type the pointer is pointing to. In this case when you add one to map you increment the location it is pointing at by four i.e. the size of a 32 bit unsigned integer.

The rule is that with this cast we are using word addresses which are byte addresses divided by 4.

Thus when we add the offsets we need to add the offset divided by 4.

With this all clear lets write a program that toggles GPIO 4 as fast as possible.

The Fastest Pulse

First we need to set it to output and GPIO 4 is controlled by FSEL0 and bits 12,13 and 14 which we want to set to 001 i.e. we need to store 0x1000 in FSEL0:

```
*paddr=0x1000;
```

With GPIO 4 set to output we now need to use the SET0 and CLR0 registers to set the line high and low. As we want to do this as fast as possible we need to precompute the addresses of SET0 and CLR0:

```
volatile uint32_t* paddr1 = map + 0x1C/4;
volatile uint32_t* paddr2 = map + 0x28/4;
for(;;){
  *paddr1=0x10;
  *paddr2=0x10;
};
```

The complete program is:

```
#include <stdio.h>
#include <stdlib.h>
#include <bcm2835.h>
#include <sys/mman.h>
#include <fcntl.h>
#include <errno.h>

int main(int argc, char** argv) {
int memfd = open("/dev/mem", O_RDWR | O_SYNC);
uint32_t * map = (uint32_t *)mmap(
                    NULL,
                    4*1024,
                    (PROT_READ | PROT_WRITE),
                    MAP_SHARED,
                    memfd,
                    0x3f200000);
 if (map == MAP_FAILED)
    printf("bcm2835_init: %s mmap failed: %s\n", strerror(errno));
close(memfd);

volatile uint32_t* paddr = map;
*paddr=0x1000;
volatile uint32_t* paddr1 = map + 0x1C/4;
volatile uint32_t* paddr2 = map + 0x28/4;
for(;;){
 *paddr1=0x10;
 *paddr2=0x10;
};
    return (EXIT_SUCCESS);
}
```

If you run this program you will discover that it generates pulses that are as small as 0.25 microseconds (Zero/2). This is as fast as you can go using memory mapped file access. As before the quality of the pulses is such that it is difficult to measure an exact pulse width.

Because of all of the complexities and differences between the Pi 1 and P2 you are much better off using the bcm2835 library which uses exactly these technique to work with the GPIO and isn't much slower than a custom code approach.

Lets look at the lower lever functions that the library provides.

Low Level Register Access

The bcm2835 library provides a small number of functions that will access any register you need to. It makes use of the /dev/mem file and the mmap function and it works in more or less the way described above. The big advantage is that it sets things up so that the addressing is correct for the current and presumably future versions of the Pi.

There are two read and two write functions:

```
uint32_t bcm2835_peri_read (volatile uint32_t *paddr)
uint32_t bcm2835_peri_read_nb (volatile uint32_t *paddr)

void bcm2835_peri_write (volatile uint32_t *paddr, uint32_t value)
void bcm2835_peri_write_nb (volatile uint32_t *paddr, uint32_t
                                                       value)
```

The difference between them is the use of read/write barriers. This is something that has been ignored until now. The processor allows operations to occur in an almost synchronous way. This means that it is possible for results to occur in a different order to the one in which you programmed them. This can only happen on the first access to a peripheral. If you read or write to a peripheral for the first time you need to use a barrier. Subsequent reads and writes don't need a barrier. If you write to another peripheral and then go back to the first you need to use a barrier again. In short, you need a barrier at the start of any consecutive peripheral accesses.

It is always safer to use standard read/write functions that apply a barrier than the nb - non-barrier functions - however these are slightly faster.

As well as the four basic read/write functions we also have a set function:

```
void bcm2835_peri_set_bits (volatile uint32_t *paddr,
                         uint32_t value, uint32_t mask)
```

This will set the bits defined in the mask to the value specified in the corresponding bit in the value parameter.

For example:

```
bcm2835_peri_set_bits (paddr,0x01,0x01)
```

will set bit 0 to a 1 leaving all other bits unchanged and

```
bcm2835_peri_set_bits (paddr,0x00,0x01)
```

will set bit 0 to a 0 leaving all other bits unchanged.

Finally we have the problem of specifying the addresses we want to use. The problem, of course, is what is the base address? There is a useful function that will return the base address of any of the standard registers:

```
uint32_t * bcm2835_regbase (uint8_t regbase)
```

where *regbase* is one of:

BCM2835_REGBASE_ST	Base of the ST (System Timer) registers
BCM2835_REGBASE_GPIO	Base of the GPIO registers
BCM2835_REGBASE_PWM	Base of the PWM registers
BCM2835_REGBASE_CLK	Base of the CLK registers
BCM2835_REGBASE_PADS	Base of the PADS registers
BCM2835_REGBASE_SPI0	Base of the SPI0 registers
BCM2835_REGBASE_BSC0	Base of the BSC0 registers
BCM2835_REGBASE_BSC1	Base of the BSC1 registers

So to get the address in user memory of the GPIO register you can use BCM2835_REGBASE_GPIO. Alternatively you can use bcm2835_peripherals and simply add the known offsets e.g.

```
bcm2835_peripherals + BCM2835_REGBASE_GPIO/4;
```

The library also provides a set of pre-computed starting addresses for the standard sets of registers:

```
bcm2835_gpio = bcm2835_peripherals + BCM2835_GPIO_BASE/4;
bcm2835_pwm  = bcm2835_peripherals + BCM2835_GPIO_PWM/4;
bcm2835_clk  = bcm2835_peripherals + BCM2835_CLOCK_BASE/4;
bcm2835_pads = bcm2835_peripherals + BCM2835_GPIO_PADS/4;
bcm2835_spi0 = bcm2835_peripherals + BCM2835_SPI0_BASE/4;
bcm2835_bsc0 = bcm2835_peripherals + BCM2835_BSC0_BASE/4; /* I2C */
bcm2835_bsc1 = bcm2835_peripherals + BCM2835_BSC1_BASE/4; /* I2C */
bcm2835_st   = bcm2835_peripherals + BCM2835_ST_BASE/4;
```

Notice that the addresses all refer to the location in user space where the file has been mapped and all of the offsets have to be converted to word addresses by being divided by 4.

An Almost Fastest Pulse

As an example of using the low level functions let's repeat the toggling of GPIO 4 using them. This doesn't give you the fastest possible time because there is the overhead of the function calls. But it is almost as good.

This time we need to initialize the library as this is where the mapping is set up.

```
if (!bcm2835_init())
    return 1;
```

Next we can get the address of the start of the GPIO registers in user memory:

```
uint32_t* gpioBASE = bcm2835_regbase(BCM2835_REGBASE_GPIO);
```

Finally we can set GPIO 4 to output and set and clear it:

```
bcm2835_peri_write(gpioBASE, 0x1000);
for (;;) {
 bcm2835_peri_write(gpioBASE + BCM2835_GPSET0 / 4, 0x10);
 bcm2835_peri_write(gpioBASE + BCM2835_GPCLR0 / 4, 0x10);
}
```

If you run this version of the program you will find that the shortest pulses are around 0.5 microseconds (PI Zero/2), and are slightly shorter on the Pi 3. If you change the writes for non-barrier writes then the pulses do get shorter, typically 0.3 microseconds (PI Zero/2) but there is much more variability. In practice using the barrier read/writes seems adequate.

GPIO Clocks - An Example

This is an advanced topic.

The GPIO Clocks are not as well known as they deserve to be and there are no functions that let you work with them in the bcm2835 library. It is, however, fairly easy to add one.

There are three general purpose GPIO clocks and two special purpose clocks - the PWM and PCM clock, You can set any of the clocks to run at a given rate and the general purpose clocks can be routed to a subset of GPIO pins. The outputs are pulse trains of the specified frequency which can be modulated by changing the clock divider.

The frequency division can include a fractional part which, if you know your digital logic, is surprising. Dividing by 2, 4 or 8 is easy but how do you divide by 2.5? The answer is that you use a MASH filter. Explaining exactly how this works is beyond the scope of this book, but it is a digital processing technique that can generate a signal with the frequency desired. The problem is that it also generates additional error frequencies that, with luck, are outside the band required and easy to remove. If you opt for no MASH filter then you cannot use a fractional divider. Selecting one, two or three MASH filters produces the required frequency but with different properties of noise associated with the signal.

The three GPIO clocks can be used with the following GPIO lines:

GPCLK0 GPIO4 GPIO20 GPIO32 GPIO34 GPIO44
GPCLK1 GPIO5 GPIO21 GPIO42 GPCLK2 GPIO6 GPIO43

The only GPIO pin available on early Pis is GPIO4 but on later ones you can use the following:

```
GPIO4  GPCLK0 ALT0
GPIO5  GPCLK1 ALT0 (reserved for system use)
GPIO6  GPCLK2 ALT0
GPIO20 GPCLK0 ALT5
```

Each clock is controlled by two registers: a control register and a register used to specify the clock divider.

The word, multiply by 4 for byte address, offsets for the registers are:

```
#define CLK_GP0_CTL 28
#define CLK_GP0_DIV 29

#define CLK_GP1_CTL 30
#define CLK_GP1_DIV 31

#define CLK_GP2_CTL 32
#define CLK_GP2_DIV 33

#define CLK_PCM_CTL 38
#define CLK_PCM_DIV 39

#define CLK_PWM_CTL 40
#define CLK_PWM_DIV 41
```

The offsets are all relative to the start of the peripheral area using:

```
BCM2835_CLOCK_BASE  0x101000
```

or to:

```
bcm2835_clk
```

which is a word address relative to the start of the memory mapped registers.

The safest way to form the address of a clock register, GP0 control for example, is to use:

```
bcm2835_clk+CLK_GP0_CTL
```

as the bcm2835_clk is automatically adjusted to the start of the registers as mapped in memory.

The control register has a simple layout:

31-24	PASSWD	Clock Manager password "5a"	
10-9	MASH	MASH control	
		0 = integer division	
		1 = 1-stage MASH	
		2 = 2-stage MASH	
		3 = 3-stage MASH	
8	FLIP	Invert the clock generator output	
7	BUSY	Clock generator is running	
6	Unused		
5	KILL	Kill the clock generator	
		0 = no action 1 = stop	
4	ENAB	Enable the clock generator	
3-0	SRC	Clock source	
		0 = GND	
		1 = oscillator	19.2MHz
		2 = testdebug0	
		3 = testdebug1	
		4 = PLLA	0MHz
		5 = PLLC	1000MHz
		6 = PLLD	500MHz
		7 = HDMI auxiliary	216MHz
		8-15 = GND	

The important points are that you use ENAB to start and stop the clock; you don't make changes to the settings while the clock is running; and you don't make changes while enabling the clock.

The divider register has the format:

31-24	PASSWD	Clock Manager password "5a"
23-12	DIVI	Integer part of divisor
11-0	DIVF	Fractional part of divisor

and as for the control register you do not change this while BUSY=1.

So to configure the clock you:

1. Set ENAB low

2. Wait for BUSY to go low

3. Set the values you want to change including the divider register but with ENAB low

4. Set ENAB high with the same set of values so as not to change them.

Now we can put this together to write a function that will set the clock associated with GPIO 4. You can easily change this to work with any of the valid GPIO lines:

```
#define CLK_GP0_CTL 28
#define CLK_GP0_DIV 29
void bcm2835_GPIO4_set_clock_source(
          uint32_t source,
          uint32_t divisorI,
          uint32_t divisorF) {
 if (bcm2835_clk == MAP_FAILED)
      return;
 divisorI &= 0xfff;
 divisorF &= 0xfff;
 source &= 0xf;

 uint8_t mask=bcm2835_peri_read(bcm2835_clk + CLK_GP0_CTL)
                                    & 0xffffffef;

 bcm2835_peri_write(bcm2835_clk + CLK_GP0_CTL,
                        BCM2835_PWM_PASSWRD | mask);

 while ((bcm2835_peri_read(bcm2835_clk + CLK_GP0_CTL)
                             & 0x80) != 0){};

 bcm2835_peri_write(bcm2835_clk + CLK_GP0_DIV,
        BCM2835_PWM_PASSWRD | (divisorI << 12) | divisorF);
 bcm2835_peri_write(bcm2835_clk + CLK_GP0_CTL,
                    BCM2835_PWM_PASSWRD |  source|0x200);
 bcm2835_peri_write(bcm2835_clk + CLK_GP0_CTL,
                    BCM2835_PWM_PASSWRD | 0x0210 | source);
}
```

At the start of the function we make sure that the divisors and the source are withing the legal range by ANDing them with masks.

Next we read the control register so as to create a mask so that we don't change any of the bits until the clock is stopped. Notice that the enable bit of the mask is set to zero, which is why the clock stops when the mask is written back to the control register.

The while loop waits for the clock to stop and then the divisor is written to the divisor register and the source to the control register.

Finally the source is written to the control register along with an enable bit set to 1. The 0x200 selects one stage of MASH, which is necessary if you want to use the fractional divider.

Also notice that we are using the predefined BCM2835_PWM_PASSWRD for 0x5A to allow a write to the registers.

You can try this out with a main program something like:

```
if (!bcm2835_init())
        return 1;
    bcm2835_gpio_fsel(4, BCM2835_GPIO_FSEL_ALT0);
    bcm2835_GPIO4_set_clock_source(6, 50, 0);
```

If you look at the output of GPIO 4 with a logic analyzer you might be surprised how jittery the 10MHz i.e. 500MHz/50 clock is. Part of this is likely to be due to the poor wave shape at such a high frequency. If you look at the pulse stream on an oscilloscope then you should see something like:

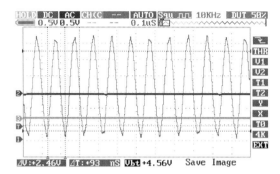

The maximum frequency that can be produced depends on the loading on the GPIO pin and stray capacitance. In theory you should be able to get up to over 100MHz in practice this is difficult. As the frequency goes up the losses due to capacitance increase and the output voltage falls. Add to this the fact that many oscilloscopes will not record a signal at 100MHz and it gets very difficult to work with dividers smaller than 20 because you can't see the output.

With a divider of 5 you can still get enough of a signal to use the output as a 100MHz FM transmitter. There are programs that make use of this effect to send an FM audio signal at by changing the frequency via the fractional divider.

Learning how to access the GPIO registers using memory mapping is important not only for using the GPIOs but also for extending what can be done to the other registers. Once you understand how Linux performs memory mapping you can see that it is a general mechanism that can be applied in other situations. However, most of the time you can start out just using the library and only think about doing anything more complicated if it proves necessary. Before implementing your own memory mapping, make sure you try the low level register functions - they are almost as fast as anything you can create.

Chapter 7

Almost Real Time Linux

You can write real time programs using standard Linux as long as you know how to control scheduling. In fact it turns out to be relatively easy and it enables the Pi to do things you might not think it capable of. There are also some surprising differences between the one and quad core Pis that make you think again about real time Linux programming.

If you are writing a real time system there are two things that should concern you - how fast the system can act and how poor this response can be in the worst case.

After learning how to generate accurate and fast pulses we now have the ability to work with I/O down in the microsecond region, but we still have the problem that our program can be interrupted at any time by the operating system. This means that our outputs and inputs can go drastically wrong. For example, if you generate a fast pulse train in the 1 microsecond range using a standard GPIO line and set a logic analyzer to trigger on a long pulse, you will eventually find one or more very long pulses - typically in the millisecond range. This problem becomes worse the more the CPU is loaded as the operating system switches between tasks to make sure that everything has an opportunity to progress.

The Scheduling Problem

If you are familiar with microcontrollers such as the PIC, AMTEL, etc, then this idea that there could be something getting between you and the hardware will be new. The majority of simple microcontrollers do nothing but run the program you download. Any talk of an "operating system" generally refers to code that does the downloading or minimal system preparation. When you write a control loop then you can safely assume that the loop will run as you wrote it and without interruption, unless of course you have coded an interrupt handler.

The point is that in many situations your program is the only program running and you are in complete charge of the processor.

In the case of running a program on the Raspberry Pi's ARM the situation is very different. Your program is just one of a number of programs running at any given time. The Raspberry Pi has up to four cores and this means that at most four programs can be running at any given time. The operating system is responsible for starting and stopping programs so that each and every program has a turn to run. This is called **scheduling** and it is a problem if you are trying to write a real time system.

The problem is, that you might write a program that toggles a GPIO line between high and low with a given timing, but whether this timing is honored depends not just on your program but on the operating system as well. You can't even be sure how the operating system will treat your program because it depends, in a fairly complex way, on what else is running on the system and exactly what the other programs are doing.

Sometime this is expressed as your program execution being **non-deterministic** whereas in a simple microcontroller it is deterministic. This means that if you run the same program twice on on the Raspberry Pi you probably don't get exactly the same result, whereas on an mcu this is a reasonable expectation.

The whole subject of multitasking operating systems, and scheduling in particular, is a large one. It is usually taught as part of a computer science degree, but generally not as it applies to real time programming. What this means is that there is often a lot of guesswork involved in getting programs with real-time demands to work properly under general operating systems such as Linux. In fact it is often stated that you can't do real-time processing under Linux because you cannot even place a bound, an upper limit, on how long your program might be suspended by the OS. This isn't true and real-time processing on standard Linux is possible, as long as you are able to live within the constraints.

As an alternative you could opt to run a specially designed real-time OS that does provide guarantees on how quickly a request will be serviced. There are specifically real-time versions of Linux that you can install but, since version 2.6, the Linux Kernel has had sufficient real time facilities for many applications, so you don't need to move to anything different to the standard Raspbian.

Before we continue, it is important to realize that there is no way that a real-time operating system can increase the speed of operation of the processor; the maximum speed of operation cannot be improved upon. In the case of the Raspberry Pi this means that you can achieve pulse times of around 1 microsecond if you are careful and no amount of real time programming is going to improve on this.

What real time provides is higher consistency of that response time. It isn't perfect, however, and after we have used all of the features of real-time Linux there will still be small periods of time when your program isn't operating and there is little to be done about this.

RT Scheduling

Every Linux thread is assigned a scheduling policy and a static priority. The normal scheduling algorithm that Linux uses, SCHED_OTHER, applies to all threads with static priority zero. If you are not using real-time scheduling then all the threads run at priority zero. In place of a static priority, each thread is assigned a dynamic priority, which increases each time it is passed over for execution by the scheduler. The scheduler gives the thread with the highest dynamic priority an opportunity to run for one quantum of time or for one time slice. A thread can be suspended before its time slice is up because it has to wait for I/O or because it is blocked in some other way. Any time a thread makes system call it is also a candidate to be suspended in favor of another thread.

You have only a little control over the computation of the dynamic priority. All you can do is set its initial value using the **nice** command or **setpriority**.

The normal scheduling algorithm doesn't provide much control over what runs. It is "fair" in the sense that all threads get a turn at running, but it isn't possible to set a thread to have a high priority so that it runs in preference to all others. To do this we need to look at the real time scheduling options. The most important for us is SCHED_FIFO and sometimes the closely related SCHED_RR. These apply to real time threads with static priorities 1(low) to 99(high).

The first thing to note is that a thread with priority greater than zero will always run in preference to a thread with priority zero and so all real-time threads will run before a thread using the normal scheduling algorithm.

What happens in FIFO is that the system maintains queues of threads that are ready to run at each priority. It then looks for the list with the highest priority with threads ready to run and it starts the thread at the head of the list. When a thread is started it is added to the back of its priority queue. Once a FIFO thread gets to run it can be preempted by a thread with a higher static priority that is ready to run.

If a FIFO thread is suspended because of a higher priority thread it goes back at the head of the queue. This makes it the next thread to resume. This is the sense in which the schedule is FIFO (First In First Out) - if a thread is suspended by another thread of higher priority that becomes runnable then it is restarted as soon as that thread that replaced it is suspended or stops running.

Finally, if a thread explicitly yields (by calling **yield**) it goes to the end of its priority queue.

Setting Scheduling Priority

This sounds like chaos, but if you think about it for a moment and start simply you will see that it provides most of what you are looking for. You are in full control of the Raspberry Pi and so you can determine exactly how many non-zero priority threads there are. By default all of the standard threads are priority zero and scheduled by the normal scheduler.

Now consider what happens if you start a FIFO scheduled thread with priority 1. It starts and is added to the end of the priority 1 queue. Of course, it is the only priority 1 process and so it starts immediately on one of the cores available. If the process never makes a call that causes it to wait for I/O or become blocked in some other way then it will execute without being interrupted by any other process. In principle this should ensure that your process never delivers anything but its fastest response time.

This is almost, but not quite, true. There are more complex situations you can invent with threads at different priorities according to how important they are but this gets complicated very quickly.

A modification to SCHED_FIFO is the Round Robin scheduler, SCHED_RR. for. In this case everything works as for SCHED_FIFO except that each running process is only allowed to run for a single time slice. When the time slice is up, the thread at the head of the priority queue is started and the current thread is added to the end of the queue. You can see that this allows each thread to run for around one time slice in turn.

In most cases for real-time programming with the Raspberry Pi, the SCHED_FIFO scheduler is what you need and in its simplest form. Its complete set of scheduling commands are:

sched_setscheduler	Set the scheduling policy and parameters of a specified thread
sched_getscheduler	Return the scheduling policy of a specified thread
sched_setparam	Set the scheduling parameters of a specified thread
sched_getparam	Fetch the scheduling parameters of a specified thread
sched_get_priority_max	Return the maximum priority available in a specified scheduling policy
sched_get_priority_min	Return the minimum priority available in a specified scheduling policy
sched_rr_get_interval	Fetch the quantum used for threads that are scheduled under the round-robin scheduling policy
sched_yield	Cause the caller to relinquish the CPU, so that some other thread be executed
sched_setaffinity	Set the CPU affinity of a specified thread
sched_getaffinity	Get the CPU affinity of a specified thread
sched_setattr	Set the scheduling policy and parameters of a specified thread
sched_getattr	Fetch the scheduling policy and parameters of a specified thread

The scheduling types supported are:

SCHED_OTHER   the standard time-sharing policy
SCHED_BATCH   for "batch" style execution of processes
SCHED_IDLE   for running very low priority background jobs
SCHED_FIFO   a first-in, first-out policy
SCHED_RR   a round-robin policy

where only the final two are real time schedulers.

Also notice that all the scheduling functions return an error code which you should check to make sure thing have worked. For simplicity the examples that follow ignore this advice.

How Bad Is The Problem?

The first question we need to answer is how bad the situation is without real time scheduling. This is not an easy question to answer because it depends on so many factors. Take, for example, a very simple program which toggles a GPIO line as fast as it can:

```
#include <bcm2835.h>
#include <stdio.h>
#include <sched.h> int main(int argc, char **argv) {
 if (!bcm2835_init())
    return 1;
 bcm2835_gpio_fsel(RPI_GPIO_P1_07 ,
 BCM2835_GPIO_FSEL_OUTP);
 while (1) {
  bcm2835_gpio_write(RPI_GPIO_P1_07 , HIGH);
  bcm2835_gpio_write(RPI_GPIO_P1_07 , LOW);
 }
bcm2835_close();
 return 0;
}
```

As we have already discovered, we can generate pulses less than 1 microsecond wide using this method. The real question is how does the scheduler change this pulse length by interrupting your program?

The Pi Zero Single Core 1GHz

The Pi Zero has a single core ARM processor so it can only do one thing at a time and makes a perfect worst case example.

If you run the program with a logic analyzer connected and with a freshly booted Pi Zero and no other tasks running then you will see the usual moderately rough pulse train with the regular 0.08 to 0.1 microsecond pulses with .5 microsecond pulses every 1.25ms.

However if you set the logic analyzer to capture long pulses even if the Pi isn't loaded you will see, after a few seconds, pulses as long as 0.5ms.

Even on a lightly loaded Pi Linux will interrupt the running task every few seconds.

On a Pi Zero running even one demanding task the story is worse.

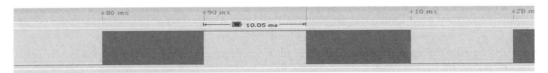

In this case the task is a simple infinite loop that will use as much of the CPUs time as it is allowed to. The result is a regular 10ms pulse. This is due to the Linux scheduler dividing up the time so that both tasks get a reasonably equal share of the single CPU. If the Pi you are using has more than one core then this behavior will occur when the number of equal priority tasks equals the number of cores.

Yes, with these conditions the program can produce 10ms pulses mixed in with the 0.1ms pulses.

Pi Zero Real Time FIFO Scheduling

Now we can try the same test but with FIFO real time scheduling selected.

To do this we need to use the sched_setscheduler function:

```
sched_setscheduler(pid,SCHED_FIFO,&priority);
```

where pid is the thread id - if zero then the calling thread is used.

The second parameter sets the type of scheduling used FIFO in this case and the final parameter is a pointer to a structure that specifies the priority.

Notice you need to include <sched.h> to make use of the scheduling functions.

The modified program is:

```c
#include <bcm2835.h>
#include <stdio.h>
#include <sched.h>
 int main(int argc, char **argv) {
  const struct sched_param priority = {1};
  sched_setscheduler(0, SCHED_FIFO, &priority);
  if (!bcm2835_init())
    return 1;
 bcm2835_gpio_fsel(RPI_GPIO_P1_07 ,BCM2835_GPIO_FSEL_OUTP);
 while (1) {
  bcm2835_gpio_write(RPI_GPIO_P1_07 , HIGH);
  bcm2835_gpio_write(RPI_GPIO_P1_07 , LOW);
 }
 bcm2835_close();
 return 0;
}
```

If you run this program you will discover that the result are very different. The first thing you might notice if you have a console open is that the response is very sluggish. The reason is that your program is hogging the CPU.

If you run a logic analyzer then there is a surprise. The program runs for one second and then it is interrupted for around 50ms.

Clearly something with a higher priority is now interrupting your program and probably keeping the console and other essentials running. If you now run a CPU hogging task you will discover that there is no change in the behavior of your program. It runs for a second and then is interrupted for 50ms. There is no 10ms switching between tasks, your program still gets a full 1 second of uninterrupted CPU time and this is irrespective of the CPU load.

You can also try locking the program's memory to stop the system from paging it if other applications need a lot of memory. In practice this isn't a common occurrence on a device like the Raspberry Pi, but if you do need to do it then all you need is a call to **mlock** in sys/mman.h and to **unlock** to unlock it. You can lock the current memory or future memory allocations. In most cases it is sufficient to lock current memory unless you are using dynamic memory allocation with:

```
mlockall(MCL_CURRENT);
```

In the case of our test program locking memory make no difference as there is plenty of real memory to go around.

Pi 2 Quad Core 900MHz

The single core Pi Zero has to share its single core even with a high priority FIFO process. The quad core Pi 2 and Pi 3 should behave differently because they have three cores to work with after you monopolize a whole core with your program.

Let's see how things work with a Pi 2. The Pi 3 running at 1.2GHz gives the same sort of results as the Pi 2, just a little faster. Comparing the Pi 2 and Zero allows us to compare the effects of one core versus four core for machines that run at roughly the same speed.

First let's try the program without real-time features. With a lightly loaded Pi 2 we have the usual 0.08 to 0.1 microsecond pulses with a 0.6 microsecond pulse every 0.125 ms and 15 microsecond pulse every 10 ms. When you add CPU hogging processes then, at about four processes, irregular 10 ms pulses start to appear

The 10 ms pulses correspond to periods of time when the program is swapped out and not running. It isn't regular because the four cores are shared between each of the processes.

If you change the program to use realtime FIFO scheduling then, with the same CPU load that produced the 10 ms pulses, you get a result that looks like a lightly loaded CPU. That is, the 10 ms pulses vanish and all you have to contend with are the 0.6 microsecond and 15 microsecond interruptions.

The reason for this behavior is fairly obvious. Now your process can be run by one of the cores while the remaining three are shared between the other non-real-time processes. Thus for a Pi 2 or 3 near realtime Linux works better than for a single core Pi Zero or Pi 1. For a Pi 2 or 3 you can reasonably expect a response within 15 microseconds.

Practical FIFO Scheduling

Adding a simple statement makes your program hog one of the available processor cores and removes the long interruptions that occur when other threads are scheduled to run. You might think at this point that the best thing to do is set a maximum priority and use FIFO scheduling as soon as your program is loaded. However, hogging a single core on a Raspberry Pi can have some undesirable effects. To avoid these it is a good idea to only enable FIFO scheduling when it is absolutely needed or to use the yield command at regular intervals.

For example, if you are writing a program that has to decode an incoming pulse stream then using FIFO scheduling for the time it actually does the decoding is the best option. After the decoding is complete, return to SCHED_OTHER.

It is true that no amount of scheduling is going to convert the Raspberry Pi into a real-time system as it is not real-time hardware nor is it configured to be. There are things the CPU has to do to keep the Pi running and these cannot be disabled.

The best you can achieve with the Pi Zero is to effectively lock your task into its single core and keep the CPU uninterrupted for a one-second period and accept the 50 ms interrupt. You can only guarantee to respond to external events in 50 ms. Of course you still have the 0.5 microsecond interrupts every 1.25 ms to take into account, but unless you are working with below 1 microsecond timings these are not usually a problem.

For the quad core Pi 2 and 3 you can use one of the cores to keep your program running and only have the 0.6 microsecond pulse every 0.125 ms and 15 microsecond pulse every 10 ms to worry about.

So we really do have near real time Linux if not actual real time Linux.

Chapter 8

Pulse Width Modulation, Servos And More

One way around the problem of getting a fast response from a microcontroller is to move the problem away from the processor. In the case of the Pi's processor there are some built-in devices that can use GPIO lines to implement protocols without the CPU being involved. In this chapter we take a close look at pulse width modulation (PWM) including, sound, driving LEDs and servos.

At their most basic output function, the GPIO lines can be set high or low by the processor. How fast they can be set high or low depends on the speed of the processor.

Using the GPIO line in its Pulse Width Modulation (PWM) mode you can generate pulse trains up to 4.8 MHz, i.e. pulses as short as just a little more than 0.08 microseconds. You can even go faster if you are prepared to do some additional work. The reason for the increase in speed is that the GPIO is connected to a pulse generator and, once set to generate pulses of a specific type, the pulse generator just gets on with it without needing any intervention from the GPIO line or the processor. In fact, the pulse output can continue after your program has ended if you forget to reset it.

Of course, even though the PWM line can generate pulses as short as 0.1 microseconds, it can only change the pulses it produces each time that the processor can modify it. For example, you can't use PWM to produce a single 0.1 microsecond pulse because you can't disable the PWM generator in just 0.1 microseconds.

Some Basic Pi PWM Facts

There are some facts worth getting clear right from the start, although some of the meanings will only become clear as we progress.

First what is PWM? The simple answer is that a Pulse Width Modulated signal has pulses that repeat at a fixed rate - say one pulse every millisecond, but the width of the pulse can be changed.

There are two basic things to specify about the pulse train that is generated, its repetition rate and the width of each pulse. Usually the repetition rate is set as a simple repeat period and the width of each pulse is specified as a percentage of the repeat period the duty cycle.

111

So, for example, a 1 ms repeat and a 50% duty cycle specifies a 1 ms period which is high for 50% of the time i.e. a pulse width of 0.5 ms. The two extremes are 100% duty cycle, i.e. the line is always high, and 0% duty cycle i.e. the line is always low.

Notice it is the duty cycle that carries the information in PWM and not the frequency. What this means is that generally you select a repeat rate and stick to it and what you change as the program runs is the duty cycle.

In many cases PWM is implemented using special PWM generator hardware that is built either into the processor chip or provided by an external chip. The processor simply sets the repeat rate by writing to a register and then changes the duty cycle by writing to another register. This generally provides the best sort of PWM with no load on the processor and generally glitch free operation. You can even buy add-on boards that will provide additional channels of PWM without adding to the load on the processor.

The alternative to dedicated PWM hardware is to implement it in software. You can quite easily work out how to do this. All you need is to set a timing loop to set the line high at the repetition rate and then set it low again according to the duty cycle. You can implement this either using interrupts or a polling loop and in more advanced ways such as using a DMA channel.

In the case of the Pi, the PWM lines are implemented using special PWM hardware.

The big problem is that, although there are two PWM implementations, both are only available on the Pi2/3 and even in this case the second PWM is used for sound generation. However as long as you don't want to use sound you can use both PWM channels on the Pi 2/3 and this is enough to run two servos or motors. The main PWM channel zero is brought out on the connector on pin12 via GPIO 18. The secondary channel which is also used by the system for sound generation is brought out on the connector on pin 35 via GPIO 13. As already mentioned, you can only use GPIO 13 if you don't want sound generation.

Both PWM lines are driven by the same clock and this sometime causes people to conclude that the two lines must work at the same repeat rate. Although there are some restrictions, each PWM line can be set to its own repeat rate.

Two PWM lines is limiting and often forces users to either use hardware expansion or implement PWM in software.

As you can guess - there are no PWM inputs, just the one output. If for some reason you need to decode or respond to a PWM input then you need to program it using the GPIO input lines and the pulse measuring techniques introduced in the previous chapters.

PWM Modes

The PWM hardware is more sophisticated than you might have encountered before. The first big difference is that it can work in two modes - **mark/space** or **balanced**. In fact there are even more options but these are the only two that have a common use.

In mark/space mode you simply have a repeat rate and a duty cycle. This is precisely what you need if you want to drive a traditional PWM device such as a servo motor. However, for other applications where the PWM signal is being used as a simple D to A converter, this is not the best way to send out a pulse train with a given duty cycle.

For example, suppose you want 1KHz pulse train with a 50% duty cycle pulse train to say deliver 50% power or voltage to a device. The mark/space way of doing this switches the GPIO line on for 500 microseconds and off for 500 microseconds. The fluctuations in voltage are very slow and this causes problems for the driven device. A better way would be to divide the time into, say, 1 microsecond blocks and spread the on and off times throughout the block. In this case the device would be high for 1 microsecond and low for 1 microsecond and the filtering problems would be much easier to solve.

This idea of distributing the duty cycle over the full repeat period is what balanced mode implements. It is much more suitable for applications such as DtoA conversion and driving loads such as LEDs or motors.

The clock that is supplied to the PWM hardware doesn't set the repeat rate, but the smallest unit of change on the PWM output line. In balanced mode it specifies the shortest high or low times for the pulse train. The way this works is that you specify a repeat rate in terms of a range parameter which is used to count down to zero at the clock rate. For example, if you set a clock rate of 1KHz and a range of 1024 then the repeat rate is 1/1024Khz, i.e. 0.99Hz because the PWM cycle starts over after 1024 clock pulses.

In mark/space mode a 50% duty cycle would simply mean holding the line high for 512 clock pulses and then low for 512 clock pulses and so on.

In balanced mode a 50% duty cycle would mean pulses 500 microseconds high and 500 microseconds low. Note that the repeat rate would still be 0,99Hz, but the signal would be much higher frequency even though it was a 50% duty cycle.

It is clear that the range sets the repeat rate. What sets the duty cycle? The answer is there is a data parameter which specifies how long the line should be held high. So, for example, if range is 1024 and data is 512 the duty cycle is 50%. In mark/space mode the line is held high for the first 512 counts and low for the remainder of the 1024 counts. In balanced mode the line is held high for 512 counts spread over the total 1024 counts.

Obviously using this way of specifying repeat rate and duty cycle means that you can select more than one range and data value for any given duty cycle. For example, a range of 4 and data of 2 is also a 50% duty cycle. So how do you choose a suitable pair of values?

The range gives you the possible number of duty cycle steps you can use. For example for a range of 2 you modify the duty cycle to 0, 50 or 100% by setting data to 0, 1 or 2. A range of 512 gives you 512 steps and is usually called 8-bit PWM and a range of 1024 gives you 1024 duty cycle steps and is usually called 16-bit PWM.

To summarize:

- The PWM clock gives the smallest unit of change of the PWM line
- The range gives the repeat rate of the pulse train
- repeat frequency = clock frequency/(2*range)
- The range gives the resolution of the duty cycle (1/range%) or the number of duty cycle steps that are available
- If you want to set duty cycle d% then data = range*d/100

You can now see why the clock frequency being supplied to the two PWM units doesn't constrain them to the same repeat rate. They can work at different rates as long as they can tolerate different duty cycle resolutions and hence range values.

PWM Functions

The bcm2835 library provides PWM in an easy to use form. Its functions allow you to set the parameters of both PWM channels, even though you can't use both on the Pi 1. The fundamental frequency of the PWM is set by:

```
void bcm2835_pwm_set_clock (uint32_t divisor)
```

You can't set the clock speed directly. Instead you have to specify a divisor to reduce the 19.2MHz clock to a lower rate. The library provides some standard settings:

```
BCM2835_PWM_CLOCK_DIVIDER_2048    9.375kHz
BCM2835_PWM_CLOCK_DIVIDER_1024   18.75kHz
BCM2835_PWM_CLOCK_DIVIDER_512    37.5kHz
BCM2835_PWM_CLOCK_DIVIDER_256    75kHz
BCM2835_PWM_CLOCK_DIVIDER_128    150kHz
BCM2835_PWM_CLOCK_DIVIDER_64     300kHz
BCM2835_PWM_CLOCK_DIVIDER_32     600.0kHz
BCM2835_PWM_CLOCK_DIVIDER_16     1.2MHz
BCM2835_PWM_CLOCK_DIVIDER_8      2.4MHz
BCM2835_PWM_CLOCK_DIVIDER_4      4.8MHz
BCM2835_PWM_CLOCK_DIVIDER_2      9.6MHz
BCM2835_PWM_CLOCK_DIVIDER_1      4.6875kHz
```

The largest divider you can specify is 0xFFF, or 4096, which gives the same frequency as specifying 1, i.e. 4.6875kHz. An important point to remember is that the clock rate is not the PWM repeat rate. How the PWM pulses are created depends on the selected mode:

```
void bcm2835_pwm_set_mode (uint8_t channel,
                           uint8_t markspace, uint8_t enabled)
```

channel has to be 0 or 1, markspace is 1 for markspace mode and 0 for balanced and enabled is 1 to start the PWM pulses running.

Finally you can set the range using:

```
void bcm2835_pwm_set_range (uint8_t channel, uint32_t range)
```

and you can set data using:

```
void bcm2835_pwm_set_data (uint8_t channel, uint32_t data)
```

The largest value of range that seems to work in practice is 0xFF FFFF, which is over 268 million clock pulses, which at the highest clock rate is around 30 seconds per repeat.

Selecting a Clock and Range

One of the basic problems in using the Pi's PWM is selecting a clock divider and range value. There is a fairly standard way of doing this. The best way to work out a configuration that gives a particular repeat rate is to start at the highest clock rate, i.e. 9.6MHz with a divider of 2, and work out the range needed.

If you need a particular repeat rate given in seconds then:

$$\text{max range} = \text{repeat time} * \text{clock frequency}$$
$$= \text{repeat time} * 9.6 * 1000$$

if the repeat time is in milliseconds.

Similarly if the repeat rate is specified as a frequency then the max range is

$$\text{max range} = \text{clock frequency} / \text{repeat frequency}$$
$$= 9.6 / \text{repeat frequency}$$

This gives you the maximum range you can use.

If you actually want a smaller range you can reduce the clock to a lower frequency and the divider you need is:

$$\text{divider} = 2 * \text{max range} / \text{desired range}$$

The two is because the smallest divider you can use is 2.

If after rounding the divider and range don't give you an accurate enough signal you have no choice but to try multiples of the range - i.e. try range*2, range*3 with the corresponding dividers i.e. divider/2, divider/3 and so on. Of course, this means you have to work with data*2, data*3 and so on but this isn't difficult.

Using PWM

So now you know how to make use of the PWM lines. All you have to do is set the frequency, range and data. You also have to set the mode of the GPIO pin that you are using the correct Alt mode. As we only have two PWM pins, you set GPIO 18 to ALT5 and GPIO 13 to ALT0:

```
bcm2835_gpio_fsel(18,BCM2835_GPIO_FSEL_ALT5 );
bcm2835_gpio_fsel(13,BCM2835_GPIO_FSEL_ALT0 );
```

The simplest PWM program you can write is:

```
#include <bcm2835.h>
int main(int argc, char** argv) {
  if (!bcm2835_init())
      return 1;
  bcm2835_gpio_fsel(18,BCM2835_GPIO_FSEL_ALT5 );
  bcm2835_pwm_set_clock(2);
  bcm2835_pwm_set_mode(0, 1, 1);
  bcm2835_pwm_set_range(0,2);
  bcm2835_pwm_set_data(0,1);
  return (EXIT_SUCCESS);
}
```

The clock is set to its fastest (9.6MHz) and PWM0 is set to mark/space mode with range 2 and data 1. This produces the fastest pulse train with one clock pulse high and one low:

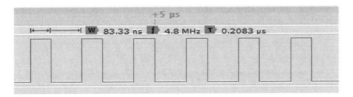

You have to set the value first and then set the period, otherwise the PWM line isn't setup properly. You also have to set the period for each pin you are using, even if it does set the same period. Notice that there is no need to put the program into an infinite loop. Once the PWM line has been set up and enabled it just gets on with generating the pulse train, no matter what the processor does. In this case the pulse generation continues long after the program has ended.

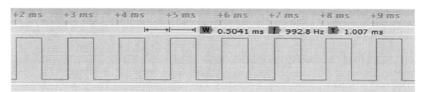

This may be fast, but as a PWM signal it is completely useless because you cannot change its duty cycle to anything useful. In practice you need to set range to something greater than .

Just to demonstrate that two PWM lines can be used independently of one another here is a program that sets each one of the PWM GPIO lines to a different duty cycle and repeat rate:

```
#include <stdio.h>
#include <stdlib.h>
#include <bcm2835.h>
int main(int argc, char** argv) {
  if (!bcm2835_init())
        return 1;
 bcm2835_gpio_fsel(18,BCM2835_GPIO_FSEL_ALT5 );
 bcm2835_gpio_fsel(13,BCM2835_GPIO_FSEL_ALT0 );

 bcm2835_pwm_set_clock(2);

 bcm2835_pwm_set_mode(0, 1, 1);
 bcm2835_pwm_set_range(0,2);
 bcm2835_pwm_set_data(0,1);

 bcm2835_pwm_set_mode(1, 1, 1);
 bcm2835_pwm_set_range(1,8);
 bcm2835_pwm_set_data(1,2);
 return (EXIT_SUCCESS);
}
```

You can see the result in the following logic analyzer display:

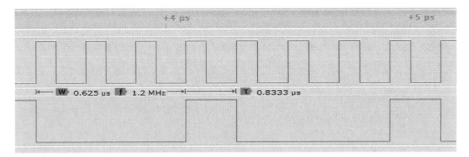

How Fast Can You Modulate?

In most cases the whole point is to vary the duty cycle or the period of the pulse train, for reasons that will be discussed later. This means that the next question is how fast can you change the characteristic of a PWM line? In other words, how fast can you change the duty cycle, say? There is no easy way to give an exact answer and in most applications an exact answer isn't of much value. The reason is that for a PWM signal to convey information it generally has to deliver a number of complete cycles with a given duty cycle. This is because of the way pulses are often averaged in applications.

We also have another problem – synchronization. There is no way to swap from one duty cycle to another exactly when a complete duty cycle has just finished. What this means is that there is going to be a glitch when you switch from one duty cycle to another. Of course, this glitch becomes less important as you slow the rate of duty cycle change and exactly what is usable depends on the application. For example, if you try changing the duty cycle about every 200 microseconds and the repeat is 25 microseconds then you are going to see roughly three to four pulses per duty cycle:

```
bcm2835_gpio_fsel(18, BCM2835_GPIO_FSEL_ALT5);
bcm2835_pwm_set_clock(2);
bcm2835_pwm_set_mode(0, 1, 1);
bcm2835_pwm_set_range(0, 256);
for (;;) {
    bcm2835_pwm_set_data(0, 10);
    bcm2835_delayMicroseconds(10);
    bcm2835_pwm_set_data(0, 200);
    bcm2835_delayMicroseconds(10);
}
```

This results in a fairly irregular pulse pattern:

Notice that now we are using an 8 bit duty cycle resolution and setting the duty cycle from 10/256 to 200/256.

The timing of the change and the time it takes to make the change cause the glitches between duty cycles so sometimes we get two and sometimes just one cycle of each duty cycle. The point is that there is time lost in changing the duty cycle and you simply cannot use PWM with modulation that involves just a few cycles. If you change and generate duty cycle changes every 500 microseconds or so, the pattern looks a lot better because you are going to see 19 to 20 pulses before each change.

What all this is really about is trying to lower your expectation of how sophisticated you can be in using PWM.

The fastest PWM repetition rate that you can use is about 25 microseconds for an 8 bit resolution and to minimize the glitches you need to leave the duty cycle stable for 10 to 20 pulses i.e. about 200-600 microseconds. In many applications this is very acceptable but don't expect to use PWM to send coded data and using it for waveform synthesis as a DtoA converter is limited to around 4KHz.

Uses of PWM - DtoA

What sorts of things do you use PWM for? There are lots of very clever uses for PWM. However, there are two use cases which account for most PWM applications - voltage or power modulation and signaling to servos.

The amount of power delivered to a device by a pulse train is proportional to the duty cycle. A pulse train that has a 50% duty cycle is delivering current to the load only 50% of the time and this is irrespective of the pulse repetition rate. So duty cycle controls the power but the period still matters in many situations because you want to avoid any flashing or other effects. A higher frequency smooths out the power flow at any duty cycle.

If you add a low pass filter to the output of a PWM signal then what you get is a voltage that is proportional to the duty cycle. This can be looked at in many different ways, but it is again the result of the amount of power delivered by a PWM signal. You can also think of it as using the filter to remove the high frequency components of the signal leaving only the slower components due to the modulation of the duty cycle.

How fast you can work depends on the duty cycle resolution you select. If you work with 8 bit resolution your DtoA will have 256 steps which at 3.3V gives a potential resolution of 3.3/256 or about 13mV. This is often good enough. At the fastest clock rate this gives a repetition rate of 37.5KHz which sounds as if it should be enough for audio synthesis.

The PWM output in this configuration mimics the workings of an 8-bit AtoD converter. You set the duty cycle using the data value 0 to 256 and you get a voltage output that is 3.3*data/256V. The repetition rate is around 25 microseconds and the usual rule of thumb is that you need 10 pulses to occur per conversion, i.e. the maximum frequency you can produce is pulse rate/10. This means that the fastest signal you can create about 3KHz, which isn't fast enough for a great many applications and you can't use it for sound synthesis, in particular.

To demonstrate the sort of approach that you can take to DtoA conversion, the following program creates a triangle or ramp waveform:

```
for (;;) {
    for (i = 0; i < 256; i = i + 10) {
        bcm2835_pwm_set_data(0, i);
        bcm2835_delayMicroseconds(100);
    }
}
```

The inner for loop sets a value of 0 to 256 in steps of 10, i.e. 300mV per step, and the delay of 100 microseconds produces a total loop time of over 106 microseconds. This means that around three or four pulses of each 25 microsecond duty cycle should be produced. This is far too few, but it is interesting to see what happens. The waveform repeats after around 2.5 ms, which makes the frequency around 400Hz. Using an oscilloscope, the measured repeat is more like 2.3ms or 430Hz.

To see the analog wave form we need to put the digital output into a low pass filter. A simple resistor and capacitor work reasonably well:

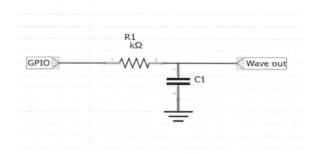

The filter's cutoff is 17KHz and might be a little on the high side for this low frequency output.

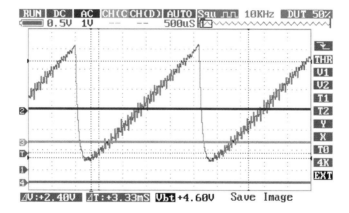

You can create a sine wave, or any other waveform you need, using the same techniques, but 400-800Hz is a practical upper limit on what you can manage.

If you already know that the PWM outputs are used to create audio on the Pi, you might be wondering how this is possible with an 800Hz upper limit? The answer is that there are other clock sources, up to 500MHz, that can be used to drive the PWM lines. If you change to mode 0, i.e. balanced output, the oscilloscope trace looks little different but there is a lot more spurious RF interference generated.

Music?

So how can the Pi generate musical notes? The simplest solution is not to try to generate anything other than a square wave. That is, use the pulse period rather than duty cycle.

As the frequency of middle C is 281.6Hz, using a clock rate of 9.6Mhz you would have set range to a period of 34091 to get the correct frequency:

```
range= clock frequency/target frequency=34091
```

So to generate middle C you could use:

```
bcm2835_gpio_fsel(18, BCM2835_GPIO_FSEL_ALT5);
bcm2835_gpio_fsel(13, BCM2835_GPIO_FSEL_ALT0);
bcm2835_pwm_set_clock(2);
bcm2835_pwm_set_mode(0, 1, 1);
int C=34091;
bcm2835_pwm_set_range(0, C);
bcm2835_pwm_set_data(0, C/2);
```

The resulting output is a square wave with a measured frequency of 281.5Hz, which isn't particularly nice to listen to. You can improve it by feeding it though a simple low pass filter like the one used above for waveform synthesis.

You can lookup the frequencies for other notes and use a table to generate them.

Controlling An LED

You can also use PWM to generate real world physical quantities such as the brightness of an LED or the rotation rate of a DC motor. The only differences required by these applications are to do with the voltage and current you need and the way duty cycle relates to whatever the physical effect is. In other words, if you want to change some effect by 50%, how much do you need to change the duty cycle?

For example how do we "dim an LED"?

By changing the duty cycle of the PWM pulse train you can set the amount of power delivered to an LED, or any other device, and hence change its brightness. In the case of an LED the connection between duty cycle and brightness is a complicated matter but the simplest approach uses the fact that the perceived brightness is roughly proportional to the cube of the input power. The exact relationship is more complicated but this is good enough for most applications. As the power supplied to the LED is proportional to the duty cycle we have:

$$b=kd^3$$

where b is the perceived brightness and d is the duty cycle. The constant k depends on the LED.

Notice that as the LED when powered by a PWM signal is either full on or full off, there is no effect of the change in LED light output with current - the LED is always run at the same current.

What all of this means is that if you want an LED to fade in a linear fashion you need to change the duty cycle in a non-linear fashion. Intuitively it means that changes when the duty cycle is small produce bigger changes in brightness than when the duty cycle is large.

For a simple example we need to connect a standard LED to the PWM line.

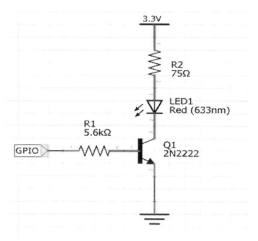

Given that all of the Pi's GPIO lines work at 3.3V and ideally only supply a few milliamps, we need a transistor to drive the LED which typically draws 20mA.

You could use a Field Effect Transistor (FET) of some sort, but for this sort of application an old-fashioned Bipolar Junction Transistor (BJT) works very well and is cheap and available in a through-hole mount, i.e. it comes with wires.

Almost any general purpose npn transistor will work, but the 2N2222 is very common:

R1 restricts the current to 0.48mA, which is very low, and assuming that the transistor has a minimum gain (hfe) of 50, this provides 24mA to power it.

R2 limits the current to 20mA. Notice that all of these values are for a red LED with forward voltage drop of 1.8V and typical current 20mA. LEDs of different colors have different forward voltage drops and currents.

If you are using the 2N2222 then the pinouts are:

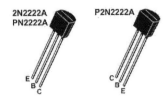

And of course, as always the positive terminal on the LED is the long pin.

Assuming that you have this circuit constructed then a simple PWM program to modify its brightness from low to high and back to low in a loop is:

```
if (!bcm2835_init())
    return 1;
bcm2835_gpio_fsel(18, BCM2835_GPIO_FSEL_ALT5);
bcm2835_pwm_set_clock(2);
bcm2835_pwm_set_mode(0, 1, 1);
bcm2835_pwm_set_range(0, 1024);
int w = 1;
int inc = 1;
for (;;) {
    bcm2835_pwm_set_data(0, w);
    w = w + inc;
    if (w > 1024 || w <= 0)inc = -inc;
    bcm2835_delayMicroseconds(5000);
}
```

The basic idea is to set up a pulse train with a period of 1ms. Next, in the for loop, the duty cycle is set to 0% to 100% and then back down to 0%.

If you watch the flashing you will see that it changes brightness very quickly and then seems to spend a long time "stuck" at almost full brightness and then suddenly starts to dim rapidly. This is a consequence of the way the human eye perceives light output as a function of input power.

Changing the LED brightness

What about a linear change in brightness?

To achieve this reasonably accurately isn't difficult all we need to do is increase the power, or equivalently the duty cycle, in steps that are cubic. If we just use 0 to 10 cubed we get a pulse width of 0 to 1000, which is ideal for our 1024 pulse range used in the previous example, i.e. a duty cycle going from 0 to close to 100%.

If you need the ultimate speed you could precompute the powers, but for simplicity we will just use integer multiplication:

```
int w = 0;
   int inc = 1;
   for (;;) {
       bcm2835_pwm_set_data(0, w*w*w);
       w = w + inc;
       if (w > 10 || w <= 0)inc = -inc;
       bcm2835_delayMicroseconds(50000);
   }
```

As this produces 10 cubic steps, a bcm2835_delayMicroseconds of 50,000 makes each step last 50 ms, and so it takes 500 ms to go from low to high. If you try the program you should find that you see the LED increase steadily towards a maximum and then decrease steadily to a minimum.

If you replace the delay with a value of 100,000 then you will get a 1 second cycle, which using only ten steps starts to look a little too flashy. You can increase the number of steps by simply dividing by a suitable factor. If you cube 1 to 20 you get 1 to 8000 and dividing by 8 gives 0 to 1000. Dividing by 8 is just a matter of three right shifts and, while not very accurate, does allow fast computation with integer arithmetic:

```
int w = 0;
int inc = 1;
for (;;) {
    bcm2835_pwm_set_data(0, (w*w*w)>>3);
    w = w + inc;
    if (w > 20 || w <= 0)inc = -inc;
    bcm2835_delayMicroseconds(50000);
}
```

Notice that now as there are twice as many steps. we only need each one to last half the time, i.e. 50,000 microseconds.

You can also set the PWM to mode 0, i.e. balanced mode:

```
bcm2835_pwm_set_mode(0, 0, 1);
```

This does make the LED look even smoother, but the increase in RF noise makes it essential to put the Pi in a metal case.

In most cases it is irrelevant exactly how linear the response of the LED is; a rough approximation looks as smooth to the human eye. The only exception is when you are trying to drive LEDs to create a gray level or color display when color calibration is another level of accuracy.

Controlling a Servo

Hobby servos, the sort used in radio control models, are very cheap and easy to use and the Pi has enough PWM lines to control two of them without much in the way of extras.

A basic servo has just three connections, ground, a power line and a signal line. The colors used vary, but the power line is usually red, ground is usually black or brown and the signal line is white, yellow or orange.

The power wire has to be connected to 5V supply capable of providing enough current to run the motor - anything up to 500mA or more depending on the servo. In general you cannot power a full size servo from the Pi's 5V pin; you need a separate power supply. You can power some micro servos directly from the Pi's 5V, line but you need to check the specifications. The good news is that the servo signal line generally needs very little current, although it does need to be switched between 0 and 5V using a PWM signal.

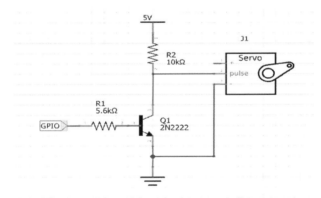

You can assume that the signal line needs to be driven as a voltage load and so the appropriate way to drive the servo is:

- The servo's + line needs to be connected to an external 5V power supply unless it is a micro servo when it might be possible to power it from the Pi's 5V line.

- The 10K resistor R1 can be a lot larger for most servos - 47K often works. The 5.6K resistor limits the base current to slightly less than 0.5mA.

Now all we have to do is set the PWM line to produce 20ms pulses with pulse widths ranging from 0.5 to 2.5 ms.

As described earlier, the best way to work out a configuration that gives a particular repeat rate is to start at the highest clock rate and work out the range needed. For example, with a clock of 9.6MHz the range needed to give a 20ms repeat rate is:

```
max range = repeat time*clock frequency = 192000
```

This gives you the maximum range you can use. If you actually want a smaller range you can reduce the clock to a lower frequency and the divider you need is:

```
divider =2* max range/desired range
```

because the smallest divider you can use is 2.

So, to get a range of 1024, i.e. a 16 bit resolution we need a clock divider of:

```
divider=2*192000/1024= 375
```

If you use a divider of 375 and a range of 1024 you will find that the repetition rate is, as promised, 20ms.

Most servos work on a pulse width ranging from 500 microseconds to 2.5 milliseconds, or a duty cycle of 2.5% to 12.5%, but this varies quite a lot according to the servo.

Using a range of 1024 this corresponds to values of data from 25 to 128.

The simplest servo program you can write is something like:

```
if (!bcm2835_init())
        return 1;

    bcm2835_gpio_fsel(18, BCM2835_GPIO_FSEL_ALT5);
    bcm2835_pwm_set_clock(375);
    bcm2835_pwm_set_mode(0, 1, 1);
    bcm2835_pwm_set_range(0, 1024);

    for(;;){
     bcm2835_pwm_set_data(0,25);
     bcm2835_delayMicroseconds(2000000);
     bcm2835_pwm_set_data(0, 50);
     bcm2835_delayMicroseconds(2000000);
     bcm2835_pwm_set_data(0, 128);
     bcm2835_delayMicroseconds(2000000);
    }
```

This moves the servo to three positions, pausing between each. If you run the program using the circuit given earlier, you will discover that the servo does nothing at all - apart perhaps from vibrating.

The reason is that the transistor voltage driver is an inverter. When the PWM line is high the transistor is fully on and the servo's pulse line is effectively grounded. When the PWM line is low the transistor is fully off and the servo's pulse line is pulled high by the resistor.

A common solution to this problem is to drive the servo using an emitter-follower configuration, but in this case this isn't possible because the maximum voltage an emitter-follower configuration would generate is

$$3.3-0.6=2.7V$$

which is too low to drive most servos.

The standard solution in this case is to use two transistors to generate a non-inverted pulse, but it is possible to use a single transistor in a non-inverting configuration.

The simplest solution of all is to ignore the problem in hardware and solve the problem in software.

This is generally a good approach to take - before you consider modifying the hardware always see if there is an easier software fix.

Instead of generating 20ms pulses with pulse widths 0.5 to 2.5ms, you can generate an inverted pulse with 20ms pulses with widths in the range 17.5 to 19 ms. The principle is that if the servo needs a 10% duty cycle we supply it with a 90% duty cycle which the inverter converts back to a 10% duty cycle.

The range of duty cycles we need goes from 17.5 ms to 19.5 ms which in percentages is 87.5% to 97.5% or as values 895 to 997.

Simple math can convert an angle T to a value in the range 895 to 997:

```
value = (997-895)/180*T+895 = 138*T/180+895
```

To make sure this works with all servos, it is a good to restrict the range to 1ms to 2ms or inverted 18ms to 19ms and hence values from 920 to 972

```
value=52*T/190+920
```

So we can write the same testing program as:

```
if (!bcm2835_init())
        return 1;
  bcm2835_gpio_fsel(18, BCM2835_GPIO_FSEL_ALT5);
  bcm2835_pwm_set_clock(375);
  bcm2835_pwm_set_mode(0, 1, 1);
  bcm2835_pwm_set_range(0, 1024);

  for(;;){
   bcm2835_pwm_set_data(0,52 * 0 / 180 + 920);
   bcm2835_delayMicroseconds(2000000);
   bcm2835_pwm_set_data(0, 52 * 90 / 180 + 920);
   bcm2835_delayMicroseconds(2000000);
   bcm2835_pwm_set_data(0, 52 * 180/ 180 + 920);
   bcm2835_delayMicroseconds(2000000);
  }
```

If you run this program you should find that the servo moves as promised. However, it might not reach its limits of movement.

Servos differ in how they respond to the input signal and you might need to calibrate the pulse widths. Many robot implementations, for example, calibrate the servos to find their maximum movement using either mechanical switches to detect when the servo is at the end of its range or a vision sensor.

You can see from the logic analyzer plot that the PWM pulse train at the GPIO pin is "inverted" as desired.

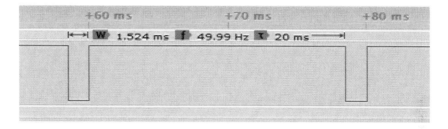

Non-Inverting Drivers

The software solution to driving a servo via a simple inverting buffer is elegant, although slightly messy when it comes to computing the duty cycle needed. The traditional solution is to use two transistors to create a non-inverting buffer:

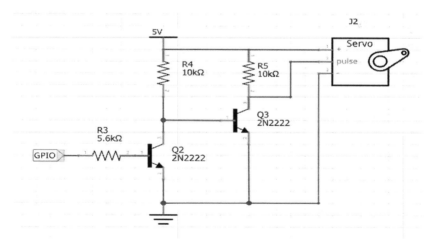

There is a way to use a single transistor as a non-inverting buffer using a common base configuration:

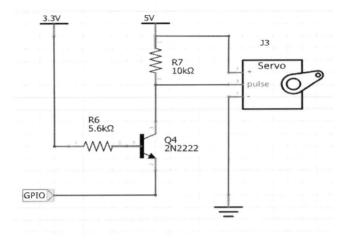

In this variation on a common base mode, the transistor's base is connected to the 3.3V line and its collector to the 5V supply. Note that the two power supplies have to share a common earth.

If the GPIO output is low then R6 sets the base emitter voltage to 0.6V and the transistor is hard on, pulling the output to the servo low.

If the GPIO output is high the base emitter voltage is zero and the transistor is cut off, making the output to the servo high.

You can see that this is non-inverting, but the problem is that the current that flows through R7 is also the emitter current, which is the current the GPIO line has to sink. What this means is that the current in R7 is limited to around 1mA and this circuit provides no amplification. Of course, you could add another transistor to provide current amplification, but in this case you would be better off going back to the standard 2-transistor arrangement.

This circuit does, however, work with most servos so in this role it is useful. The current in the GPIO line is 1mA and this is well within the drive power of a standard GPIO line.

Here is a "non-inverted" version of the test program given earlier. The range of duty cycle is limited to make sure it works with all servos. Change the range or center value to make it work with your servo:

```
if (!bcm2835_init())
      return 1;
  bcm2835_gpio_fsel(18, BCM2835_GPIO_FSEL_ALT5);
  bcm2835_pwm_set_clock(375);
  bcm2835_pwm_set_mode(0, 1, 1);
  bcm2835_pwm_set_range(0, 1024);

  for(;;){
   bcm2835_pwm_set_data(0,30);
   bcm2835_delayMicroseconds(2000000);
    bcm2835_pwm_set_data(0, 70);
    bcm2835_delayMicroseconds(2000000);
    bcm2835_pwm_set_data(0, 110);
    bcm2835_delayMicroseconds(2000000);
  }
```

What Else Can You Use PWM For?

PWM lines are incredibly versatile and it is always worth asking the question "could I use PWM?" when you are considering almost any problem.

The LED example shows how you can use PWM as a power controller. You can extend this idea to a computer controlled switch mode power supply. All you need is a capacitor to smooth out the voltage and perhaps a transformer to change the voltage.

You can also use PWM to control the speed of a DC motor and if you add a simple bridge circuit you can control its direction and speed.

Finally, you can use a PWM signal as a modulated carrier for data communications. For example, most infrared controller make use of a 38KHz carrier, which is roughly a 26 microseconds. This is switched on and off for 1 ms and this is well within the range that the PWM can manage. So all you have to do is replace the red LED in the previous circuit with an infrared LED and you have the start of a remote control or data transmission link.

Some Hardware Details

Advanced Topic

The PWM hardware is more complicated than what is required just to produced a simple PWM signal. It also has a serialize mode, which can clock a 32-bit word out of a register to create a pulse train with the characteristic you require. To make this even more useful, it also supports the use of DMA to keep the serialization queue full. These features are beyond the scope of this book, but if you understand how things work they are not difficult to use.

The PWM has a large number of registers associated with it including a control register and status register for both channels and a pair of data and range registers for each channel, plus a DMA and a FIFO register for serialization.

The offsets from bcm2835_pwm as word addresses are:

```
BCM2835_PWM_CONTROL 0
BCM2835_PWM_STATUS  1
BCM2835_PWM_DMAC    2
BCM2835_PWM0_RANGE  4
BCM2835_PWM0_DATA   5
BCM2835_PWM_FIF1    6
BCM2835_PWM1_RANGE  8
BCM2835_PWM1_DATA   9
```

There is also a single clock which has the same registers as the GP clocks described in the previous chapter with word offset from bcm2835_clk given by:

```
BCM2835_PWMCLK_CNTL    40
BCM2835_PWMCLK_DIV     41
```

You can look up the details of the control and status registers and write your own functions to make use of the addition modes of operation.

One easy to implement and useful addition is to modify the PWM clock source and rate. The function given at the end of the previous chapter is easy to modify to work with the PWM clock:

```
void bcm2835_pwm_set_clock_source(
        uint32_t source,
        uint32_t divisorI,
        uint32_t divisorF) {

if (bcm2835_clk == MAP_FAILED
        || bcm2835_pwm == MAP_FAILED)
  return;
divisorI &= 0xfff;
divisorF &= 0xfff;
source &= 0xf;
uint8_t mask = bcm2835_peri_read(bcm2835_clk +
                    BCM2835_PWMCLK_CNTL) & 0xffffffef;
bcm2835_peri_write(bcm2835_clk + BCM2835_PWMCLK_CNTL,
                    BCM2835_PWM_PASSWRD | mask);
while ((bcm2835_peri_read(bcm2835_clk +
                    BCM2835_PWMCLK_CNTL) & 0x80) != 0) {};
bcm2835_peri_write(bcm2835_clk + BCM2835_PWMCLK_DIV,
        BCM2835_PWM_PASSWRD|(divisorI << 12) | divisorF);
bcm2835_peri_write(bcm2835_clk + BCM2835_PWMCLK_CNTL,
                BCM2835_PWM_PASSWRD|source| 0x200);
bcm2835_peri_write(bcm2835_clk + BCM2835_PWMCLK_CNTL,
                BCM2835_PWM_PASSWRD 0x210|source);
}
```

This works in the same way as the previous function. If first disables the clock, then sets the new divisor and source and then enables the clock again.

If you use PLLD then the clock can be as high as 500MHz. This allows you to set a range of 256 and get an effective repeat frequency of 1.9MHz which means you can get a PWM sample every half a microsecond.

Repeating the previous triangle wave generator given earlier but at this new frequency pushes the upper limit on audio generation using this method to around 20KHz.

```
bcm2835_gpio_fsel(18, BCM2835_GPIO_FSEL_ALT5);
bcm2835_pwm_set_clock_source(6, 2, 0);
bcm2835_pwm_set_mode(0, 1, 1);
bcm2835_pwm_set_range(0, 256);
int i;
  for (;;) {
   for (i = 0; i < 256; i = i + 10) {
      bcm2835_pwm_set_data(0, i);
      bcm2835_delayMicroseconds(2);
   }
  }
```

Using the same filter circuit given earlier, the output looks a better when you take into account the frequency is now 20KHz:

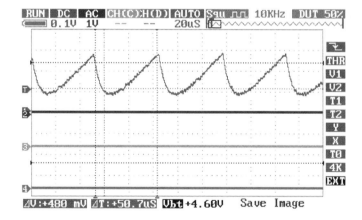

There are more sophisticated coding methods that can create higher quality audio than this simple approach. However, this at least gives you the basic tools to do the job.

Chapter 9

Using the I2C Bus

The I-Squared-C (I2C) bus is one of the most useful ways of connecting moderately sophisticated sensors and peripherals to the any processor. The only problem is that it can seem like a nightmare confusion of hardware, low level interaction and high level software. There are few general introductions to the subject because at first sight every I2C device is different, but here we present one.

The I2C bus is a serial bus that can be used to connect multiple devices to a controller. It is a simple bus that uses two active wires: one for data and one for a clock. Despite there being lots of problems in using the I2C bus because it isn't well standardized and devices can conflict and generally do things in their own way, it is still commonly used and too useful to ignore.

The big problem in getting started with the I2C bus is that you will find it described at many different levels of detail, from physical bus characteristics, the protocol, the details of individual devices. It can be difficult to relate all of this together and produce a working project. In fact you only need to know the general workings of the I2C bus, some general features of the protocol and know the addresses and commands used by any particular device.

To explain and illustrate these idea we really do have to work with a particular device to make things concrete. However the basic stages of getting things to work, the steps, the testing and verification, are more or less the same irrespective of the device.

I2C Hardware Basics

The I2C bus is very simple from the hardware point of view. It has just two signal lines, SDA and SCL, the data and clock lines respectively. Each of these lines is pulled up by a suitable resistor to the supply line at whatever voltage the devices are working at - 3.3V and 5V are common choices. The size of the pullup resistors isn't critical, but 4.7K is typical as shown in the circuit diagram.

You simply connect the SDA and SCL pins of each of the devices to the pull up resistors. Of course, if any of the devices have built-in pullup resistors you can omit the external resistors. More of a problem is if multiple devices each have pullups. In this case you need to disable all but one set.

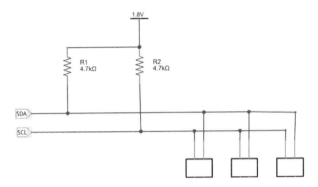

The I2C bus is an open collector bus. This means that it is actively pulled down by a transistor set to on. When the transistor is off, however, the bus returns to the high voltage state via the pullup resistor. The advantage of this approach is that multiple devices can pull the bus low at the same time. That is an open collector bus is low when one or more devices pulls it low and high when none of the devices is active.

The SCL line provides a clock which is used to set the speed of data transfer; one data bit is presented on the SDA line for each pulse on the SCL line. In all cases the master drives the clock line to control how fast bits are transferred. The slave can however hold the clock line low if it needs to slow down the data transfer. In most cases the I2C bus has a single master device, the Pi in our case, which drives the clock and invites the slaves to receive or transmit data. Multiple masters are possible, but this is advanced and not often necessary.

At this point we could go into the details of how all of this works in terms of bits. However, the bcm2835 library handles these details for us. All you really need to know is that all communication occurs in 8-bit packets. The master sends a packet, an address frame, which contains the address of the slave it wants to interact with. Every slave has to have a unique address which is usually 7 bits, but it can be 11 bits and the Pi does support this.

One of the problems in using the I2C bus is that manufacturers often use the same address or same set of selectable addresses and this can make using particular combinations of devices on the same bus difficult or impossible.

The 7-bit address is set as the high order 7 bits in the byte and this can be confusing as an address that is stated as 0x40 in the data sheet results in 0x80 being sent to the device. The low order bit of the address signals a write or a read operation depending on whether it is a 0 or a 1 respectively. After sending an address frame it then sends or receives data frames back from the slave. There are also special signals used to mark the start and end of an exchange of packets, but the library functions take care of these.

This is really all you need to know about I2C in general to get started, but it is worth finding out more of the details as you need them - you almost certainly will need them as you debug I2C programs.

The Pi I2C

The processor has three built in I2C masters referred to as BCS controllers. The Broadcom Serial controller is essentially an implementation of the I2C bus and in general you don't have to worry about incompatibilities. BSC2, is dedicated to working with the HDMI interface, and therefore isn't available for use. BSC1 is brought out on the main connector at pin 3 (GPIO2/SDA1) and pin 5 (GPIO3/SCL1). BSC0 is brought out on pin 27 (GPIO0/SDA0) and pin 28 (GPIO1/SCL0).

There are 1.6K pull-up resistors on BSC1 and this means you have to disable any provided by modules you connect to it. BSC0 is used for HAT expansion card identification and it is best avoided if possible.

The bcm2835 library only supports BSC1, but it isn't difficult to extend it to support BSC0 if required.

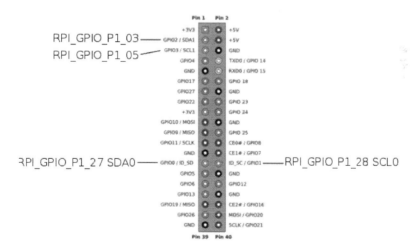

137

To summarize:

- There is one easy to use I2C bus available on pins 3 and 5 complete with 1.6K pullup resistors.
- There is an additional I2C bus on pins 27 and 28 but it is allocated to expansion EPROM use and best avoided if possible. There are no pullup resistors fitted.
- The bcm2835 library only supports the bus on pins 3 and 5.

The hardware can work at 100kHz up to 250MHz and while it supports clock stretching you have to know how to make it work, see later.

The I2C Functions

There are two initialization functions:

```
int bcm2835_i2c_begin (void)
void bcm2835_i2c_end (void)
```

The **begin** function changes pins 3 and 5 to ALT0 which gets things ready for I2C data transfer. The **end** function restores them to default GPIO inputs.

You also have to set the speed of the bus if you don't want to accept the default 100KHz and there are two functions to set the clock:

```
void bcm2835_i2c_setClockDivider(uint16_t divider)

void bcm2835_i2c_set_baudrate(uint32_t baudrate)
```

There following constants to set the clock to common frequencies.

BCM2835_I2C_CLOCK_DIVIDER_2500	*10us*	*= 100 kHz*
BCM2835_I2C_CLOCK_DIVIDER_626	*2.504us*	*= 399.3610 kHz*
BCM2835_I2C_CLOCK_DIVIDER_150	*60ns*	*= 1.666 MHz default*
BCM2835_I2C_CLOCK_DIVIDER_148	*59ns*	*= 1.689 MHz*

Note the frequencies quoted all assume a standard 250MHz clock rate.

The baud rate function is used to mimic the action of the Linux driver settings. As the library doesn't use the Linux driver, this is purely for convenience of transferring software. The baud rate is simply the clock speed in Hz.

There is also a function to set the slave devices address for subsequent read/write operations.

```
void bcm2835_i2c_setSlaveAddress(uint8_t addr)
```

Simply specify the slave's address as specified in its data sheet, noting that the 7-bit address is sent as the high order bits in the byte and that when you specify a device address the library will convert the address according to whether the operation is a write or a read. For example, a device might report an address of 0x40 on its data sheet. On the bus this would translate to a write address of 0x80 and a read address of 0x81.

Write

While there are two write functions, the basic one is:

```
uint8_t bcm2835_i2c_write(const char * buf, uint32_t len)
```

This performs a simple write of the buffer to the previously selected slave.

When you use it, first an address frame, a byte containing the address of the device you specified, is transmitted. Notice that the 7-bit address has to be shifted into the topmost bits and the first bit has to be zeroed for a write operation. So to when you write to a device with an address of 0x40 you will see 0x80 on a logic analyzer i.e. 0x40<<1. After the address frame as many data frames are sent as you specified in buf and len.

If you know about the I2C protocol, it is worth saying that the library functions deal with the start sequence and the address frame, check the NAK/ACK bit from the slave, send the data bits, check the NAK/ACK bit from the slave and send the stop sequence. That is, the usual write transaction sending n bytes is:

```
START|ADDR|ACK|DATA0|ACK|
            DATA1|ACK|
              ....
            DATAn|ACK|STOP
```

Notice that it is the slave that sends the ACK bit and if the data is not received correctly it can send NACK instead. Also notice that the Pi sends a single STOP bit when the entire transaction is complete.

A multibyte transfer is quite different from sending n single bytes one at a time.

```
START|  ADDR  |ACK|DATA0|ACK|STOP
START|  ADDR  |ACK|DATA1|ACK|STOP
      . . .
START|  ADDR  |ACK|DATAn|ACK|STOP
```

Notice that there are now multiple ADDR frames sent as well as multiple START and STOP bits. What this means in practice is that you have to look at a device's data sheet and send however many bytes it needs as a single operation. You cannot send the same number of bytes broken into chunks.

Write To A Register

A very standard interaction between master and slave is writing data to a register. This isn't anything special and, as far as the I2C bus is concerned, you are simply writing raw data. However, data sheets and users tend to think in terms of reading and writing internal storage locations i.e. registers in the device. In fact many devices have lots of internal storage, indeed some I2C devices, for example I2C EPROMS, are nothing but internal storage. In this case a standard transaction to write to a register is:

1. Send address frame
2. Send a data frame with the command to select the register
3. Send a data frame containing the byte or word to be written to the register

So, for example, you might use:

```
char buf[]={registerAddress,data};
bcm2835_i2c_write(buf,2);
```

Notice the command that has to be sent depends on the device and you have to look it up in its datasheet. Also notice that there is a single START and STOP bit at the beginning and end of the transaction.

Read

There are two read functions and the simplest follows the logic of the corresponding write function:

```
uint8_t bcm2835_i2c_read (char *buf, uint32_t len)
```

This sends an address frame and then reads as many bytes from the slave as specified. As in the case of write, the address supplied is shifted up one bit and the lower order bit set to 1 to indicate a read operation. So if the current slave is at address 0x40 the read sends a read address of 0x81.

The read transaction is:

```
START|ADDR|ACK|DATA0|ACK|
              |DATA1|ACK|
        . . .
              |DATAn|NACK|STOP
```

The master sends the address frame and the slave sends the ACK after the address to acknowledge that it has been received and it is ready to send data. Then the slave sends bytes one at a time and the master sends ACK in response to each byte. Finally master sends a NACK to indicate that the last byte has been read and then a STOP bit. That is, the master controls how many bytes are transferred.

As in the case of the write functions a block transfer of n bytes is different from transferring n bytes one at a time.

Read A Register

As for writing to a register, reading from a register is a very standard operation, but it is slightly more complicated in that you need a write and a read operation. That is. to read a register you need a write operation to send the address of the register to the device and then a read operation to get the data that the device sends as the contents of the register. So, for example, to read a register you would use something like:

```
char buf[]={registerAddress};
bcm2835_i2c_write(buf,1);
bcm2835_i2c_read(buf,1);
```

If the register sends multiple bytes then you can usually read these one after another without sending an address frame each time as a block transfer.

This write/read combination is so common that there is a second read function designed just for this application, but with an extra feature. The **read_register_rs** function will read any number of bytes from a register specified by its address.

```
uint8_t bcm2835_i2c_read_register_rs(char *regaddr,
                                     char *buf, uint32_t len)
```

In other words, this combines writing the registers address with reading it.

In theory, and mostly in practice, a register read of this sort can work with a stop-start separating the write and the read operation, which is what you get if you use separate write and read function calls:

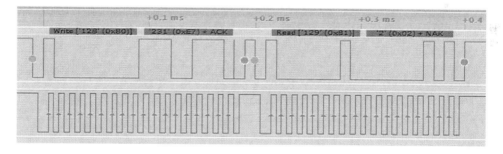

That is the transfer sequence is:

```
START|ADDR|ACK|REGADDR|ACK|STOP|
START|ADDR|ACK|DATA1|ACK|
                |DATA2|ACK|
      . . .
                |DATAn|NACK|STOP
```

If you look at the end of the write and the start of the read you will see that there is a STOP and START bit between them. For some devices this is a problem. A STOP bit is a signal that another transaction can start and this might allow another master to take over the bus. To avoid this some devices demand a repeated START bit between the write and the read and no STOP bit. This is referred to as a repeated start bit transaction. That is the sequence for a repeated start bit register read is:

```
START|ADDR|ACK|REGADDR|ACK|
START|ADDR|ACK|DATA0|ACK|
              |DATA1|ACK|
    . . .
              |DATAn|NACK|STOP
```

Notice that there is only one STOP bit.

In theory either form of transaction should work but in practice you will find that some slave devices state that they need a repeated start bit and no stop bits in continued transactions. In this case you need to be careful how you send and receive data. For example to read a register from a device that requires repeated START bits but no STOP bit you would use:

```
char buf[] = {0xE7};
bcm2835_i2c_setSlaveAddress(0x40);
bcm2835_i2c_read_register_rs(buf,buf,1);
```

You can see in the logic analyzer display that there is now just a single START bit between the write and the read.

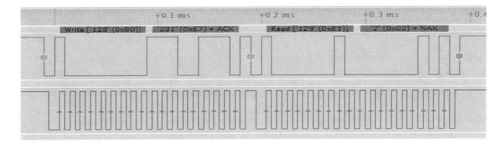

The read_register_rs function sends a single byte to select the register and then reads back as many bytes as the slave device specifies as a response.

What if you need to send more than one byte to the slave?

You can of course use separate write and read function calls, but there is a special function which will suppress the STOP bits between the write and read of any number of bytes:

```
uint8_t bcm2835_i2c_write_read_rs(char * cmds,
               uint32_t cmds_len,
               char * buf,
               uint32_t buf_len
)
```

This writes cmd_len bytes from buf and then reads buf_len bytes from the slave without putting a STOP bit between the write and read. Of course:

```
bcm2835_i2c_write_read_rs(buf,1,buf,1);
```

is the same as:

```
bcm2835_i2c_read_register_rs(buf,buf,1);
```

Very few devices need a repeated START transaction. The documentation mentions the MLX90620 IR array, but this is hardly a common peripheral. In practice it usually doesn't make any difference if you send a STOP bit in the middle of a write/read transaction but you need to know about it just in case.

Slow Read

The I2C clock is mostly controlled by the master and this raises the question of how we cope with the speed that a slave can or cannot respond to a request for data.

There are two broad approaches to waiting for data on the I2C bus.

The first is simply to request the data and then perform reads in a polling loop. If the device isn't ready with the data then it sends a data frame with a NACK bit set.

The I2C functions return one of the following codes:

BCM2835_I2C_REASON_OK	Success
BCM2835_I2C_REASON_ERROR_NACK	Received a NACK
BCM2835_I2C_REASON_ERROR_CLKT	Received Clock Stretch Timeout
BCM2835_I2C_REASON_ERROR_DATA	Not all data is sent / received

So all we have to do is test for an ERROR_NACK response. Of course, the polling loop doesn't have to be "tight". The response time is often long enough to do other things and you can use the I2C bus to work with other slave devices while the one you activated gets on with trying to get the data you requested. All you have to do is to remember to read its data at some later time.

The second way is to allow the slave to hold the clock line low after the master has released it – so called clock stretching. In most cases the master will simply wait before moving on to the next frame while the clock line is held low. This is very simple and it means you don't have to implement a polling loop but also notice that your program is frozen until the slave releases the clock line.

The Pi's implementation of I2C clock stretching has a flaw in that it fails if the clock stretching is very short. However, there is also a problem with the Linux driver and with the bcm2835 library that may account for many of the reports that I2C doesn't work at all.

143

There is a clock stretch timeout register that isn't much discussed and as there isn't a library function to set it, it tends to be ignored and this causes clock stretching to appear not to work. By default it is set to 40, but the units are I2C clock pulses. If you are using a high clock rate then 40 clock pulses can be a very short time period and not long enough for devices such as AtoD converters to complete their tasks. To make clock stretching work you have to set the timeout and you can see how to do this in the example that follows.

Many devices implement both types of slow read protocol and you can use whichever suits your application.

A Real Device

Using an I2C device has two problems - the physical connection between master and slave and figuring out what the software has to do to make it work. Here we'll work with the SparkFun HTU21D/Si7021 and the information in its data sheet to make a working temperature humidity sensor using the I2C functions we've just met.

First the hardware. The HTU21D Humidity and Temperature sensor is one of the easiest of I2C devices to use. Its only problem is that it is only available in a surface mount package. To overcome this you could solder some wires onto the pads or buy a general breakout board. However, it is much simpler to buy the SparkFun HTU21D breakout board because this has easy connections and built-in pullup resistors. The HTU21D has been replaced by the Si7021 which is more robust than the original and works the same.

If you decide to work with some other I2C device you can still follow the steps given, modifying what you do to suit it. In particular, if you select a device that only works at 5V you might need a level converter.

Wiring the HTU21D

Given that the HTU21D has pullup resistors we really should disable them for use on the Pi's internal I2C bus which already has pullups. In practice the additional pullups don't seem to make much difference to the waveforms and you can leave them in place while testing.

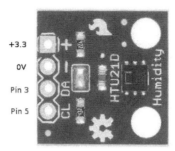

You can use a prototype board to make the connections and this makes it easier to connect other instruments such as a logic analyzer.

A First Program

After wiring up any i2C device the first question that needs to be answered is, does it work?

Unfortunately for most complex devices finding out if it works is a multi-step process. Our first program aims to read some data back from the HTU21D - any data will do.

If you look at the data sheet you will find that the device address is 0x40 and its supports the following commands/registers:

Command	Code	Comment
Trigger Temperature Measurement	0xE3	Hold master
Trigger Humidity Measurement	0xE5	Hold master
Trigger Temperature Measurement	0xF3	No Hold master
Trigger Humidity Measurement	0xF5	No Hold master
Write user register	0xE6	
Read user register	0xE7	
Soft Reset	0xFE	

The easiest of these to get started with is the Read user register command. The user register gives the current setup of the device and can be used to set the resolution of the measurement.

Notice that the codes that you send to the device can often be considered addresses or commands. In this case you can think of sending 0xE7 as a command to read the register or the read address of the register, it makes no difference. In most cases the term command is used when sending the code makes the device do something, and the term address is used when it simply makes the device read or write specific data.

To read the user register we have to write a byte containing 0xE7 and then read the byte the device sends back. This involves sending an address frame, a data frame, and then another address frame and reading a data frame. The device seems to be happy if you send a stop bit between each transaction or just a new start bit.

A program to read the user register is fairly easy to put together. The address of the device is 0x40 so its write address is 0x80 and its read address is 0x81. As the I2C functions adjust the address as needed, we simply use 0x40 as the device's address, but it does affect what you see if you sample the data being exchanged:

```
#include <stdio.h>
#include <stdlib.h>
#include <bcm2835.h>
int main(int argc, char** argv) {
if (!bcm2835_init())
        return 1;
 char buf[] = {0xE7};
 bcm2835_i2c_begin ();
 bcm2835_i2c_setSlaveAddress (0x40);
 bcm2835_i2c_write (buf,1);
 bcm2835_i2c_read (buf,1);
 printf("User Register = %X \r\n",buf[0]);
 bcm2835_i2c_end ();
 return (EXIT_SUCCESS);
}
```

This sends the address frame 0x80 and then the data byte 0xE7 to select the user register. Next it sends an address frame 0x81 to read the data.

If you run the program you will see:

```
Register= 02
```

This is the default value of the register and it corresponds to a resolution of 12 and 14 bits for the humidity and temperature respectively and a supply voltage greater than 2.25V.

The I2C Protocol in Action

If you have a logic analyzer that can interpret the I2C protocol connected, what you will see is:

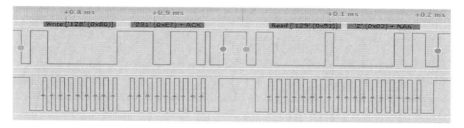

You can see that the write_byte function sends an address packet set to the device's 7-bit address 0x40 as the high order bits with the low order bit set to zero to indicate a write, i.e 0x80. After this you get a data packet sent containing 0xE7, the address of the register. After a few microseconds it sends the address frame again, only this time with the low order bit set to 1 to indicate a read. It then receives back a single byte of data from the device, 0x02. This demonstrates that the external device is working properly and we can move on to getting some data of interest.

Reading the raw temperature data

Now we come to reading one of the two quantities that the device measures – temperature. If you look back at the command table you will see that there are two possible commands for reading the temperature:

Command	Code	Comment
Trigger Temperature Measurement	0xE3	Hold master
Trigger Temperature Measurement	0xF3	No Hold master

What is the difference between Hold master and No Hold master? This was discussed earlier in a general context. The device cannot read the temperature instantaneously and the master can either opt to be held waiting for the data, i.e. hold master, or released to do something else and poll for the data until it is ready.

The hold master option works by allowing the device to stretch the clock pulse by holding the line low after the master has released it. In this mode the master will wait until the device releases the line. Not all masters support this mode but the Pi does and this makes this the simplest option. To read the temperature using the Hold master mode you simply send 0xE3 and then read three bytes.

```
char buf[4] = {0xE3};
bcm2835_i2c_read_register_rs(buf, buf, 3);
uint8_t msb = buf[0];
uint8_t lsb = buf[1];
uint8_t check = buf[2];
printf("msb %d \n\r lsb %d \n\r checksum %d \n\r", msb, lsb, check);
```

The buffer is unpacked into three variables with more meaningful names: msb most significant byte; lsb - least significant byte; and check(sum).

If you try this you will find that it doesn't work. This is almost certainly, because it times out given the default setting of 40 clock pulses for the clock stretching timeout. At the default clock speed of 1.666MHz, this gives a timeout of 24 microseconds, which is very short. The HTU21D takes 40 milliseconds or more to complete a temperature conversion so a timeout is inevitable.

Setting The Clock Stretching Timeout

In most cases when using clock stretching, we have to modify the clock stretching timeout. Unfortunately the bcm2835 library doesn't provide a function to do this. It is however fairly easy to create one:

```
void setTimeout(uint16_t timeout) {
 volatile uint32_t* stimeout = bcm2835_bsc1 + BCM2835_BSC_CLKT / 4;
 bcm2835_peri_write(stimeout, timeout);
}
```

This simply writes to the timeout register using the address constants created by the library.

Now we can make clock stretching work by disabling the timeout by setting a value of zero.

```
bcm2835_i2c_begin();
bcm2835_i2c_setClockDivider(BCM2835_I2C_CLOCK_DIVIDER_150);

setTimeout(0);
char buf[4] = {0xE3};
uint8_t status = bcm2835_i2c_read_register_rs(buf, buf, 3);
uint8_t msb = buf[0];
uint8_t lsb = buf[1];
uint8_t check = buf[2];
printf("msb %d \n\r lsb %d \n\r checksum %d \n\r", msb, lsb, check);
```

If you try this out you should find that it works and it prints something like

```
msb 97
lsb 232
checksum 217
```

with the temperature in the 20C range.

The logic analyzer reveals what is happening. First we send the usual address frame and write the 0xE3. Then, after a short pause, the read address frame is sent and the clock line is held low by the device (lower trace):

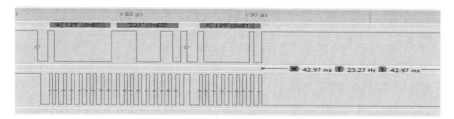

The clock line is held low by the device for over 42ms while it gets the data ready. It is released and the three data frames are sent:

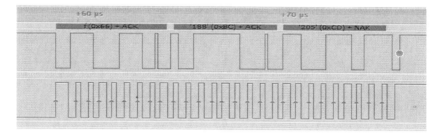

This response is a long way down the logic analyzer trace so keep scrolling until you find it.

Working with a clock stretch timeout disabled isn't a good idea for a production program, but at the default clock rate the longest timeout that can be set using 16 bits is 24.5 milliseconds, which is not long enough. To set a timeout of 100 milliseconds the clock has to be at most 1.5 microseconds. A standard clock rate of BCM2835_I2C_CLOCK_DIVIDER_626 gives a clock time of 2.5 microseconds and a timeout count of 40,000 for 100ms.

The complete program extract is:

```
bcm2835_i2c_begin();
bcm2835_i2c_setClockDivider(BCM2835_I2C_CLOCK_DIVIDER_626);
setTimeout(40000);
bcm2835_i2c_setSlaveAddress(0x40);
char buf[4] = {0xE3};
uint8_t status = bcm2835_i2c_read_register_rs(buf, buf, 3);
printf("status=%d\n\r",status);
uint8_t msb = buf[0];
uint8_t lsb = buf[1];
uint8_t check = buf[2];
printf("msb %d \n\r lsb %d \n\r checksum %d \n\r", msb, lsb, check);
```

This now works reliably and will timeout if anything goes wrong with the slave.

Processing the data

Our next task isn't really directly related to the problem of using the I2C bus, but it is a very typical next step. The device returns the data in three bytes, but the way that this data relates to the temperature isn't simple.

If you read the data sheet you will discover that the temperature data is the 14-bit value that results from putting together the most and least significant byte and zeroing the bottom two bits. The bottom two bits are used as status bits, bit zero currently isn't used and bit one is a 1 if the data is a humidity measurement and a 0 if it is a temperature measurement.

To put the two bytes together we use:

```
unsigned int data16=((unsigned int) msb << 8) |
                              (unsigned int) (lsb & 0xFC);
```

This zeros the bottom two bits, shifts the msb up eight bits and ORs the two together. The result is a 16-bit temperature value with the bottom two bits zeroed.

Now we have raw temperature value but we have still have to convert it to standard units. The datasheet gives the formula:

```
Temp in C = -46.85 + 175.72 * data16 / 2¹⁶
```

The only problem in implementing this is working out 2^{16}. You can work out 2^x with the expression 1<<x, i.e. shift 1 x places to the right.

This gives:

```
float temp = (float)(-46.85 +(175.72 * data16 /(float)(1<<16)));
```

As 2^{16} is a constant that works out to 65536 it is more efficient to write:

```
float temp = (float)(-46.85 +(175.72 * data16 /(float)65536));
```

Now all we have to do is print the temperature:

```
printf("Temperature %f C \n\r", temp);
```

The final program extract is:

```
if (!bcm2835_init()) return 1;
bcm2835_i2c_begin();
bcm2835_i2c_setClockDivider(BCM2835_I2C_CLOCK_DIVIDER_626);
setTimeout(40000);
bcm2835_i2c_setSlaveAddress(0x40);
char buf[4] = {0xE3};
uint8_t status = bcm2835_i2c_read_register_rs(buf, buf, 3);
printf("status=%d\n\r",status);
uint8_t msb = buf[0];
uint8_t lsb = buf[1];
uint8_t check = buf[2];
printf("msb %d \n\r lsb %d \n\r checksum %d \n\r", msb, lsb, check);
unsigned int data16 = ((unsigned int) msb << 8) |
                                    (unsigned int) (lsb & 0xFC);
float temp = (float) (-46.85 + (175.72 * data16 / (float) 65536));
printf("Temperature %f C \n\r", temp);
```

Reading the humidity

The nice thing about I2C and using a particular I2C device is that it gets easier. Once you have seen how to do it with one device the skill generalizes and once you know how to deal with a particular device other aspects of the device are usually similar.

While clock stretching is the most simple it sometimes doesn't work with some slave and master combinations. It is worth knowing how the alternative polling method works. For this reason let's implement the humidity reading using polling. We also find out how to use the No hold master mode of reading the data which is sometimes useful.

In this case we can't use the read_register_ns command to read and the master because we don't want to keep sending the 0xF5 command. We write it once to the slave and then repeatedly attempt to read the three byte response. If the slave isn't ready it simply replies with a NACK.

```
buf[0] = 0xF5;
bcm2835_i2c_write(buf, 1);
while (bcm2835_i2c_read(buf, 3) == BCM2835_I2C_REASON_ERROR_NACK)
      bcm2835_delayMicroseconds(500);
};
```

This polls repeatedly until the slave device returns an ACK when the data is loaded into the buffer.

Once we have the data, the formula to convert the 16-bit value to percentage humidity is:

```
RH= -6 + 125 * data16 / 2^16
```

Putting all this together and reusing some variables from the previous parts of the program we have:

```
buf[0] = 0xF5;
bcm2835_i2c_write(buf, 1);
while (bcm2835_i2c_read(buf, 3) == BCM2835_I2C_REASON_ERROR_NACK) {
        bcm2835_delayMicroseconds(500);
    };
msb = buf[0];
lsb = buf[1];
check = buf[2];
printf("msb %d \n\r lsb %d \n\r checksum %d \n\r",
                                            msb, lsb, check);
printf("crc = %d\n\r", crcCheck(msb, lsb, check));
data16 = ((unsigned int) msb << 8) | (unsigned int) (lsb & 0xFC);
float hum = -6 + (125.0 * (float) data16) / 65536;
printf("Humidity %f %% \n\r", hum);
bcm2835_i2c_end();
```

The only unusual part of the program is using %% to print a single % character, which is necessary because % means something in printf.

Checksum calculation

Although computing a checksum isn't specific to I2C, it is another common task. The datasheet explains that the polynomial used is:

$$X8+X5+X4+1$$

Once you have this information you can work out the divisor by writing a binary number with a one in each location corresponding to a power of X in the polynomial. In this case the 8th, 5th, 4th and 1st bit. Hence the divisor is:

0x0131

What you do next is roughly the same for all CRCs. First you put the data that was used to compute the checksum together with the checksum value as the low order bits:

```
uint32_t data32 = ((uint32_t)msb << 16)|
                    ((uint32_t) lsb <<8) |
                    (uint32_t) check;
```

Now you have three bytes, i.e 24 bits in a 32-bit variable. Next you adjust the divisor so that its most significant non-zero bit aligns with the most significant bit of the three bytes. As this divisor has a 1 at bit eight it needs to be shifted 15 places to the right to move it to be the 24th bit:

```
uint32_t divisor = ((uint32_t) 0x0131) <<15;
```

Now that you have both the data and the divisor aligned, you step through the top-most 16 bits, i.e. you don't process the low order eight bits which is the received checksum. For each bit you check to see if it is a 1 - if it is you replace the data with the data XOR divisor. In either case you shift the divisor one place to the right:

```
for (int i = 0 ; i < 16 ; i++){
  if( data32 & (uint32_t)1<<(23 - i) )
                  data32 =data32 ^ divisor;
  divisor=divisor >> 1;
};
```

When the loop ends, if there was no error, the data32 should be zeroed and the received checksum is correct and as computed on the data received.

A complete function to compute the checksum with some optimizations is:

```
uint8_t crcCheck(uint8_t msb, uint8_t lsb, uint8_t check){
 uint32_t data32 = ((uint32_t)msb << 16)|((uint32_t) lsb <<8)|
             (uint32_t) check;
 uint32_t divisor = 0x988000;
 for (int i = 0 ; i < 16 ; i++){
  if( data32 & (uint32_t)1<<(23 - i) ) data32 ^= divisor;
  divisor>>= 1;
 };
 return (uint8_t) data32;
}
```

It is rare to get a crc error on an I2C bus unless it is overloaded or subject to a lot of noise.

Complete Listing

The complete program including crc checks is:

```c
#include <stdio.h>
#include <stdlib.h>
#include <bcm2835.h>

uint8_t crcCheck(uint8_t msb, uint8_t lsb, uint8_t check);

int main(int argc, char** argv) {
    if (!bcm2835_init())
        return 1;
    bcm2835_i2c_begin();
    bcm2835_i2c_setClockDivider(BCM2835_I2C_CLOCK_DIVIDER_626);
    setTimeout(40000);
    bcm2835_i2c_setSlaveAddress(0x40);
    char buf[4] = {0xE3};
    uint8_t status = bcm2835_i2c_read_register_rs(buf, buf, 3);
    printf("status=%d\n\r",status);
    uint8_t msb = buf[0];
    uint8_t lsb = buf[1];
    uint8_t check = buf[2];
    printf("msb %d\n\rlsb %d\n\rchecksum %d\n\r",msb, lsb,check);
    printf("crc = %d\n\r", crcCheck(msb, lsb, check));
    unsigned int data16 = ((unsigned int) msb << 8) |
                                    (unsigned int) (lsb & 0xFC);
    float temp = (float) (-46.85 + (175.72 *
                                    data16 / (float) 65536));
    printf("Temperature %f C \n\r", temp);

    buf[0] = 0xF5;
    bcm2835_i2c_write(buf, 1);
    while (bcm2835_i2c_read(buf, 3)==BCM2835_I2C_REASON_ERROR_NACK){
      bcm2835_delayMicroseconds(500);
    };
    msb = buf[0];
    lsb = buf[1];
    check = buf[2];
    printf("msb %d\n\rlsb%d\n\rchecksum %d\n\r",msb,lsb,check);
    printf("crc = %d\n\r", crcCheck(msb, lsb, check));

    data16 = ((unsigned int) msb << 8) | (unsigned int)(lsb & 0xFC);
    float hum = -6 + (125.0 * (float) data16) / 65536;
    printf("Humidity %f %% \n\r", hum);
    bcm2835_i2c_end();
    return (EXIT_SUCCESS);
}
```

```c
uint8_t crcCheck(uint8_t msb, uint8_t lsb, uint8_t check) {
    uint32_t data32 = ((uint32_t) msb << 16) |
            ((uint32_t) lsb << 8) |
            (uint32_t) check;
    uint32_t divisor = 0x988000;
    int i;
    for (i = 0; i < 16; i++) {
        if (data32 & (uint32_t) 1 << (23 - i))
            data32 ^= divisor;
        divisor >>= 1;
    };
    return (uint8_t) data32;
}

void setTimeout(uint16_t timeout) {
    volatile uint32_t* stimeout = bcm2835_bsc1+BCM2835_BSC_CLKT/4;
    bcm2835_peri_write(stimeout, timeout);
}
```

Of course this is just the start.

Once you have the device working and supplying data it is time to write your code in the form of functions that return the temperature and the humidity and generally make the whole thing more useful and easier to maintain.

This is often how this sort of programming goes - at first you write a lot of inline code so that it works as fast as it can then you move blocks of code to functions to make the program more elegant and easy to maintain checking at each refactoring that the programming still works.

Not all devices used standard bus protocols. Next we looks at a custom serial protocol that we have to implement for ourselves.

Chapter 10

The DHT22 Sensor
Implementing A Custom Protocol

In this chapter we make use of all the ideas introduced in earlier chapters to create a raw interface with the low cost DHT11/22 temperature and humidity sensor. It is an exercise in implementing a custom protocol directly in C.

The DHT22

The DHT22 is a more accurate version of the DHT11 and it is used in this project, but the hardware and software will work with both versions and with the AM2302 which is similar to the DHT22.

```
Model AM2302/DHT22
Power supply 3.3-5.5V DC
Output signal digital signal via 1-wire bus
Sensing element Polymer humidity capacitor
Operating range
  humidity 0-100%RH;
  temperature -40~80Celsius
Accuracy
  humidity +-2%RH(Max +-5%RH);
  temperature +-0.5Celsius
Resolution or sensitivity
  humidity 0.1%RH;
  temperature 0.1Celsius
Repeatability
  humidity +-1%RH;
  temperature +-0.2Celsius
```

The device will work at 3.3V and it makes use of a 1-wire open collector style bus, which makes it very easy to make the physical connection to the Pi.

The one wire bus used isn't standard and is only used by this family of devices, so we have little choice but to implement the protocol in C.

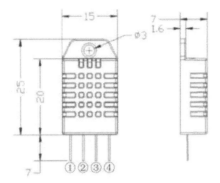

The pinouts are:

1. VDD
2. SDA serial data
3. not used
4. GND

and the standard way of connecting the device is:

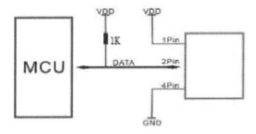

Although the recommended pull up resistor is 1K, a higher value works better with the Pi - typically 4.7K, but larger will work.

The serial protocol is also fairly simple:

1. The host pulls the line low for between 0.8 and 29 ms, usually 1ms.

2. It then releases the bus which is pulled high.

3. After between 20 and 200 microseconds, usually 30 microseconds, the device starts to send data by pulling the line down for around 80 microseconds and then lets it float high for another 80 microseconds.

4. Next 40 bits of data are sent using a 70-microsecond high for a 1 and a 26-microsecond high for a 0 with the high pluses separated by around 50 microsecond low periods.

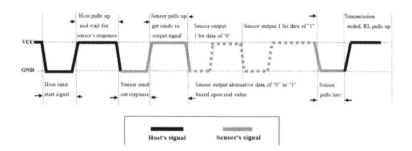

What we have to do is pull the line low for 1 ms or so to start the device sending data and this is very easy. Then we have to wait for the device to pull the line down and let it pull up again for about 160 microsecond and then read the time that the line is high 80 times.

A 1 corresponds to 70 microseconds and a 0 corresponds to 26 microseconds. This is within the range of pulse measurement that can be achieved using standard library functions. There is also a 50-microsecond period between each data bit and this can be used to do some limited processing. Notice that we are only interested in the time that the line is held high.

When trying to work out how to decode a new protocol it often helps to try to answer the question,

"how can I tell the difference between a 0 and a 1?"

If you have a logic analyzer it can help to look at the wave form and see how you work it out manually. In this case, despite the complex looking timing diagram, the difference comes down to a short versus a long pulse!

The Electronics

Exactly how you build the circuit is a matter of preference. The basic layout can be seen below.

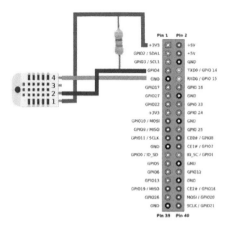

It is very easy to create this circuit using a prototyping board and some jumper wires. You can also put the resistor close to the DHT22 to make a sensor package connected to the Pi using three cables.

The Software

With the hardware shown above connected to the Pi the first thing that we need to do is establish that the system is working. The simplest way to do this is to pull the line down for 1ms and see if the device responds with a stream of pulses. These can be seen on a logic analyzer or an oscilloscope - both are indispensable tools. If you don't have access to either tool then you will just have to skip to the next stage and see if you can read in some data.

The simplest code that will do the job is:

```
void GetDHT22data(uint8_t pin) {
    bcm2835_gpio_fsel(pin, BCM2835_GPIO_FSEL_OUTP);
    bcm2835_gpio_write(pin, LOW);
    bcm2835_delayMicroseconds(1000);
    bcm2835_gpio_fsel(pin, BCM2835_GPIO_FSEL_INPT);
    return;
}
```

Setting the line initially high, to ensure that it is configured as an output, we then set it low, wait for around 1000 microseconds and then change its direction to input by reading the data.

There is no need to set the lines pull up mode because it is the only device driving the line until it releases the line by changing direction to input. When a line is in input mode it is high impedance and this is why we need an external pull up resistor in the circuit.

As long as the circuit has been correctly assembled and you have a working device you should see something like:

Reading The Data

With preliminary flight checks complete it is time to read the 40-bit data stream. The first thing to do is wait for the low that the device sends before the start bit:

```
int i;
for (i = 1; i < 2000; i++) {
  if (bcm2835_gpio_lev(pin)==0)break;
};
```

Next we can start to read in the bit stream. When doing this there are two things to keep in mind. The first is that it is only the time the line is high that matters and you need to measure just this accurately - you don't care so much about how long the line is low for. The second is that it is usually better to collect the bits and only later process them and extract the data. To this end it is usually a good idea to save the data in a buffer:

```
uint64_tbuf[41];
int j;
 for(j=0;j<41;j++){
   for(i=1;i<2000;i++){
    if(bcm2835_gpio_lev(pin)==1)break;
   };
   t=bcm2835_st_read();
   for(i=1;i<2000;i++){
    if(bcm2835_gpio_lev(pin)==0) break;
   }
   buf[j]=(bcm2835_st_read()-t);
}
```

You should be able to see how this works. The outer for loop, indexed on j, repeats to read in all 41 bits, i.e. 40 data bits and the initial start bit. The first inner loop waits for the line to go high and its final count gives us a measure of how long the line has been low. This is of no interest because the device keeps the line low for the same length of time for a 0 or a 1. Next the second for loop waits for the line to go low. Its final count is now proportional to the time the line was high. For machines that don't have a microsecond

161

clock this would be enough to decode the data. In this case we can use the low order 32 bits of the Pi's clock as returned by bcm2835_st_read(). We just need the difference between the time the clock went high and returned to low to work out if the data is a 1 or a 0.

If you add:

```
for(j=0;j<=40;j++){
 printf("%d %d \n",j,buf[j]);
}
```

to the end of the program you will be able to see the counts and you should quickly be able to work out the value halfway between the long 1 pulses and the short 0 pulses. Examining the data reveals that short pulses returned 26 to 27 microseconds and long pulses returned 73 to 74 microseconds. Thus the threshold halfway between the two is approximately 50 microseconds.

With a threshold of 50 we can classify the pulses into long and short and store 1s and 0s in the buffer.

```
int buf[41];
int j;
for(j=0;j<41;j++){
 for(i=1;i<2000;i++){
  if(bcm2835_gpio_lev(pin)==1)break;
 };
 t=bcm2835_st_read();
 for(i=1;i<2000;i++){
  if(bcm2835_gpio_lev(pin)==0) break;
 }
 buf[j]=(bcm2835_st_read()-t)>50;
}
```

You can afford to include this extra processing in the data collection loop because it happens while the line is low and we aren't interested in measuring this time accurately. If we were then it would be a good idea to put off all processing until the loop had finished. Notice that now we can use an integer buffer because we aren't storing the 64-bit time in it, just the result of the conditional expression which is 0 or 1.

There is a small bug in this program as it stands but probably one that we can live with. The time difference will be wrong if the clock rolls over to zero. You can fix this by doing the arithmetic mod the size of the clock, or you can simply put up with the fact that, very rarely, you will get a checksum error.

Extracting The Data

Now we have the data in the buffer as 0s and 1s. All that remains is to decode it into temperature and humidity readings. But first we will convert the bits into five bytes of data.

The simplest way of doing this is to write a function that will pack eight bits into an uint:

```
uint8_t getByte(int b,int buf[]){
  int i;
  uint8_t result=0;
  b=(b-1)*8+1;
  for(i=b;i<=b+7;i++){
   result= result<<1;
   result=result | buf[i];
  }
  return result;
}
```

The b parameter can be set to the byte that you want to extract from the array. For example, if b=2 then the for loop runs from i=9 to i=16, i.e. the second byte stored in the array. Notice that we skip the first bit because this just signals the start of the data. The bit manipulation in the for loop is a fairly standard shift left and OR the least significant bit into the result.

Using this function getting the five bytes is trivial:

```
int byte1 = getByte(1, buf);
int byte2 = getByte(2, buf);
int byte3 = getByte(3, buf);
int byte4 = getByte(4, buf);
int byte5 = getByte(5, buf);
```

The first two bytes are the humidity measurement, the second two the temperature, and the final byte is the checksum. The reason for the cast to int rather than keeping the data as bytes is that it makes computing the checksum easier.

The checksum is just the sum of the first four bytes reduced to eight bits and we can test it using:

```
printf("Checksum %hho %d\n",byte5,(byte1+byte2+byte3+byte4)&0xFF);
```

If the two values are different, there has been a transmission error. The addition of the bytes is done as a full integer and then it is reduced back to a single byte by the AND operation. If there is a checksum error, the simplest thing to do is get another reading from the device. Notice, however, that you shouldn't read the device more than once every 2 seconds.

The humidity and temperature data are also easy to reconstruct as they are transmitted high byte first and 10 times the actual value.

Extracting the humidity data is easy:

```
float humidity= (float) (byte1<<8 |byte2)/10.0;
printf("Humidity= %f \n",humidity);
```

The temperature data is slightly more difficult in that the top most bit is used to indicate a negative temperature. This means we have to test for the most significant bit and flip the sign of the temperature if it is set:

```
float temperature;
int neg=byte3 & 0x80;
byte3=byte3 & 0x7F;
temperature= (float) (byte3<<8 |byte4)/10.0;
if(neg>0)temperature=-temperature;
printf("Temperature= %f \n",temperature);
```

This complete the data processing.

A main program to call the measuring function is just:

```
int main(int argc, char** argv) {
 const struct sched_param priority = {5};
 sched_setscheduler(0, SCHED_FIFO, &priority);
 mlockall(MCL_CURRENT | MCL_FUTURE);
 if (!bcm2835_init())
     return 1;
 bcm2835_gpio_fsel(RPI_GPIO_P1_07, BCM2835_GPIO_FSEL_INPT);
 bcm2835_delayMicroseconds(1000);

 GetDHT22data(RPI_GPIO_P1_07);
 return 0;
}
```

You can, of course modify GetDHT22data to not print any results and to return the temperature and humidity.

You need to add a test on the checksum to take the measurement again if there is an error, but you need to keep in mind the 2 second maximum reading rate. Using a static variable you could even slow down the rate that the GetDHT22 function was used to more than 2 seconds per call.

The point is that we have a simple and reliable program that reads the DHT22 without the need for drivers or a third party library. Decoding protocols of this sort is easy and makes your program self-contained.

Complete Listing

That's all we need to do and the final program, complete with some minor tidying up can be seen below:

```
#include <bcm2835.h>
#include <stdio.h>
#include <sched.h>
#include <sys/mman.h>

uint8_t getByte(int b, int buf[]);
void GetDHT22data(uint8_t pin);

int main(int argc, char** argv) {
    const struct sched_param priority = {1};
    sched_setscheduler(0, SCHED_FIFO, &priority);
    mlockall(MCL_CURRENT | MCL_FUTURE);
    if (!bcm2835_init())
        return 1;
    bcm2835_gpio_fsel(RPI_GPIO_P1_07, BCM2835_GPIO_FSEL_INPT);
    bcm2835_delayMicroseconds(1000);
    GetDHT22data(RPI_GPIO_P1_07);
    return 0;
}

void GetDHT22data(uint8_t pin) {
    bcm2835_gpio_fsel(pin, BCM2835_GPIO_FSEL_OUTP);
    bcm2835_gpio_write(pin, LOW);
    bcm2835_delayMicroseconds(1000);
    bcm2835_gpio_fsel(pin, BCM2835_GPIO_FSEL_INPT);
    int i;
    for (i = 1; i < 2000; i++) {
        if (bcm2835_gpio_lev(pin) == 0)break;
    };
    uint64_t t;
    int buf[41];
    int j;
    bcm2835_delayMicroseconds(1);
    for (j = 0; j < 41; j++) {
        for (i = 1; i < 2000; i++) {
            if (bcm2835_gpio_lev(pin) == 1)break;
        };
        t = bcm2835_st_read();
        for (i = 1; i < 2000; i++) {
            if (bcm2835_gpio_lev(pin) == 0) break;
        }
        buf[j] = (bcm2835_st_read() - t) > 50;
    }
```

```
        printf("Checksum %d %d \n\r", byte5,
                (byte1 + byte2 + byte3 + byte4) & 0xFF);
        float humidity = (float) (byte1 << 8 | byte2) / 10.0;
        int byte1 = getByte(1, buf);
        int byte2 = getByte(2, buf);
        int byte3 = getByte(3, buf);
        int byte4 = getByte(4, buf);
        int byte5 = getByte(5, buf);
        printf("Humidity= %f \n\r", humidity);
        float temperature;
        int neg = byte3 & 0x80;
        byte3 = byte3 & 0x7F;
        temperature = (float) (byte3 << 8 | byte4) / 10.0;
        if (neg > 0)temperature = -temperature;
        printf("Temperature= %f \n\r", temperature);
        return;
}

uint8_t getByte(int b, int buf[]) {
        int i;
        uint8_t result = 0;
        b = (b - 1)*8 + 1;
        for (i = b; i <= b + 7; i++) {
            result = result << 1;
            result = result | buf[i];
        }
        return result;
}
```

The DHT11/22 is a useful device but when it comes to low cost temperature measurement the DS18D20 is a very popular choice and it is more accurate than the DHT11/22. It is also an example of a standard 1-wire device, which gives us access to a range of sensors that work in the same way. This is the subject of the next four chapters.

Chapter 11

Exploring 1-Wire Bus Basics

The Raspberry Pi is fast enough to be used to directly interface to 1-Wire bus without the need for drivers. The advantages of programming our own 1-wire bus protocol is that it doesn't depend on the uncertainties of a Linux driver.

The Maxim 1-Wire bus is a proprietary bus that is very easy to use and has a lot of useful devices you can connect to it including the iButton security devices. However, probably the most popular of all 1-wire devices is the DS18B20 temperature sensor - it is small, very cheap and very easy to use. The next two chapters show you how to use both of these, but first let's deal with the general techniques needed to work with the 1-wire bus.

There are 1-wire drivers for Linux and these are most commonly used in Python and other programs that work with the bus. However, to make these work you have to install the drivers and occasionally there are compatibility problems. If you are programming in C then you have more than enough speed to write your own 1-wire protocol functions and this has the advantage of not requiring any interaction with Linux to work. You are also free to modify and extend the 1-wire functions without having to become involved in writing Linux modules.

The Hardware

One wire devices are very simple and only use a single wire to transmit data, hence the name.

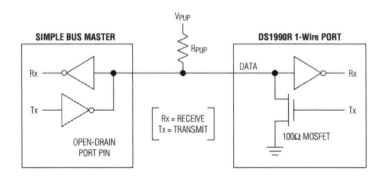

The 1-wire device can pull the bus low using its Tx line and can read the line using its Rx line. The reason for the pullup resistor is that both the bus master and the slave can pull the bus low and it will stay low until they both release the bus. The device can even be powered from the bus line by drawing sufficient current through the pullup resistor - so called parasitic mode. Low power devices work well in parasitic mode, but some devices have such a heavy current draw that the master has to provide a way to connect them to the power line - so called strong pullup. In practice parasitic mode can be difficult to make work reliably for high power devices.

In normal powered mode there are just three connections, V power, usually 3.3V for the Pi; Ground and Data:

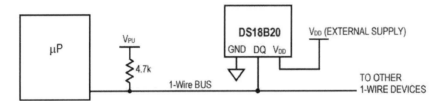

The pullup resistor varies according to the device, but anything from 2.2K to 4.7K Ohms works. There can be multiple devices on the bus and each one has a unique 64-bit lasered ROM code, which can be used as an address to select the active devices.

For simplicity, it is better to start off with a single device and avoid the problem of enumerating the devices on the bus, although once you know how everything works this isn't difficult to implement.

So to get started select a 1-wire device that you want to work with and set it up ready to talk to the Pi of your choice. In the next chapter we show how to work with an iButton and in the following chapter the DS18B20 is explained. The functions described in this chapter should work with any 1-wire device.

Initialization

Every transaction with the a 1-wire device starts with an initialization handshake. First we have to work out how to configure the GPIO line. This example assumes that the 1-wire device is connected to pin 7. If this isn't the case change the pin enumeration to the correct pin. For a full practical example, see either of the next two chapters.

You might think that we have to initialize the GPIO line so that it works in pullup mode. This isn't necessary and the default push-pull mode will do. The reason is that, in the case of the 1-wire bus, the master controls when other devices send their data. Typically the master sends a pulse and then the slaves respond by pulling the line low. As long as the master doesn't drive the line during the period when the slaves are responding, everything is fine.

What we do in practice is to configure the GPIO line for output only when the master needs to drive the line. Once the master is finished the GPIO line is set back to input and the pullup resistor is allowed to pull the line back up. After this, any slave wanting to send data is free to pull the line low.

The first transaction we need is the initialization pulse. This is simply a low pulse that lasts at least 480 microseconds, a 15 to 60-microsecond pause follows and then any and all of the devices on the bus pull the line low for 60 to 240 microseconds.

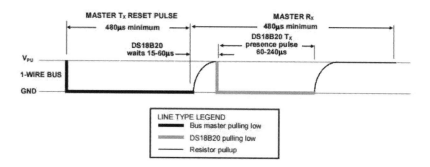

The suggested timings are set the line low for 480 microseconds and read the line after 70 microseconds followed by a 410-microsecond pause.

This is fairly easy to implement as a function:

```
int presence(uint8_t pin) {
    bcm2835_gpio_fsel(pin, BCM2835_GPIO_FSEL_OUTP);
    bcm2835_gpio_write(pin, LOW);
    bcm2835_delayMicroseconds(480);
    bcm2835_gpio_fsel(pin, BCM2835_GPIO_FSEL_INPT);
    bcm2835_delayMicroseconds(70);
    uint8_t b = bcm2835_gpio_lev(pin);
    bcm2835_delayMicroseconds(410);
    return b;
}
```

We pull the line low for 480 microseconds and then let it be pulled back up by changing the line to input, i.e. high impedance. After a 70-microsecond wait, which is right at the start of the guaranteed period when the line should be low, if there is an active device on the bus we read the input line and then wait another 410 microseconds to complete the data slot.

The timings in this case are not critical as long as the line is read while it is held low by the slaves, which is never less than 60 microseconds and is typically as much as 100 microseconds.

The actual pulse timings with the values given are a 483-microsecond reset and a total slot time of 632 microseconds. If there is a device the function should return a 0 and if there are no devices it should return a 1.

```
if(presence(RPI_GPIO_P1_07)==1){
 printf("No device \n");
}
```

If you try this partial program and have a logic analyzer with a 1-wire protocol analyzer you will see something like:

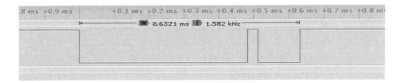

Seeing a presence pulse is the simplest and quickest way to be sure that your hardware is working.

Writing Bits

Our next task is to implement the sending of some data bits to the device.

The 1-wire bus has a very simple data protocol. All bits are sent using a minimum of 60 microseconds for a read/write slot. Each slot must be separated from the next by a minimum of 1 microsecond.

The good news is that timing is only critical within each slot. You can send the first bit in a time slot and then take your time before you send the next bit as the device will wait for you. This means you only have to worry about timing within the functions that read and write individual bits.

To send a 0 you have to hold the line low for most of the slot. To send a one you have to hold the line low for just between 1 and 15 microseconds and leave the line high for the rest of the slot. The exact timings can be seen below:

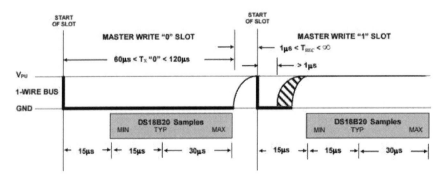

It seems reasonable to use the typical timings given in the data sheets. So for a 0 we hold the line low for 60 microseconds then let it go high for the remainder of the slot, 10 microseconds. To send a 1 we hold the line for 6 microseconds and then let it go high for the remainder of the slot, 64 microseconds. As the only time critical operations are the actual setting of the line low and then back to high, there is no need to worry too much about speed of operation of the entire function so we might as well combine writing 0 and 1 into a single writeBit function:

```
void writeBit(uint8_t pin,int b) {
    int delay1, delay2;
    if (b == 1) {
        delay1 = 6;
        delay2 = 64;
    } else {
        delay2 = 60;
        delay2 = 10;
    }
    bcm2835_gpio_fsel(pin, BCM2835_GPIO_FSEL_OUTP);
    bcm2835_gpio_write(pin, LOW);
    bcm2835_delayMicroseconds(delay1);
    bcm2835_gpio_fsel(pin, BCM2835_GPIO_FSEL_INPT);
    bcm2835_delayMicroseconds(delay2);
}
```

The code at the start of the function simply increases the time between slots slightly. Notice that once again we return the GPIO line to input, i.e. high impedance, rather than driving the line high at the end of the transaction. This allows the line to be pulled high ready for any response from the slave.

You can see two 1s followed by two 0s in the following logic analyzer trace:

A First Command - Writing Bytes

After discovering that there is at least one device connected to the bus, the master has to issue a ROM command. In many cases the ROM command used first will be the Search ROM command, which enumerates the 64-bit codes of all of the devices on the bus. After collecting all of these codes, the master can use Match ROM commands with a specific 64-bit code to select the device the master wants to talk to.

While it is perfectly possible to implement the Search ROM procedure, it is simpler to work with the single device by using commands which ignore the

171

64-bit code and address all of the devices on the bus at the same time. Of course. this only works as long as there is only one device on the bus. If there is only one device then we can use the Skip ROM command 0xCC to tell all the devices on the bus to be active.

We now need a function that can send a byte. As we have a writeBit function this is easy:

```
void sendskip(uint8_t pin){
writeBit(pin,0);
writeBit(pin,0);
writeBit(pin,1);
writeBit(pin,1);
writeBit(pin,0);
writeBit(pin,0);
writeBit(pin,1);
writeBit(pin,1);
}
```

Notice that 0xCC is 1100 1100 in binary and the 1-wire bus sends the least significant bit first. If you try this out you should find it works but device doesn't respond because it is waiting for another command. Again as the time between writing bits isn't critical we can take this first implementation of the function and write something more general if slightly slower.

The writeByte function will write the low 8 bits of an int to the device:

```
void writeByte(uint8_t pin,int byte) {
    int i;
    for (i = 0; i < 8; i++) {
        if (byte & 1) {
            writeBit(pin,1);
        } else {
            writeBit(pin,0);
        }
        byte = byte >> 1;
    }
}
```

Using this we can send a Skip ROM command using:

```
writeByte(RPI_GPIO_P1_07,0xCC);
```

You can see the pattern of bits sent on a logic analyzer:

Reading Bits

We already know how the master sends a 1 and a 0. The protocol for the slave device is exactly the same except that the master still provides the slot's starting pulse. That is the master starts a 60-microsecond slot by pulling the bus down for a bit more than 1 microsecond. Then the slave device either holds the line down for a further 15 microseconds minimum, or it simply allows the line to float high. See below for the exact timings:

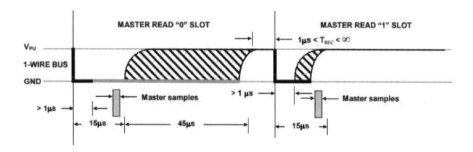

So all we have to do to read bits is to pull the line down for just a bit more than 1 microsecond and then sample the bus after a pause. The data sheet gives 6 microseconds for the master's pulse and a 9 microsecond pause. In practice, a final delay of 8 microseconds seems to work best and allows for the time to change the line's direction.

```
uint8_t readBit(uint8_t pin) {
    bcm2835_gpio_fsel(pin, BCM2835_GPIO_FSEL_OUTP);
    bcm2835_gpio_write(pin, LOW);
    bcm2835_delayMicroseconds(6);
    bcm2835_gpio_fsel(pin, BCM2835_GPIO_FSEL_INPT);
    bcm2835_delayMicroseconds(8);
    uint8_t b = bcm2835_gpio_lev(pin);
    bcm2835_delayMicroseconds(55);
    return b;
}
```

A logic analyzer shows the typical pattern of bits from the device:

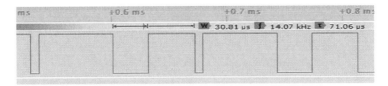

Finally we need a function that will read a byte. As in the case of writing a byte there is no time criticality in the time between reading bits so we don't need to take extra special care in constructing the function.

```c
int readByte(uint8_t pin) {
    int byte = 0;
    int i;
    for (i = 0; i < 8; i++) {
        byte = byte | readBit(pin) << i;
    };
    return byte;
}
```

The only difficult part is to remember that the 1-wire bus sends the least significant bit first and so this has to be shifted into the result from the right.

Now we can:

- Test to see if a device is present:
  ```c
  presence(uint8_t pin)
  ```

- Write a byte:
  ```c
  void writeByte(uint8_t pin,int byte)
  ```

- Read a byte:
  ```c
  int readByte(uint8_t pin)
  ```

These functions will be used in the next two chapters to work with two real 1-wire devices.

These are not the only functions we need to work with the 1-wire bus.

We need to be able to compute the CRC error checks that are commonly used to confirm that data has been transmitted correctly and we need to perform a ROM search to discover what devices are connected to the bus.

Chapter 12

Using iButtons

If you haven't already discovered iButtons then you are about to find lots of uses for them. At its simplest, an iButton is an electronic key providing a unique code stored in its ROM, which can be used to unlock or simply record the presence of a particular button. The good news is that they are easy to interface to a Pi.

A basic iButton is small can that can be placed into a simple contact reader. Often it is placed in a fob that makes it possible to keep on a key ring:

A typical reader is just a two contact receptacle:

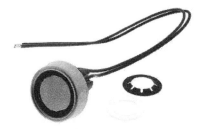

iButtons are cheap and robust and they are easy to use, as long as you have some 1-wire software.

You can get very simple iButtons that store a unique serial number for a few dollars. These are suitable for security applications. You could design a reader to open a door, arm an alarm or record comings and goings. The main advantage of iButtons over swipe cards and similar id devices is that they are almost indestructible. The small stainless steel can is tough and water proof.

There are also more sophisticated iButtons that come with sensors and data loggers. These are more expensive and slightly more difficult to read, but after you have seen how to work with the basic security button there should be no problem in extending the software.

The Hardware

A typical iButton is used in parasitic mode, meaning it derives its operating power from the data line and has such a low current drain that you don't need to do anything to make it work properly. All that is needed is a pullup resistor, typically 2.2KOhms, a 3.3V supply, ground and a GPIO line, pin 7 in this example but it could be any other you care to use.

The circuit really couldn't be simpler:

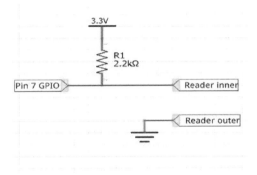

You can realize this in many ways. A prototype board allows you to check that things are working with a logic analyzer, but you can wire it directly to the Pi's connector.

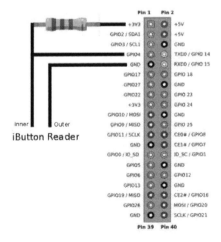

Is There a Button?

The first thing you want to try with any 1-wire device is to discover if the bus is working and to do this you send an initialization pulse. We created a function to do just this in the previous chapter so we can just use it.

However iButtons have a particular problem. You want to detect when an iButton is pressed into the reader so you need a loop something like:

```
uint8_t b = 1;
for (;;) {
  b = presence(RPI_GPIO_P1_07);
  if (b == 0) {
    read iButton
  }
}
```

where **presence** is a function from the previous chapter.

In practice there is also the problem that the iButton is likely to make intermittent contact and so you have to implement error checking and some way of "debouncing" the iButton so you only read it once. For the moment we can ignore this problem and just read the iButton.

Read the Serial Number

The DS1990R and similar are very simple 1-wire devices and they only support a few commands. If it is the only device on the bus then only one of these commands is actually useful. After the initialization pulse and the device has sent its presence pulse back, it waits for a command byte to be transmitted from the master. In most cases the only command you need to send is Read ROM which is either 0x33 or 0x0F. In response the slave then sends the unique serial number stored in its memory.

Normally you would have to send the Skip ROM command or Match ROM command to select the slave device but in this case it isn't necessary because the iButton is usually the only device on the bus.

To send the Read ROM command you use the writeByte function introduced in the previous chapter:

```
writeByte(RPI_GPIO_P1_07, 0x33);
```

Now you can read the data that the slave is read to send. The slave sends eight bytes. The first byte is the family code which identifies the type of device for a simple iButton this is a 0x01. Next it sends the six bytes of the serial number and finally a CRC check byte. Often you can ignore the check byte because the transmission is reliable and getting it wrong isn't important. In this case you can't because the connection with the iButton is subject to a lot of noise.

8-BIT CRC CODE	48-BIT SERIAL NUMBER	8-BIT FAMILY CODE (01h)

Reading the eight bytes is easy:

```
uint8_t code[8];
int i;
for (i = 0; i < 8; i++) {
  code[i] = readByte(RPI_GPIO_P1_07);
}
```

Now we have all of the data we need but it does need to be checked for transmission errors.

Computing The CRC

A CRC (Cyclic Redundancy Checksum) is often regarded as a tough problem. However once you know the basic idea you should be able implement any CRC calculation, perhaps not in the most efficient way but it will work. For low data rate applications high efficiency isn't needed and you can make use of a direct implementation. The data sheet specifies the CRC used as a shift register:

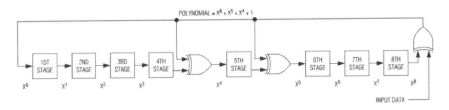

The first thing to notice is the generator polynomial that defines the CRC.

In this case it is:

$$X^8 + X^5 + X^4 + 1$$

The first question to answer is what is the connection between binary values and polynomials? The answer is that you can treat a binary number as the coefficients of a polynomial, for example 101 is $1*X^2+0*X+1$. Each bit position corresponds to a power of X. Using this notation creates a very simple relationship between multiplying by X and a left shift. For example:

$$(1*X^2 + 0*X+ 1)*X = 1*X^3 + 0*X^2 + 1X + 0$$

corresponds to:

$$101 <<1 == 1010$$

You can see that this extends to multiplying one polynomial by another and even polynomial division, all accomplished by shifting and XOR (eXclusive OR).

The CRC is the remainder when you divide the polynomial that represents the data by the generator polynomial. The computation of the remainder is what the shift register specified on the data sheet does. The fact that the division can be implemented so simply in hardware is what makes this sort of CRC computation so common. All the hardware has to do is zero the shift register and feed the data into it. When all the data has been shifted in, what is left in the shift register is the CRC i.e. the remainder.

To check the data you have received all you have to do is run it through the shift register again and compare the computed CRC with the one received. A better trick is also to run the received CRC though the shift register. If there have been no errors this will result in 0.

You can look into the theory of CRCs, bit sequences and polynomials further, it is interesting and practically useful, but we now know everything we need to if we want to implement the CRC used by the iButton. All we have to do is implement the shift register in software.

From the diagram, what we have to do is take each bit of the input data and XOR it with the least significant bit of the current shift register. If the input bit is 0 then the XORs in the shift register don't have any effect and the CRC just has to be moved one bit to the right. If the input bit is 1, you have to XOR bits at positions 3 and 4 with 1 and we have to put a 1 in at position 7 to simulate shifting a 1 into the register, i.e. XOR the shift register with 10001100.

So the algorithm for a single byte is:

```
for (j = 0; j < 8; j++) {
        temp = (crc ^ databyte) & 0x01;
        crc >>= 1;
        if (temp)
            crc ^= 0x8C;
        databyte>>= 1;
    }
}
```

First we XOR the data with the current CRC and extract the low order bit into temp. Then we right shift the CRC by 1 place. If the low order result, stored in temp was a 1, you have to XOR the CRC with 0x8C to simulate the XORs in the shift register and shift in a 1 at the most significant bit. Then shift the data one place right and repeat for the next data bit.

With this worked out we can now write a function that computes the CRC for the entire 8 byte data:

```
uint8_t crc8(uint8_t *data, uint8_t len) {
    uint8_t i;
    uint8_t j;
    uint8_t temp;
    uint8_t databyte;
    uint8_t crc = 0;
    for (i = 0; i < len; i++) {
        databyte = data[i];
        for (j = 0; j < 8; j++) {
            temp = (crc ^ databyte) & 0x01;
            crc >>= 1;
            if (temp)
                crc ^= 0x8C;
            databyte >>= 1;
        }
    }
    return crc;
}
```

With this in place we can now check the CRC and print the results:

```
uint8_t crc = crc8(code, 8);
 printf("CRC %hhX  ", crc);
 for (i = 0; i < 8; i++) {
     printf("%hhX ", code[i]);
 }
 printf("\n\r");
 fflush(stdout);
}
bcm2835_delayMicroseconds(100000);
```

iButton Function

Putting the functions together we can create a single function that returns a 0 if there is no iButton or if the CRC is incorrect and 1 if an iButton has been read and the CRC is OK.

```
int readiButton(uint8_t pin, uint8_t *data) {
    int b = presence(pin);
    if (b != 0) return 0;
    writeByte(pin, 0x33);

    int i;
    for (i = 0; i < 8; i++) {
        data[i] = readByte(pin);
    }
    uint8_t crc = crc8(data, 8);
    if (crc == 0) return 1;
    return 0;
}
```

180

Notice that if it returns a 1 then the serial number is in the second parameter which has to be passed an 8-byte array.

For example:

```
int i;
  uint8_t code[8];
  for (;;) {

      int p = readiButton(RPI_GPIO_P1_07, code);
      if (p == 1) {
          for (i = 0; i < 8; i++) {
              printf("%hhX ", code[i]);
          }
          printf("\n\r");
          fflush(stdout);
      }
      bcm2835_delayMicroseconds(100000);
  };
```

Complete Program Listing

```c
#include <bcm2835.h>
#include <stdio.h>
#include <sched.h>
#include <sys/mman.h>

int presence(uint8_t pin);
void writeByte(uint8_t pin, int byte);
uint8_t crc8(uint8_t *data, uint8_t len);
int readByte(uint8_t pin);
int readiButton(uint8_t pin, uint8_t *data);

int main(int argc, char **argv) {
    const struct sched_param priority = {1};
    sched_setscheduler(0, SCHED_FIFO, &priority);
    mlockall(MCL_CURRENT | MCL_FUTURE);

    if (!bcm2835_init())
        return 1;
    bcm2835_gpio_fsel(RPI_GPIO_P1_07, BCM2835_GPIO_FSEL_INPT);

    int i;
    uint8_t code[8];
    for (;;) {
        int p = readiButton(RPI_GPIO_P1_07, code);
        if (p == 1) {
            for (i = 0; i < 8; i++) {
                printf("%hhX ", code[i]);
            }
            printf("\n\r");
            fflush(stdout);
        }
        bcm2835_delayMicroseconds(100000);
    };
    bcm2835_close();
    return 0;
}

int presence(uint8_t pin) {
    bcm2835_gpio_fsel(pin, BCM2835_GPIO_FSEL_OUTP);
    bcm2835_gpio_write(pin, LOW);
    bcm2835_delayMicroseconds(480);
    bcm2835_gpio_fsel(pin, BCM2835_GPIO_FSEL_INPT);
    bcm2835_delayMicroseconds(70);
    uint8_t b = bcm2835_gpio_lev(pin);
    bcm2835_delayMicroseconds(410);
    return b;
}
```

```c
void writeBit(uint8_t pin, int b) {

    int delay1, delay2;
    if (b == 1) {
        delay1 = 6;
        delay2 = 64;
    } else {
        delay1 = 80;
        delay2 = 10;
    }
    bcm2835_gpio_fsel(pin, BCM2835_GPIO_FSEL_OUTP);
    bcm2835_gpio_write(pin, LOW);
    bcm2835_delayMicroseconds(delay1);
    bcm2835_gpio_fsel(pin, BCM2835_GPIO_FSEL_INPT);
    bcm2835_delayMicroseconds(delay2);
}

uint8_t readBit(uint8_t pin) {
    bcm2835_gpio_fsel(pin, BCM2835_GPIO_FSEL_OUTP);
    bcm2835_gpio_write(pin, LOW);
    bcm2835_delayMicroseconds(6);
    bcm2835_gpio_fsel(pin, BCM2835_GPIO_FSEL_INPT);
    bcm2835_delayMicroseconds(9);
    uint8_t b = bcm2835_gpio_lev(pin);
    bcm2835_delayMicroseconds(55);
    return b;
}

void writeByte(uint8_t pin, int byte) {
    int i;
    for (i = 0; i < 8; i++) {
        if (byte & 1) {
            writeBit(pin, 1);
        } else {
            writeBit(pin, 0);
        }
        byte = byte >> 1;
    }
}

int readByte(uint8_t pin) {
    int byte = 0;
    int i;
    for (i = 0; i < 8; i++) {
        byte = byte | readBit(pin) << i;
    };
    return byte;
}
```

```c
uint8_t crc8(uint8_t *data, uint8_t len) {

    uint8_t i;
    uint8_t j;
    uint8_t temp;
    uint8_t databyte;
    uint8_t crc = 0;
    for (i = 0; i < len; i++) {
        databyte = data[i];
        for (j = 0; j < 8; j++) {
            temp = (crc ^ databyte) & 0x01;
            crc >>= 1;
            if (temp)
                crc ^= 0x8C;

            databyte >>= 1;
        }
    }

    return crc;
}

int readiButton(uint8_t pin, uint8_t *data) {
    int b = presence(pin);
    if (b != 0) return 0;
    writeByte(pin, 0x33);
    int i;
    for (i = 0; i < 8; i++) {
        data[i] = readByte(pin);
    }
    uint8_t crc = crc8(data, 8);
    if (crc == 0) return 1;
    return 0;
}
```

Chapter 13

DS18B20 Temperature Sensor

Using the software developed in previous chapters we show how to connect and use the very popular DS18B20 temperature sensor without the need for external drivers.

The Hardware

The DS18B20 is available in a number of formats but the most common makes it look just like a standard BJT (Bipolar Junction Transistor) which can sometimes be a problem when you are trying to find one. You can also get them made up into waterproof sensors complete with cable.

No matter how packaged, they will work at 3.3V or 5V.

The basic specification of the DS18B20 is:

- Measures Temperatures from -55°C to +125°C (-67°F to +257°F)
- ±0.5°C Accuracy from -10°C to +85°C
- Thermometer Resolution is User Selectable from 9 to 12 Bits
- Converts Temperature to 12-Bit Digital Word in 750ms (Max)

It can also be powered from the data line, making the bus physically need only two wires - data and ground, however this "parasitic power" mode is difficult to make work reliably and best avoided in an initial design. To supply it with enough power during a conversion the host has to essentially connect it directly to the data line by providing a "strong pullup" - essentially a transistor. In normal powered mode there are just three connections:

Ground needs to be connected to the system ground, VDD to 3.3V and DQ to the pullup resistor of an open collector bus.

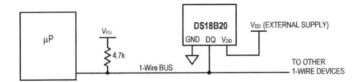

While you can have multiple devices on the same bus for simplicity, it is better to start off with a single device until you know that everything is working.

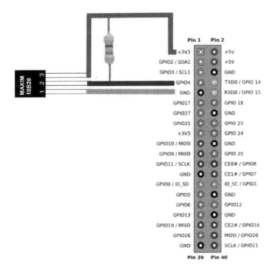

You can build the circuit in a variety of ways. You can solder the resistor to the temperature sensor and then use some longer wires with clips to connect to the Pi. You could also solder directly to the Pi, which is a good plan for the Pi Zero, or use a prototyping board.

Initialization

Every transaction with the a 1-wire device starts with an initialization handshake. The master holds the bus low for at least 480 microseconds, a 15 to 60 microsecond pause follows and then any and all of the devices on the bus pull the line low for 60 to 240 microseconds.

We have already implemented the presence function and so can simply use it again:

```
int main(int argc, char **argv) {
    const struct sched_param priority = {1};
    sched_setscheduler(0, SCHED_FIFO, &priority);
    mlockall(MCL_CURRENT | MCL_FUTURE);

    if (!bcm2835_init())
        return 1;
    bcm2835_gpio_fsel(RPI_GPIO_P1_07, BCM2835_GPIO_FSEL_INPT);

  if(presence(RPI_GPIO_P1_07)==0){
     read temperature
  };
```

If you find this doesn't work, make sure that you are running the program as root as described at the start of Chapter 2.

If you try this partial program and have a logic analyzer with a 1-wire protocol analyzer you will see something like:

Seeing a presence pulse is the simplest and quickest way to be sure that your hardware is working. From this point it is just a matter of using the functions developed in the previous chapters to work with the commands defined in the data sheet.

Initiating A Temperature Conversion

As there is only one device on the 1-wire bus so we can use the Skip ROM command (0xCC) to signal it to be active:

```
        writeByte(RPI_GPIO_P1_07, 0xCC);
```

You can see the pattern of bits sent on a logic analyzer:

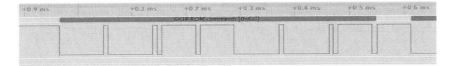

Our next task is to send a Convert command (0x44) to start the DS18B20 making a temperature measurement. Depending on the resolution selected this can take as long as 750ms.

How the device tells the master that the measurement has completed depends on the mode in which it is operating, but using an external power line, i.e. not using parasitic mode, the device sends a 0 bit in response to a bit read until it is completed when it sends a 1.

This is how 1-wire devices that need time to get data read slow down the master until they are ready. The master can read a single bit as often as it likes and the slave will respond with a 0 until it is ready with the data.

As we already have a readBit function this is easy. The software polls for the completion by reading the bus until it gets a 1 bit:

```
int convert(uint8_t pin) {
    int i;
    writeByte(pin, 0x44);
    for (i = 0; i < 1000; i++) {
        bcm2835_delayMicroseconds(100000);
        if (readBit(pin) == 1)break;
    }
    return i;
}
```

You can of course test the return value to check that the result has been obtained. If convert returns 500 then the loop timed out. When the function returns, the new temperature measurement is stored in the device's scratchpad memory and now all we have to do is read this.

Reading The Scratchpad

The scratchpad memory has nine bytes of storage in total and does things like control the accuracy of conversion and provide status information. In our simple example the only two bytes of any great interest are the first two, which hold the result of a temperature conversion. However, as we are going to check the CRC for error correction we need to read all nine bytes. All we have to do is issue a Read Scratchpad 0xBE command and then read the nine bytes that the device returns.

To send the new command we have to issue a new initialization pulse and a Skip ROM 0xCC command followed by a read scratchpad command 0xBE:

```
presence(RPI_GPIO_P1_07);
writeByte(RPI_GPIO_P1_07, 0xCC);
writeByte(RPI_GPIO_P1_07, 0xBE);
```

Now the data is ready to read. We can read all nine bytes of it or just the first two that we are interested in. The device will keep track of which bytes have been read. If you come back later and read more bytes you will continue the read from where you left off. If you issue another initialization pulse then the device aborts the data transmission.

As we do want to check the CRC for errors we will read all nine bytes:

```
int i;
uint8_t data[9];
for (i = 0; i < 9; i++) {
    data[i] = readByte(RPI_GPIO_P1_07);
}
```

Now we have all of the data stored in the scratch pad and the CRC byte. We can now check for errors:

```
uint8_t crc = crc8(data, 9);
```

As before, crc will be 0 if there are no transmission errors.

Getting the Temperature

To obtain the temperature measurement we need to work with the first two bytes, which are the least and most significant bytes of the 12-bit temperature reading:

```
int t1 = data[0];
int t2 = data[1];
```

t1 holds the low order bits and t2 the high order bits.

All we now have to do is to put the two bytes together as a 16-bit two's complement integer. As the Pi supports a 16-bit int type we can do this very easily:

```
int16_t temp1 = (t2 << 8 | t1);
```

Notice that this only works because int16_t really is a 16-bit integer. If you were to use:

```
int temp1= (t2<<8 | t1);
```

temp1 would be correct for positive temperatures but it would give the wrong answer for negative values because the sign bit isn't propagated into the top 16 bits.

If you want to use a 32-bit integer then you will have to propagate the sign bit manually:

```
if(t2 & 0x80) temp1=temp1 | 0xFFFF0000;
```

Finally we have to convert the temperature to a scaled floating point value. As the returned data gives the temperature in centigrade with the low order four bits giving the fractional part it has to be scaled by a factor of 1/16:

```
float temp = (float) temp1 / 16;
```

Now we can print the crc and the temperature:

```
printf("CRC %hho \n\r ", crc);
printf("temperature = %f C \n", temp);
```

A Temperature Function

Packaging all of this into a single function is easy:

```
float getTemperature(uint8_t pin) {
    if (presence(pin) == 1) return -1000;
    writeByte(pin, 0xCC);
    convert(pin);
    presence(pin);
    writeByte(pin, 0xCC);
    writeByte(pin, 0xBE);
    int i;
    uint8_t data[9];
    for (i = 0; i < 9; i++) {
        data[i] = readByte(pin);
    }
    uint8_t crc = crc8(data, 9);
    if(crc!=0) return -2000;
    int t1 = data[0];
    int t2 = data[1];
    int16_t temp1 = (t2 << 8 | t1);
    float temp = (float) temp1 / 16;
    return temp;
}
```

Notice that the function returns -1000 if there is no device and -2000 if there is a CRC error. These are values outside of the range of temperature that can be measured.

Other Commands

As well as the commands that we have used to read the temperature the DS18B20 supports a range of other commands. There are two command concerned with when there are more devices on the bus - Search ROM (0xF0) is used to scan the bus to discover what devices are connected and Match ROM (0x55) is used to select a particular device.

You can also read the unique 64-bit code of a device using the Read ROM command (0x33) and this works in exactly the same way as for the iButton discussed in the previous chapter. In this case the slave transmits 8 bytes, comprised of a single byte device family code, 0x28 for the DS18B20, six bytes of serial number and a single CRC byte.

You can use the read iButton function given in the previous chapter to read the serial number:

```
uint8_t code[8];
int i;
int p = readiButton(RPI_GPIO_P1_07, code);
if (p == 1) {
  for (i = 0; i < 8; i++) {
    printf("%hhX ", code[i]);
  }
  printf("\n\r");
  fflush(stdout);
}
```

As well as the Read ScratchPad command that we used to read the temperature there is also a Write ScratchPad command, 0x4E.

The format of the scratchpad is:

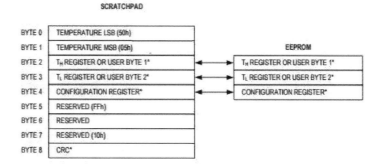

The first two bytes are the temperature that we have already used. The only writable entries are bytes 2, 3 and 4. The Write ScratchPad command transfers three bytes to these locations. Notice that there is no CRC and no error response if there is a transmission error. The data sheet suggests that you read the scratchpad after writing it to check that you have been successful in setting the three bytes.

The third byte written to the scratchpad is to the configuration register:

BIT 7	BIT 6	BIT 5	BIT 4	BIT 3	BIT 2	BIT 1	BIT 0
0	R1	R0	1	1	1	1	1

Essentially the only thing you can change is the resolution of the temperature measurement.

Configuration Register	Resolution	Time
0x1F	9 bits	93ms
0x3F	10 bits	175ms
0x5F	11 bits	375ms
0x7F	12 bits	750ms

The time quoted is the maximum for a conversion at the given precision. You can see that the only real advantage of decreasing precision is to make conversion faster. The default is 0x7F and 12 bits of precision.

The first two bytes of the write scratchpad set a high and low temperature alarm. This feature isn't much used, but you can set two temperatures that will trigger the device into alarm mode. Note you only set the top eight bits of the threshold temperatures. This is easy enough, but the alarm status is set with every read so if the temperature goes outside the set bounds and then back in the alarm is cleared.

The second problem is that to discover which devices are in alarm mode you have to use the Alarm Search command (0xEC). This works like the Search ROM command, but the only devices that respond are the ones with an alarm state. The alarm feature might be useful if you have a lot of devices and simply want to detect an out of band temperature. You could set up multiple devices with appropriate temperature limits and then simply repeatedly scan the bus for devices with alarms set. To see how this can be done see the next chapter.

You may notice that the scratchpad also has an EEPROM memory connected. You can transfer the three bytes of the scratchpad to the EEPROM using Copy Scratchpad (0x48) and transfer them back using the Recall EEPROM command (0xB8). You can use this to make the settings non-volatile.

Finally there is the Read Power Supply command (0xB4). If the master reads the bus after issuing this command a 0 indicates that there are parasitic powered devices on the bus. If there are such devices the master has to run the bus in such a way that they are powered correctly.

If you restrict yourself to a single slave device on the bus, this is more or less all there is to the DS18B20, and the 1-wire bus in general. If you want to have multiple slave devices, however, while you don't need any more hardware, you do need some more software, which is the subject of the next chapter.

Chapter 14
The Multidrop 1-Wire Bus

Sometimes it it just easier from the point of view of hardware to connect a set of 1-wire devices to the same GPIO line, but this makes the software more complex. Find out how to discover what devices are present on a multidrop bus (MDB) and how to select the one you want to work with.

The 1-wire bus has a very sophisticated addressing mechanism that lets you discover what devices are connected to a single 1-wire implementation. This is an algorithm worth knowing about for its ingenious design and in this chapter a 1-wire bus scanning function is developed. Unlike the one presented by Maxim, the company that invented of the 1-wire bus, it is recursive and as a result simpler.

Every 1-wire bus device has a unique 64-bit serial number that serves as its address on the bus. You can select just one device by writing its serial number. However how do you discover what devices are connected?

The Hardware

The first thing to clear up is that you can run multiple 1-wire devices on the same bus by simply adding them in parallel. You only need a single pullup resistor, no matter how many devices there are on the bus.

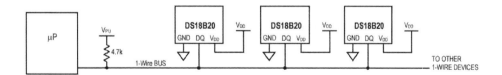

In this chapter the DS18B20 will be used as an example because it is often used in this way, but the same techniques will work with other devices and mixed devices.

The 1-Wire Search Algorithm

The serial number has a standard format. The least significant byte is a family code, i.e. what sort of device it is, the next six bytes are the serial number, and the most significant byte is a checksum.

MSB	64-Bit 'Registration' ROM Number		LSB
8-Bit CRC	48-Bit Serial Number	8-Bit Family Code	
MSB LSB	MSB LSB	MSB LSB	

All eight bytes are used as the address of the devices and this means we can check for transmission errors by simply applying the CRC function developed in earlier chapters.

If you know the serial numbers of the devices, you can simply write your program to work with them. However, this means that you need to hardcode the serial numbers into your program, which doesn't make it very portable. A better solution is to scan the bus to search for connected devices and discover their serial numbers. This is what the 1-wire search algorithm is for. It has a reputation for being difficult to understand and even more difficult to implement. The good news it that it isn't as difficult as it first appears and is very instructive.

The basic idea is that the master sends an initialization pulse on the bus and all of the connected devices respond with their presence pulse. Next the master places the search command, 0xF0, on the bus which sets all of the devices into search mode.

The master then reads two bits from the bus that together encode the first bit of the serial numbers from all of the devices. Given the nature of the 1-wire bus and the way the pullup works, what the master receives is the logical AND of all the bits sent from each of the slaves. The first bit the slaves send is their low order bit and the second bit is the logical complement, i.e NOT, of their first bit. From these two bits the master can deduce the following:

1st Bit	2nd Bit	Conclusion
0	0	There is at least one device with a 1 in this position and another with a 0
0	1	All devices have a 0 in this position
1	0	All devices have a 1 in this position
1	1	No devices are present

Obviously 1,1 is an error condition indicating something has removed the devices from the bus.

In the case of receiving either 0,1 or 1,0 the bit at that position has been determined to be a 0 or 1 respectively and all of the devices on the bus share this value in their serial numbers at this bit position. If the master receives 0,0 then there are devices with a 1 and devices with a 0 in their serial number at this position and the master can pick one of the values to explore further. Of course if the master wants to list all of the devices on the bus it has to return to this point and explore the second possibility.

The master selects which value it is going to follow by transmitting a single bit. All of the devices that do match the bit in their serial number continue to transmit bits to the master while those that do not go into a wait state until the next initialization pulse from the master.

The search algorithm determines a single bit of a serial number by reading two bits from the slaves and transmitting one bit to reduce the number of slaves participating in the scan. By repeating the "read two bits/write one" action the master eventually finds all 64 bits of one of the slave's serial number. It then has to backtrack to one of the bit locations where there was a choice of which bit to select and select the alternative. In this way the master eventually lists all of the serial numbers on the bus.

Notice that the master starts off trying to determine bit zero for a single device connected to the bus. It determines each bit where all of the devices agree on a 0 or a 1. Each time the master encounters a bit conflict, i.e. there are devices with a 0 and a 1 in that bit position, it selects one value and tells the devices with the other value to switch off. It then continues to determine the subsequent bit positions for the remaining devices. As the serial numbers are unique, the master always ends up talking to just one device.

You can probably see that this is a depth first tree search with branches where the bit values are in conflict.

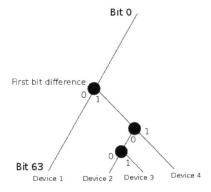

If there are four devices on the bus they must all differ in at least one bit position. When the master starts the scan, it reads all 1 or all 0 as it processes each until it comes to the first location where there is another device with a different value at that bit. The master receives a 0,0 back from the slaves and arbitrarily sends a 0 to switch off all the slaves with a 1 in that location. The master then continues to read bits and if all of the other devices have a 1 in that bit position there are no more conflict.

When the master reaches bit 63, it has the complete serial number of the first device, Device 1 in the diagram. It then backtracks to the bit position where the first conflict occurred. It now writes a 1 to switch off Device 1 and continues to read bits until it encounters another conflict. Again it arbitrarily chooses a 0 and switches off all of the devices with a 1 in that bit position.

In the example there are two devices with a 0 in that bit position and so as the master reads bits it encounters another conflict. Again it sends a 0 and switches off the other device and completes reading bits until it reaches bit 63 when it has the serial number of Device 2.

The master now backtracks to the most recent conflict, sends a 1 and continues down the next branch to get the next device's serial number and so on until there are no conflict points to backtrack to.

Make sure you understand the algorithm before moving on to consider the implementation.

A Recursive Scan

The depth first tree search described above is most easily implemented using recursion. While recursion is often considered difficult, when it fits in with the nature of the problem it is often the best way to work. A simple, but not quite complete, recursive algorithm for the depth first search described above is relatively easy to construct. If you don't follow how it works then you can just use it, but it is worth trying to understand as it is a really good example of how recursion can make things simpler.

The serial numbers of the devices found will be stored in an array of 64 bit integers:

```
int oneWireScan(uint8_t pin, uint64_t serial[]) {
```

Two static variables are needed to record a global state, **bitcount**, which records how deep in the tree we currently are; and **deviceCount**, which records how many devices we have found so far:

```
static int bitcount = 0;
static int deviceCount = 0;
```

Static variables are shared between all invocations of a function; they are only initialized once, when the program starts; and they are allocated on the heap not the stack.

The way to think about **oneWireScan**, and how to think about it if you were writing it from scratch, is that calling it will process the bit indicated by the current value of bitcount. As you increment bitcount before you call oneWireScan. it will process all of the bits down to 63 by repeatedly calling itself to process the next bit. Next we need to write starting and ending conditions. This is fairly usual with recursion. If bitcount is greater than 63 then we have a full serial number and can move deviceCount on by one and zero bitcount to start over.

```
if (bitcount > 63) {
    bitcount = 0;
    deviceCount++;
    return deviceCount;
}
```

Similarly if bitcount is zero we need to start a traverse of the tree by sending a presence pulse, and then a search command. If there are no devices on the bus, we set bitcount to zero and return as there is nothing to do.

```
if (bitcount == 0) {
    if (presence(pin) == 1) {
        bitcount = 0;
        return deviceCount;
    }
    deviceCount = 0;
    serial[deviceCount] = 0;
    writeByte(pin, 0xF0);
};
```

Now we are ready to read the first, or next, bit - it doesn't really make a lot of difference to what we have to do:

```
int b1 = readBit(pin);
int b2 = readBit(pin);
```

What we have to do, however, does depend on b1 and b2. The two simplest conditions are if there are no conflicts on the bus and we simply need to set a 0 or a 1:

```
if (b1 == 0 && b2 == 1) {
        serial[deviceCount] >>= 1;
        writeBit(pin, 0);
        bitcount++;
        oneWireScan(pin, serial);
};
if (b1 == 1 && b2 == 0) {
        serial[deviceCount] >>= 1;
        serial[deviceCount] |= 0x8000000000000000LL;
        writeBit(pin, 1);
        bitcount++;
        oneWireScan(pin, serial);

};
```

We either shift a 0 or a 1 into the serial number we are building up and then write a 0 or a 1 to keep all of the slaves in the scan. Finally, and this is where recursion comes in, we increment bitcount and call oneWireScan again to process the next bit. This is the part that worries most programmers, but as long as you understand that we get a complete new version of oneWireScan and it processes the next bit just like the previous bit, then it all works.

If we get b1 and b2 equal to one then we have an error condition and this terminates the processing of the next bit:

```
if (b1 == 1 && b2 == 1) {
    bitcount = 0;
    return deviceCount;
};
```

Notice that you have to set bitcount back to zero otherwise it will be wrong the next time you call the function.

The most difficult of the conditions to deal with is when there is a collision because you have to explore both branches of the tree. Using recursion, however, this is fairly easy:

```
if (b1 == 0 && b2 == 0) {

    serial[deviceCount] >>= 1;
    writeBit(pin, 0);
    bitcount++;
    oneWireScan(pin, serial);

    serial[deviceCount] >>= 1;
    serial[deviceCount] |= 0x8000000000000000LL;
    writeBit(pin, 1);
    bitcount++;
    oneWireScan(pin, serial);    };

    return deviceCount;
}
```

All that happens here is that first we record a 0 in the serial number and send a 0 to turn off all the devices with a 1 in this position. Next we call oneWireScan again to complete this version of the serial number. When this returns we have the completed 64-bit serial number and deviceCount is incremented. Next we follow the other branch, recording a 1 in the serial number and writing a 1 to turn off all of the devices with 0 in this position as we already have them in the array, and then call oneWireScan to find the remaining bits.

That completes the function and the final instruction is:

```
        return deviceCount;
    }
```

If you try this out you will find it doesn't work.

The reason is very simple. In the conflict-handling part of the function it is assumed that, when the first call to oneWireScan returns, it is exactly where it was before the call, i.e. at the same bit position, and is ready to continue down the new branch of the tree. This is true as far as the function is concerned but the devices on the bus have physically moved on and are no longer at the same bit positions.

In fact the scan has completed; we are at bit 63 and we need to start a new scan. Not only do we need to start a new scan we need to restore the hardware to the position it was in just before the call to oneWireScan.

This is the reason that most programmers don't implement the scan as a recursive function - the function is recursive but the hardware isn't. If we had a hardware stack we could simply push the state just before the call and then pop it when the call returned. We don't have a hardware stack, but it is very easy to restore the state of the hardware.

In fact the only thing we need to record is the current bit position in a local, rather than a static, variable, **bitposition**:

```
        int bitposition = bitcount;
        bitcount++;
        oneWireScan(pin, serial);
```

Now when the oneWireScan returns, bitposition holds the number of the bit that it was working on before the call. We can now restore bitcount and start a completely new scan:

```
        bitcount = bitposition;
        if (presence(pin) == 1){
            bitposition=0;
            return 0;
        }
        writeByte(pin, 0xF0);
```

This starts us off at bit zero of the scan, but to restore the state we want to be at the bit position stored in bitposition. If you think about it, the bits of the next serial number up to bitposition are going to be the same as the just retrieved serial number, they will only differ after this point. So we can retrieve the first part of the serial number from the previous serial number. The only difference is that the last bit that we want isn't going to be a 0. It now needs to be a 1 to take us down the next branch of the tree.

We can do this in one go:

```
uint64_t temp = serial[deviceCount - 1] | (0x1LL << (bitcount));
```

Now we need to walk the hardware through all of the bits in **temp** from bit zero to bitcount:

```
int i;
uint64_t bit;
for (i = 0; i < bitcount+1; i++) {
    bit = temp & 0x01LL;
    temp >>= 1;
    b1 = readBit(pin);
    b2 = readBit(pin);
    writeBit(pin, bit);
    serial[deviceCount] >>= 1;
    serial[deviceCount] |= (bit << 63);
}
```

The hardware is now restored to its state just before the first call to oneWireScan and we have sent a 1 in place of the 0 for the current bit. We can now call oneWireScan again to explore the alternative branch of the tree:

```
        bitcount++;
        oneWireScan(pin, serial);

    };
```

That's the final step for a recursive scan of the 1-wire bus.

oneWireScan

The complete function is:

```
int oneWireScan(uint8_t pin, uint64_t serial[]) {
    static int bitcount = 0;
    static int deviceCount = 0;

    if (bitcount > 63) {
        bitcount = 0;
        deviceCount++;
        return deviceCount;

    }

    if (bitcount == 0) {
        if (presence(pin) == 1) {
            bitcount = 0;
            return deviceCount;
        }
        deviceCount = 0;
        serial[deviceCount] = 0;
        writeByte(pin, 0xF0);
    };

    int b1 = readBit(pin);
    int b2 = readBit(pin);

    if (b1 == 0 && b2 == 1) {
        serial[deviceCount] >>= 1;
        writeBit(pin, 0);
        bitcount++;
        oneWireScan(pin, serial);
    };

    if (b1 == 1 && b2 == 0) {
        serial[deviceCount] >>= 1;
        serial[deviceCount] |= 0x8000000000000000LL;
        writeBit(pin, 1);
        bitcount++;
        oneWireScan(pin, serial);

    };
```

```
    if (b1 == 1 && b2 == 1) {
            bitcount = 0;
            return deviceCount;
    };
    if (b1 == 0 && b2 == 0) {
            serial[deviceCount] >>= 1;
            writeBit(pin, 0);
            int bitposition = bitcount;
            bitcount++;
            oneWireScan(pin, serial);

            bitcount = bitposition;
            if (presence(pin) == 1){
                bitposition=0;
                return 0;
            }

            writeByte(pin, 0xF0);
            uint64_t temp = serial[deviceCount - 1] |
                                    (0x1LL << (bitcount));
            int i;
            uint64_t bit;
            for (i = 0; i < bitcount+1; i++) {
                bit = temp & 0x01LL;
                temp >>= 1;
                b1 = readBit(pin);
                b2 = readBit(pin);
                writeBit(pin, bit);
                serial[deviceCount] >>= 1;
                serial[deviceCount] |= (bit << 63);
            }
            bitcount++;
            oneWireScan(pin, serial);
    };

    return deviceCount;
}
```

Scanning The Bus

Scanning the 1-wire bus is a strange thing to do. The reason is that in most cases the devices on the bus don't change. You set up a group of slaves and unless one or more of them fail the serial numbers don't change.

So why bother scanning the bus? As long as you program the serial numbers into your code, it will all work.

It is not uncommon to find people using 1-wire bus scanners to discover what is connected and then transcribing the serial numbers to the program, sometimes even if there is only one device on the bus! However discovering the devices on the bus dynamically does allow you to write programs that are robust against failures and auto configuring. So instead of scanning the bus and hardcoding the serial numbers, why not scan the bus each time there is a restart, or even sooner? Now we come to the problems of scanning the bus.

The 1-wire bus isn't very robust. Its use of pullup resistors at such high speeds means that it doesn't take much capacitance to make the pulses look more like a capacitor charging up. Getting the wiring right for a 1-wire bus with multiple devices isn't easy. What is more, scanning the bus is the only time, apart from the presence pulse, when multiple devices control the bus. A setup that works perfectly well with a single device often has problems when there is more than one device. In fact, a standard 1-wire bus debugging technique is to remove all but one device and see if what wasn't working suddenly works.

You can get around some of the problems by lowering the value of the pullup resistor, but this does increase the load on the driving GPIO lines and the slave devices. You can reduce the pull up to 2K or even less to account for the reduced working voltage of 3.3V. The 1-wire bus works best as 5V when the lines are long, but it is usually not worth the trouble to add a 3.3V to 5V driver.

If you want to drive a very long line, or just need the highest possible performance, there is a technique which, while it might not be worth using in many situations, is worth knowing about. It is called by a number of names but "controllable slew rate" is close enough. The idea is that when the master releases the bus, we have to wait for it to pullup via the resistor.

The transistor associated with SPU is related to the strong pullup needed for

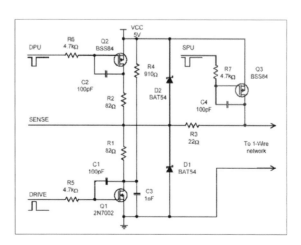

parasitic power power mode and you can ignore it.

The principle used is that we can put a transistor in parallel with the pullup resistor and use it to pull the line up faster when appropriate. For example, when the master pulls the line low for a presence pulse, it can trigger the pullup transistor when the pulse ends to get the line back up faster than just via the resistor.

The fast pullup transistor is switched off just before the slaves start to pull the line low. You can use the fast pullup transistor in the same way when the master writes a 0 or reads or writes a 1. Of course, you don't need to use it when the master reads a 0 because the slave holds the line low for the whole time slot and there is no need for a fast pullup. It is claimed that lines as long as 500m can work in this mode. Notice that you now need an additional GPIO line to drive the fast pullup transistor. If you want to know more then refer to the Maxim design notes.

In practice you have to face up to the fact that you will get errors when working with the 1-wire bus and especially so with multiple devices. The problem is particularly bad if you are testing a circuit using a protoboard. Things often work better when you move to properly soldered connections and cables, but you will still get errors. However, even with the best wiring possible, you are still going to get errors due to the inevitable occasional interrupt that Linux will force on your program.

The only reasonable solution is to add error checking to validate the serial numbers using the standard CRC function.

Error Checking

Error checking a bus scan is fairly easy. The only problem is exactly how respond when you detect an error.

When the oneWireScan function returns we have an array with serial numbers ready to check. Each serial number is a 64-bit integer, but the CRC checking function accepts an 8-byte array. At this point you might be starting to think about repacking the bits into an array, but there is a much simpler solution.

The layout in memory for an 8-byte array and a 64-bit integer is the same so all we have to do is cast the array to a suitable pointer type and pass the 64-bit integer as if it was an 8-byte array. That is:

```
uint64_t serial[15];
uint8_t *code;
int crc;
int d;
d = oneWireScan(RPI_GPIO_P1_11, serial);
crc = 0;
for (i = 0; i < d; i++) {
    code = (uint8_t*) & serial[i ];
    crc += crc8(code, 8);
}
```

When you call oneWireScan you have to provide it with an array of 64-bit integers it can use to store serial numbers. It returns d, the number of devices it has found, and you need to check for CRC errors in each of them. As there is no CRC error if they are all 0 we can check for any CRC errors by summing the crc values for each serial number.

The important line to explain is:

```
code = (uint8_t*) & serial[i ];
```

This takes the address of the ith element of serial and casts it to a pointer to uint8_t, i.e. unsigned bytes. The function can use this as if it was an array of unsigned bytes and everything works without having to do any bit manipulation, such is the power, and danger, of programming in C. Everything works as long as the basic assumption, that a 64-bit unsigned integer and an 8-byte array are stored in memory in the same way, holds. They usually are, but there is no guarantee.

This short piece of code allows you to scan the bus and detect if there is an error. If there is then you can scan it again. Generally speaking you will mostly get a scans without error, but in scans of configurations with small numbers, up to about 8, of devices you will get errors in about one in ten scans. Notice that a scan transfers a lot of data and how long it takes depends on how many devices are connected to the bus.

How Many Devices?

Unfortunately there are other ways that a bus scan can go wrong. It can fail to detect one or more devices. It only takes a single bit error and the scan will fail to get the serial number for that device. If it is the first device in the scan and there are no backtrack points as yet, the entire scan is canceled. More usually, however, just one device goes missing during a scan. This will not be detected as an error because the serial numbers returned will not be in error and hence will not trigger a CRC error.

There are a number of solution to this problem. You could add error detection to the scanning function, but even if you did this correctly there are times when a device simply doesn't respond at all, presumably because it misses the initialization pulse, and hence goes missing without triggering an error.

In practice there are two easy things you can do to deal with missing devices. You can scan the bus more than once and take the maximum number of correct serial numbers you find as the number of devices on the bus; and you can set the number of devices as a constant and only accept scans that return that number.

In practice it is normal to know how many devices there are on the bus and as such enforcing the scan to find that number is the best solution. For example, here is an error-proof bus scan for exactly four devices:

```
for (j = 0; j < 100; j++) {
        d = oneWireScan(RPI_GPIO_P1_11, serial);
        if (d != 4)continue;
        crc = 0;
        for (i = 0; i < d; i++) {
            code = (uint8_t*) & serial[i ];
            crc += crc8(code, 8);
        }
        if (crc == 0)break;
        bcm2835_delayMicroseconds(30000);
    }
```

You can adjust the retries and time delays to suit your application. The delay is included to give time for any noise or instability in the system to subside. If you don't use twisted pair cable then 1-wire is prone to RF interference. The scan is retried 100 times over a 3 second period. If you don't get a good scan in that time something is seriously wrong and most likely one of the devices has failed.

Reading Specific Devices

Now that we have an array of serial numbers, we can use them to read the devices they correspond to. Before you do this you should check the family codes, i.e. the first byte of the serial number, to discover what kind of device you are about to work with. In practice you usually already know. In this example it is assumed that all of the devices are DS18B20 temperature sensors.

To read a specific device all you have to do is send a Match ROM command (0x55) in place of a Skip ROM command (0xCC) and then send the 64-bit serial number to select a single device. After this the transaction is the same and you can, in the case of the DS18B20, initiate a conversion and then read the scratchpad.

The new function to read a specific device is very similar to the original that read a single device on the bus. First we have to issue a convert command after selecting the device:

```
float getDeviceTemperature(uint8_t pin, uint64_t device) {
    if (presence(pin) == 1) return -1000;
    writeByte(pin, 0x55);
    int i, bit;
    uint64_t d = device;
    for (i = 0; i < 64; i++) {
        bit = d & 0x01;
        d = d >> 1;
        writeBit(pin, bit);
    }
    convert(pin);
```

After sending Match ROM, we send all the 64 bits of the device serial number, low order bits first. This causes all the devices that do not match the serial number to go into an idle state. The convert function waits for the active device to complete its conversion. Now we have to read the scratchpad. This works in the same way, but we have to select the device a second time because the initialization pulse activates all the devices.

This may seem a nuisance, but you can use it to your advantage if you have set of devices in that you could first set each one to convert and then read each one after waiting long enough for them to settle:

```
presence(pin);
writeByte(pin, 0x55);
d = device;
for (i = 0; i < 64; i++) {
    bit = d & 0x01;
    d = d >> 1;
    writeBit(pin, bit);
}
writeByte(pin, 0xBE);
uint8_t data[9];
for (i = 0; i < 9; i++) {
    data[i] = readByte(pin);
}
```

The final part of the function is identical to the original read temperature function. The entire function, using a new matchROM function to select the device, is:

```
float getDeviceTemperature(uint8_t pin, uint64_t device) {
    if (presence(pin) == 1) return -1000;

    matchROM(pin, device);
    convert(pin);
    presence(pin);
    matchROM(pin, device);
    writeByte(pin, 0xBE);
    uint8_t data[9];
    int i;
    for (i = 0; i < 9; i++) {
        data[i] = readByte(pin);
    }
    uint8_t crc = crc8(data, 9);
    if (crc != 0) return -2000;
    int t1 = data[0];
    int t2 = data[1];
    int16_t temp1 = (t2 << 8 | t1);
    float temp = (float) temp1 / 16;
    return temp;
}
```

```
      void matchROM(uint8_t pin, uint64_t device) {
          writeByte(pin, 0x55);
          int i, bit;
          for (i = 0; i < 64; i++) {
              bit = device & 0x01;
              device >>= 1;
              writeBit(pin, bit);
          }
      }
```

An example main program that scans the bus and reads the devices found is:

```
int main(int argc, char **argv) {
    const struct sched_param priority = {5};
    sched_setscheduler(0, SCHED_FIFO, &priority);
    mlockall(MCL_CURRENT | MCL_FUTURE);
    if (!bcm2835_init())
        return 1;
    bcm2835_gpio_fsel(RPI_GPIO_P1_07, BCM2835_GPIO_FSEL_INPT);
    uint64_t serial[15];
    int i, j;
    uint8_t *code;
    int crc,d;
    for (;;) {
        for (j = 0; j < 1000; j++) {
            d = oneWireScan(RPI_GPIO_P1_07, serial);
            if (d != 4)continue;
            crc = 0;
            for (i = 0; i < d; i++) {
                code = (uint8_t*) & serial[i ];
                crc += crc8(code, 8);
            }
            printf("%hho %d %d\n\r", crc, d, j);
            fflush(stdout);
            if (crc == 0)break;
            bcm2835_delayMicroseconds(30000);
        }
        for (i = 0; i < d; i++) {
        printf("%llX \n", serial[i]);
        float temp = getDeviceTemperature(RPI_GPIO_P1_07,
                                          serial[i]);
        printf("temperature = %f C \n", temp);
        }
    }
```

Alarm Scan

You can use the same technique to pick out devices with an alarm set. The DS18B20 discussed in the previous chapter, for example, can have a high and low limit temperature set by writing data to the scratchpad. If the temperature goes outside these limits an alarm is set. You can obtain the serial numbers of all devices with an alarm set by scanning the bus using Alarm Search (0xEC) rather than Match ROM (0x55). Just change the code sent in the function. In this case you will get a list of serial numbers corresponding to devices with alarms set and you can continue to process just these.

This seems like an attractive option but, given the propensity for errors, it isn't particularly robust and you could easily miss a device with an alarm set. If possible it is better to perform a manual scan of each device on the bus and read its alarm status.

Final Thoughts

The 1-wire bus is simple and immensely useful - as long as you don't try to push it too far. Problems start to arise when you use long, over 2 or 4m connections or try to put lots of devices on the same bus. With the price of a Pi Zero and the number of GPIO lines available this seems like an unnecessary complication.

Chapter 15

Getting Started With The SPI Bus

The Serial Peripheral Interface (SPI) bus can be something of a problem because it doesn't have a well defined standard that every device conforms to. Even so if you only want to work with one specific device it is usually easy to find a configuration that works - as long as you understand what the possibilities are.

SPI Bus Basics

The SPI bus is commonly encountered as it is used to connect all sorts of devices from LCD displays, through real time clocks and AtoD converters, but as different companies have implemented it in different ways, you have to work harder to implement it in any particular case. However it does usually work, which is a surprise for a bus with no standard or clear specification.

The reason it can be made to work is that you can specify a range of different operating modes, frequencies and polarities. This makes the bus slightly more complicated to use but generally it is a matter of looking up how the device you are trying to work with implements the SPI bus and then getting the Pi to work in the same way.

The bus is odd in another way - it does not use bidirectional serial connections. There is a data line for the data to go from the master to the slave and a separate data line from the slave back to the master. That is instead of a single data line that changes its transfer direction there is one for data out and one for data in. It is also worth knowing that the drive on the SPI bus is push-pull and not open collector/drain. This provides higher speed and more noise protection as the bus is driven in both directions. There is a bidirectional mode where a single wire is used for the data, but the Pi doesn't support this.

In the configuration used for the Pi, there is a single master and, at most, two slaves. The signal lines are:

- MOSI (Master Output Slave Input), i.e. data to the slave
- MISO (Master Input Slave Output), i.e. data to the master
- SCLK (Serial Clock), which is always generated by the master

In general, there can also be any number of SS (Slave Select) or CE (Chip Select) lines, which are usually set low to select which slave is being addressed. Notice that, unlike other buses I2C for example, there are no SPI commands or addresses only bytes of data. However, slave devices do interpret some of the data as commands to do something or send some particular data.

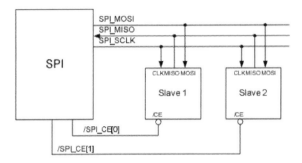

The Pi has only a single SPI bus exposed on the GPIO connector and only two SS lines. This means that in principle you can only connect two SPI devices to the Pi, although this is a restriction that is easy to overcome.

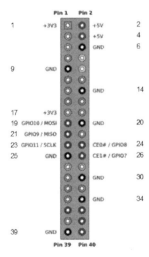

The pins that are used for the Pi's SPI bus are:

MOSI   GPIO 10 19 Out
MISO   GPIO 9   21 In
SCLK   GPIO 11 23 Out
CE0   GPIO 8   24 Out
CE1   GPIO 7   26 In

The data transfer on the SPI bus is also slightly odd. What happens is that the master pulls one of the chip selects low, which activates a slave. Then the master toggles the clock SCLK and both the master and the slave send a single bit on their respective data lines. After eight clock pulses, a byte has been transferred from the master to the slave and from the slave to the master. You can think of this as being implemented as a circular buffer, although it doesn't have to be.

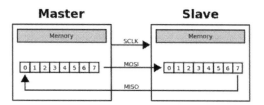

This full duplex data transfer is often hidden by the software and the protocol used. For example, there is a read function that reads data from the slave and sends zeros or data that is ignored by the slave. Similarly there is a write function that sends valid data, but ignores whatever the slave sends. The transfer is typically in groups of eight bits, usually most significant bit first, but this isn't always the case. In general as long as the master supply clock pulses data is transferred.

Notice this circular buffer arrangement allows for slaves to be daisy chained with the output of one going to the input of the next. This makes the entire chain one big circular shift register. This can make it possible to have multiple devices with only a single chip select but it also means any commands sent to the slaves are received by each one in turn. For example, you could send a convert command to each AtoD converter in turn and receive back results from each one.

The final odd thing about the SPI bus is that there are four modes which define the relationship between the data timing and the clock pulse. The clock can be either active high or low - clock polarity CPOL and data can be sampled on the rising or falling edge of the clock - clock phase CPHA.

All combinations of these two possibilities gives the four modes:

SPI Mode*	Clock Polarity CPOL	Clock Edge CPHA	Characteristics
0	0	0	Clock active high data output on falling edge and sampled on rising
1	0	1	Clock active high data output on rising edge and sampled on falling
2	1	0	Clock active low data output on falling edge and sampled on rising
3	1	1	Clock active low data output on rising edge and sampled on falling

*The way that the SPI modes are labeled is common but not universal.

There is often a problem trying to work out what mode a slave device uses. The clock polarity is usually easy and the Clock phase can sometimes be worked out from the data transfer timing diagrams and:

- First clock transition in the middle of a data bit means CPHA=0

- First clock transition at the start of a data bit means CPHA=1

So to configure the SPI bus to work with a particular slave device:

1. Select the clock frequency - anything from 125MHz to 3.8KHz

2. Set the CS polarity - active high or low

3. Set the clock mode Mode0 thru Mode3

Now we have to find out how to do this using the bcm2835 library.

The SPI Functions

Initialization

There are two functions concerned with enabling and disabling the SPI bus:

```
bcm2835_spi_begin ()
bcm2835_spi_end ()
```

Before you make use of the SPI bus you have to initialize it using:

```
bcm2835_spi_begin ()
```

This returns 1 if successful and 0 otherwise. After this the pins allocated to the SPI bus no longer work as general purpose GPIO pins. If this function fails the most likely reason is that you are not running the program as root.

When you are finished using the SPI bus you can return the pins to general GPIO lines by calling:

```
bcm2835_spi_end ()
```

Configuration

There are a number of functions that you can use to configure the way the bus works.

```
bcm2835_spi_setClockDivider (uint16_t divider)
bcm2835_spi_setBitOrder (uint8_t order)
bcm2835_spi_setDataMode (uint8_t mode)
bcm2835_spi_chipSelect (uint8_t cs)
bcm2835_spi_setChipSelectPolarity (uint8_t cs,uint8_t active)
```

setClockDivider sets the speed of data transfer as a fraction of the back Pi clock speed. The documentation indicates that only powers of two can be used for the divider and provides a predefined enumeration:

```
BCM2835_SPI_CLOCK_DIVIDER_powerof2
```

In fact you can use any value for the clock divider.

The clock speed is given by:

```
clock speed=250/divider MHz
```

You can ignore the BitOrder function because the Pi's SPI bus doesn't support it.

setDataMode can be used to set the data transfer to one of:

BCM2835_SPI_MODE0	CPOL = 0, CPHA = 0
BCM2835_SPI_MODE1	CPOL = 0, CPHA = 1
BCM2835_SPI_MODE2	CPOL = 1, CPHA = 0
BCM2835_SPI_MODE3	CPOL = 1, CPHA = 1

chipSelect sets which chip select line will be involved in all data transfer operations until it is changed. You can set any of:

BCM2835_SPI_CS0	Chip Select 0
BCM2835_SPI_CS1	Chip Select 1
BCM2835_SPI_CS2	Chip Select 2 (i.e. pins CS1 and CS2 are asserted)
BCM2835_SPI_CS_NONE	No CS, control it yourself

Finally **setChipSelectPolarity** can be used to set either of the chip select lines to active high or active low.

In general you should configure the operation of the SPI bus completely but the defaults are:

Mode 0
divider 65536 i.e. approx 3.81 kHz the slowest clock possible
chip select CS0
chip select polarity active low
Bit order most significant bit first

Just to make sure that you get the configuration you want you should get in the habit of including:

```
bcm2835_spi_setBitOrder(BCM2835_SPI_BIT_ORDER_MSBFIRST);
bcm2835_spi_setDataMode(BCM2835_SPI_MODE0);
bcm2835_spi_setClockDivider(BCM2835_SPI_CLOCK_DIVIDER_65536);
bcm2835_spi_chipSelect(BCM2835_SPI_CS0);
bcm2835_spi_setChipSelectPolarity(BCM2835_SPI_CS0, LOW);
```

This sets the defaults but you can modify the settings as you need.

Data Transfer functions

Because of the way the SPI bus uses a full duplex transfer things are a little different from other buses when it comes to implementing functions to transfer data:

```
uint8_t bcm2835_spi_transfer (uint8_t value)
bcm2835_spi_writenb (char *buf, uint32_t len)
bcm2835_spi_transfern (char *buf, uint32_t len)
bcm2835_spi_transfernb (char *tbuf, char *rbuf, uint32_t len)
```

If you recall that the data transfer sends a byte of data out of the register while shifting in a byte of data then the transfer functions will make sense.

The most basic of this set of functions is **transfer** which sends a single byte to the slave while receiving a single byte sent back. Unlike the underlying protocol it doesn't overwrite the original value with the slaves data. So, for example, to send and receive data you would use something like:

```
uint8_t SendData=0x55;
uint8_t ReadData;
Read_data = bcm2835_spi_transfer(Send_data);
```

Of course, you can always simply throw away the data from the slave or send meaningless data to the slave to create something that looks like a read/write pair.

The remaining functions all send multiple bytes of data stored in a buffer. The differ in how they treat the data returned by the slave - **writenb** ignores it; **transfernb** stores it in a new buffer; and **transfern** overwrites the send buffer with it. Let's look at each one in turn.

If you just want to write data to the slave and ignore what it sends back then you need to use the **writenb** function. This takes a char buffer and a length specification and transfers each byte in turn throwing away any data that slave sends back. For example:

```
char buf[] = {'A','B','C'};
bcm2835_spi_writenb(buf,3);
```

will send three bytes, containing the ASCII codes for A B and C, to the slave ignoring any data sent back. Notice that you need to get the size of the buffer correct in the function call to avoid buffer overflow.

The **transfern** function will send the number of bytes you specify and return the slaves data in the same buffer. For example:

```
char buf[] = {'A','B','C'};
bcm2835_spi_transfern(buf,3);
```

sends the ASCII codes for A, B C but overwrites each element of the array with whatever the slave transferred, i.e. buf no longer contains A B C.

Finally the transfernb function uses two buffers, one for the data to send and one for the received data. For example:

```
char buf[] = {'A','B','C'};
char readBuf[3];
bcm2835_spi_transfernb(buf,readBuf,3);
```

sends A B C to the slave and stores the three bytes sent back into readBuf.

Using just these functions you should be able to deal with most SPI slaves.

Now we come to a subtle point. What is the difference between transferring multiple bytes using transfernb, transfern or writeb and simply sending the bytes individually using multiple transfer calls? The answer is that each time you make a transfer call the chip select line is activated, the data transferred and then it is deactivated. Using the buffer transfers the chip select is left active for the entire transfer, i.e. it isn't deactivated between each byte. Sometimes this difference isn't important and you can transfer three bytes using three calls to transfer or one call to tranfernb. However, some slaves will abort the current multibyte operation if the chip select line is deactivated in the middle of a multibyte transfer.

It is important to realize that the nature of the transfer is that the first byte is sent at the same time that the first byte is received. That is, unlike other protocols, the whole of the send buffer isn't sent before the received data comes back. The whole transfer works a byte at a time - first byte is sent while the first byte is being received, then the second byte is sent at the same time as the second byte is being received and so on. Not fully understanding this idea can lead to some interesting bugs.

A Loopback Example

Because of the way that data is transferred on the SPI bus, it is very easy to test that everything is working without out having to add any components. All you have to do is connect MOSI to MISO so that anything sent it also received in a loopback mode.

First connect pin 19 to pin 20 using a jumper wire and start a new NetBeans project. The program is very simple. First we initialize the library and the SPI bus:

```
if (!bcm2835_init()) {
 return 1;
}
if (!bcm2835_spi_begin()) {
 return 1;
}
```

If either call fails the chances are you aren't running as root as explained in Chapter 2.

As this is a loopback test we really don't need to configure the bus but for completeness:

```
bcm2835_spi_setBitOrder(BCM2835_SPI_BIT_ORDER_MSBFIRST);
bcm2835_spi_setDataMode(BCM2835_SPI_MODE0);
bcm2835_spi_setClockDivider(BCM2835_SPI_CLOCK_DIVIDER_65536);
bcm2835_spi_chipSelect(BCM2835_SPI_CS0);
bcm2835_spi_setChipSelectPolarity(BCM2835_SPI_CS0, LOW);
```

Next we can send some data and receive it right back:

```
uint8_t read_data = bcm2835_spi_transfer(0xAA);
```

The hex value AA is useful in testing because it generates the bit sequence 10101010 which is easy to see on a logic analyzer.

Check that the received data matches the sent data:

```
if( read_data== 0xAA) printf("data received correctly");
```

Finally we close the bus and the library:

```
bcm2835_spi_end();
bcm2835_close();
return (EXIT_SUCCESS);
```

Putting all of this together gives us the complete program:

```c
#include <stdio.h>
#include <stdlib.h>
#include <bcm2835.h>

int main(int argc, char** argv) {

 if (!bcm2835_init()) {
  return 1;
 }
 if (!bcm2835_spi_begin()) {
  return 1;
 }

 bcm2835_spi_setBitOrder(BCM2835_SPI_BIT_ORDER_MSBFIRST);
 bcm2835_spi_setDataMode(BCM2835_SPI_MODE0);
 bcm2835_spi_setClockDivider(BCM2835_SPI_CLOCK_DIVIDER_65536);
 bcm2835_spi_chipSelect(BCM2835_SPI_CS0);
 bcm2835_spi_setChipSelectPolarity(BCM2835_SPI_CS0, LOW);

 uint8_t read_data = bcm2835_spi_transfer(0xAA);
 if( read_data== 0xAA) printf("data received correctly");
 bcm2835_spi_end();
 bcm2835_close();
 return (EXIT_SUCCESS);
}
```

If you run the program and don't get the "data received correctly" message then the most likely reason is that you have connected the wrong two pins together or not connected them at all.

If you connect a logic analyzer to the four pins involved - 19,21, 23 and 24 you will see the data transfer:

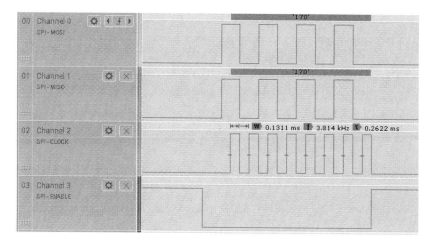

219

If you look carefully you will see the CS0 line go low before the master places the first data bit on the MOSI and hence on the MISO lines. The documentation states that the CS line is held for at least three core clock cycles before transfer starts and held for at least one clock cycle when the transfer is complete. Notice that the clock rises in the middle of each data bit making this a mode 0 transfer. You can also see that the clock is measured to be 3.8KHz as promised.

Problems

The SPI bus is often a real headache because of the lack of a definitive standard, but in most cases you can make it work. The first problem is in discovering the characteristics of the slave device you want to work with. In general this is solved by a careful reading of the data sheet or perhaps some trial and error, see the next chapter for an example.

If you are working with a single slave then generally things work once you have the SPI bus configuration set correctly. Things are more difficult when there are multiple devices on the same bus. The Pi can only directly support two devices, but this is enough to make the task more difficult. Typically you will find SPI devices that don't switch off properly when they are not being addressed. In principle, all SPI devices should present high impedance outputs (i.e. tristate buffers) when not being addressed but some don't. If you encounter a problem you need to check that the selected slave is able to control the MISO line properly.

Another problem, which is particularly bad for the Pi, is noise. If you are using a USB, or some other power supply that isn't able to supply sufficient instantaneous current draw to the Pi, you will see noise on any or all of the data lines - the CS0/1 lines seem to be particularly sensitive. The solution is to get a better power supply.

If you really need more than two SPI devices, you might be tempted to look at the possibility of enabling the other SPI buses. This sounds good in theory, but in practice it seems to be difficult. The documentation advises not to use the SPI bus used for EEPROM I/O in HAT boards in the Pi 2 and later.

A better solution is to multiplex the CS0/1 lines to create additional chip selects. For example, you can use standard GPIO lines as chip selects and connect more than two SPI slaves.

Summary

- The SPI bus is often problematic because there is no SPI standard
- Unlike other serial buses it makes use of unidirectional connections.
- The data lines are MOSI master output slave input and MISO master input slave output.
- In addition there is a clock line, output from master, and a number of select lines, two in the case of the Pi.
- Data is transferred from the master to the slave and from the slave to the master on each clock pulse, arranged as a circular buffer.
- The bcm2835 library provides all the functions you need to set up the SPI bus and transfer data one byte or multiple bytes at a time.
- You can test the SPI bus using a simple loopback connection.
- Working with a single slave is usually fairly easy, working with multiple slaves can be more of a problem.

Chapter 16

AtoD With The SPI Bus

The SPI bus can be difficult to make work at first, but once you know what to look for about how the slave claims to work it gets easier. To demonstrate how its done, let's add eight channels of 12 bit AtoD using the MCP3008.

The Raspberry Pi doesn't have any analog inputs or outputs. You can buy expansion boards, HATs, that add multiple interfaces including analog I/O, but sometimes you just don't need that many new features. The MCP3000 family of AtoD converters provides a simple, cheap and low cost alternative to fitting an entire expansion board. Although the MCP3008 with 8 AtoD inputs and the MCP3004 with 4 AtoD inputs at 10-bit precision are the best known, there are other devices in the family including 12- and 13-bit precision and differential inputs at around the same sort of cost $1 to $2.

In this chapter the MCP3008 is used because it is readily available and provides a good performance at low cost but the other devices in the family work in the same way and could be easily substituted.

The MCP3008

The MCP3008 is available in a number of different packages but the standard 16 pin PDIP is the easiest to work with using a prototyping board. You can buy it from the usual sources including Amazon if you need one in a hurry. Its pin outs are fairly self explanatory:

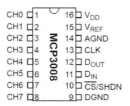

You can see that the analog inputs are on the left and the power and SPI bus connections are on the right. The conversion accuracy is claimed to be 10 bits, but how many of these bits correspond to reality and how many are noise depends on how you design the layout of the circuit.

You need to take great care if you need high accuracy. For example, you will notice that there are two voltage inputs VDD and VREF. VDD is the supply voltage that runs the chip and VREF is the reference voltage that is used to compare the input voltage. Obviously, if you want highest accuracy VREF, which has to be lower than or equal to VDD, should be set by an accurate low noise voltage source. However in most applications VREF and VDD are simply connected together and the usual, low quality, supply voltage is used as the reference. If this isn't good enough then you can use anything from a Zener diode to a precision voltage reference chip such as the TL431. At the very least, however, you should add a 1uF capacitor to ground connected to the VDD pin and the VREF pin.

The MC3000 family is a type of AtoD called a successive approximation converter. You don't need to know how it works to use it, but it isn't difficult. The idea is that first a voltage is generated equal to VREF/2 and the input voltage is compared to this. If it is less then the most significant bit is a 0 and if it is more or equal then it is a 1. At the next step the voltage generated is VREF/2+VREF/4 and the comparison is repeated to generate the next bit.

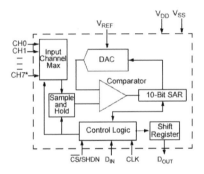

You can see that successive approximation fits in well with a serial bus as each bit can be obtained in the time needed to transmit the previous bit. However, the conversion is relatively slow and a sample and hold circuit has to be used to keep the input to the converter stage fixed. The sample and hold takes the form of a 20pF capacitor and a switch. The only reason you need to know about this is that the conversion has to be complete in a time that is short compared to the discharge time of the capacitor. So for accuracy there is a minimum SPI clock rate as well as a maximum.

Also, to charge the capacitor quickly enough for it to follow a changing voltage, it needs to be connected to a low impedance source. In most cases this isn't a problem, but if it is you need to include an op amp.

If you are using an op amp buffer then you might as well implement an anti-aliasing filter to remove frequencies from the signal that are too fast for the AtoD to respond to. How all this works takes us into the realm of analog electronics and signal processing and well out of the core subject matter of this book.

You can also use the AtoD channels in pairs - differential mode - to measure the voltage difference them. For example, in differential mode you measure the difference between CH0 and CH1, i.e. what you measure is CH1-CH0. In most cases you want to use all eight channels in single-ended mode.

In principle you can take 200K samples per second, but only at the upper limit of the supply voltage VDD=5V falling to 75K samples per second at its lower limit of VDD=2.7V.

The SPI clock limits are a maximum of 3.6MHz at 5V and 1.35MHz at 2.7V. The clock can go slower but because of the problem with the sample and hold mentioned earlier it shouldn't go below 10kHz.

How fast we can take samples is discussed later in this chapter.

Connecting MCP3008 To The Pi

The connection to the PI's SPI bus is very simple and can be seen in the diagram below.

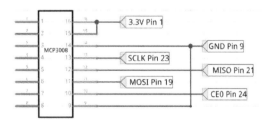

The only additional component that is recommended is a 1uF capacitor connected between pins 15 and 16 to ground mounted as close to the chip as possible. As discussed in the previous section you might want a separate voltage reference for pin 15 rather than just using the 3.3V supply.

Basic Configuration

Now we come to the configuration of the SPI bus. We have some rough figures for the SPI clock speed - 10kHz to a little more than 1.35MHz. So an initial clock divider of 4096 giving a frequency of 61kHz seems a reasonable starting point.

From the data sheet, the chip select has to be active low and data is sent most significant bit first is the default for both the master and the slave. The only puzzle is what mode to use? This is listed in the data sheet if you look really carefully and it can be mode 0,0 with clock active high or mode 1,1 with clock active low. For simplicity we can use mode 0,0 which is mode0 in the bcm2835 library.

We now have enough information to initialize the slave:

```
bcm2835_spi_setDataMode(BCM2835_SPI_MODE0);
bcm2835_spi_setClockDivider(BCM2835_SPI_CLOCK_DIVIDER_4096);
bcm2835_spi_chipSelect(BCM2835_SPI_CS0);
bcm2835_spi_setChipSelectPolarity(BCM2835_SPI_CS0, LOW);
bcm2835_spi_setBitOrder(BCM2835_SPI_BIT_ORDER_MSBFIRST);
```

The Protocol

Now we have the SPI initialized and ready to transfer data but what data do we transfer? The SPI bus doesn't have any standard commands or addressing structure. Each device responds to data sent in different ways and sends data back in different ways. You simply have to read the data sheet to find out what the commands and responses are.

Reading the data sheet might be initially confusing because it says that what you have to do is send five bits to the slave - a start bit; a bit that selects its operating mode single or differential; and a 3-bit channel number. The operating mode is 1 for single--ended and 0 for differential.

So to read Channel 3 i.e. 011, in single--ended mode you would send the slave:

```
11011xxx
```

where xxx means don't care. The response from the slave is that it holds its output in a high impedance state until the sixth clock pulse it then sends a zero bit on the seventh followed by bit 9 of the data on clock eight.

That is the slave sends back:

```
xxxxxx0b9
```

where x means indeterminate. The remaining 9-bits are sent back in response to the next nine clock pulses. This means you have to transfer three bytes to get all ten bits of data. This all makes reading the data in 8-bit chunks confusing.

The data sheet suggests a different way of doing the job that delivers the data more neatly packed into three bytes. What it suggests is, to send a single byte:

```
00000001
```

the slave transfers random data at the same time which is ignored. The final 1 is treated as the start bit. If you now transfer a second byte with most significant bit indicating single or differential mode, then a 3-bit channel address and the remaining bits set to 0, the slave will respond with the null and the top two bits of the conversion. Now all you have to do to get the final eight bits of data is to read a third byte:

This way you get two neat bytes containing the data with all the low order bits in their correct positions.

Using this information we can now write some instructions that read a given channel. For example, to read Channel 0 we first send a byte set to 0x01 as the start bit and ignore the byte the slave transfers. Next we send 0x80 to select single--ended and channel zero and keep the byte the slave sends back as the high order two bits. Finally, we send a zero byte so that we get the low order bits from the slave i.e.

```
char buf[] = {0x01,0x80,0x00};
char readBuf[3];
bcm2835_spi_transfernb(buf,readBuf,3);
```

Notice you cannot send the three bytes one at a time using transfer because that results in the CS line being deactivated between the transfer of each byte.

To get the data out of readBuf we need to do some bit manipulation:

```
int data=((int)readBuf[1] & 0x03) << 8 |(int) readBuf[2];
```

The first part of the expression extracts the low three bits from the first byte the slave sent and as these are the most significant bits they are shifted up eight places. The rest of the bits are then ORed with them to give the full 10-bit result. To convert to volts we use:

```
float volts=(float)data*3.3f/1023.0f;
```

assuming that VREF is 3.3V.

In a real application you would also need to convert the voltage to some other quantity like temperature or light level.

Some Packaged Functions

This all works, but it would be good to have a function that read the AtoD on a specified channel:

```
int readADC(uint8_t chan){
 char buf[] = {0x01,(0x08|chan)<<4,0x00};
 char readBuf[3];
 bcm2835_spi_transfernb(buf,readBuf,3);
 return ((int)readBuf[1] & 0x03) << 8 | (int) readBuf[2];
}
```

Notice that this only works if the SPI bus has been initialized and set up correctly. An initialization function is something like:

```
void SPI_init(){
  bcm2835_spi_setDataMode(BCM2835_SPI_MODE0);
  bcm2835_spi_setClockDivider(BCM2835_SPI_CLOCK_DIVIDER_4096);

  bcm2835_spi_chipSelect(BCM2835_SPI_CS0);
  bcm2835_spi_setChipSelectPolarity(BCM2835_SPI_CS0, LOW);
  bcm2835_spi_setBitOrder(BCM2835_SPI_BIT_ORDER_MSBFIRST);
}
```

How Fast

Once you have the basic facilities working, the next question is always how fast does something work. In this case we need to know what sort or data rates we can achieve using this AtoD converter. The simplest way of finding this out is to use the fastest read loop, for Channel 5 say:

```
for(;;){
  int data=readADC(0x5);
}
```

With the clock divider we used earlier:

```
BCM2835_SPI_CLOCK_DIVIDER_4096
```

This gives a measured clock rate of 61kHz and the sampling rate is measured to be 2.26kHz. This is perfectly reasonable as it takes at least 24 clock pulses to read the data. Most of the time in the loop is due to the 24 clock pulses so there is little to be gained from optimization.

Increasing the clock rate to around 900kHz by setting the divider to 256 pushes the sampling rate to 36kHz, which is just fast enough to digitize audio as long as you don't waste too much time in the loop in processing. Changing the clock rate to 2Mhz, divider 128, pushes the sampling up to 70kHz, which is fast enough for most audio.

The fastest sample rate achieved with the samples of the device to hand was a clock rate of 4Mhz, divider 32, and a sampling rate of 216kHz. However the readings became increasingly unreliable in the low order bits.

This could perhaps br improved with the use of a buffer and careful layout, but for a prototype board a sampling rate of 70kHz is the limit. Also notice that as the clock rate goes up you have to ensure that the voltage source is increasingly low impedance to allow the sample-and-hold to charge in a short time.

Summary

Making SPI work with any particular device has four steps

1. Discover how to connect the device to the SPI put this is a matter of identifying pin outs and mostly what chip selects are supported.

2. Find out how to configure the Pi's SPI bus to work with the device. This is mostly a matter of clock speed and mode.

3. Identify the commands that you need to send to the device to get it to do something and what data it sends back as a response.

4. Find, or workout, the relationship between the raw reading, the voltage and the quantity the voltage represents.

Chapter 17

The Serial Port

The serial port is one of the oldest of ways of connecting devices together, but it is still very useful as it provides a reasonably fast communication channel that can be used over a larger distance than most other connections such as USB. Today, however, its most common and important use is in making connections with small computers and simple peripherals.

Serial Protocol

The serial protocol is very simple. It has to be because it was invented in the days when it was generated using electro-mechanical components, motors and the like. It was invented to make early teletype machines work and hence you will often find abbreviations such as **TTY** used in connection with it. As the electronic device used to work with serial is called a Universal Asynchronous Receiver/Transmitter, the term **UART** is also often used.

The earliest standards are **V24** and **RS232**. Notice, however, that early serial communications worked between plus and minus 24V and later ones ±12V. Today's serial communications work at logic, or **TTL** levels of 0 to 5V or 0 to 3.3V. This voltage difference is a problem we will return to later. What matters is that, irrespective of the voltage, the protocol is always the same.

For the moment let's concentrate on the protocol. As already mentioned, the protocol is simple. The line rests high and represents a 0. When the device starts to transmit it first pulls the line low to generate a start bit. The width of this start bit sets the transmission speed - all bits are the same width as the start bit. After the start bit there are a variable number, usually seven or eight, data bits, an optional single parity bit, and finally one or two 0 stop bits.

Originally the purpose of the start bit was to allow the motors etc to get started and allow the receiving end to perform any timing corrections. The stop bits were similarly there to give time for the motors to come back to their rest position. In the early days the protocol was used at very slow speeds; 300 baud, i.e. roughly 300 bits per second, was considered fast enough.

Today the protocol is much the same but there is little need for multiple stop bits and communications is often so reliable that parity bits are dispensed with. Transmission speeds are also higher - typically 9600 or 115200 baud.

To specify what exact protocol is in use, you will often encounter a short form notation. For example, 9600 8 data bits, no parity, one stop bit, will be written as 9600 8n1. Here you can see the letter A (01111101) transmitted using 8n1:

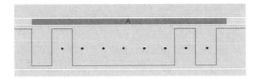

The first low is the start bit, then the eight dots show the ideal sampling positions for the receiver. The basic decoding algorithm for receiving serial is to detect the start of the start bit and then sample the line at the center of each bit time. Notice that the final high on the right is the stop bit.

For a serial connection to work, it is essential that the transmitter and the receiver are set to the same speed, data bits and parity. Serial interfaces most often fail because they are not working with the same settings.

A logic analyzer with a serial decoder option is an essential piece of equipment if you are going to do anything complicated with serial interfacing.

What is a baud? Baud rate refers to the basic bit time. That is, 300 baud has a start bit that is 1/300s wide. For 9600 this means a bit is 1/9600 wide or roughly 104 microseconds. At 115200 baud a bit is 1/115200 or roughly 8.6 microseconds. Notice baud rate doesn't equate to speed of sending data because there is an overhead in stop, start and perhaps parity bits to include in the calculation.

Hardware

A simple serial interface has a transmit pin **Tx** and a receive pin **RX**. That is, a full serial interface uses two wires for two-way communications. Typically you connect the Tx pin on one device to the Rx pin on the other and vice versa. The only problem is that some helpful manufacturers label the pins by what they should be connected to not what they are and you have to connect Rx to Rx and Tx to Tx - not really helpful. You generally need to check with a scope, logic probe or meter which pin is which if you are in any doubt.

In addition to the Tx and Rx pins, a full serial interface also has a lot of control lines. Most of these were designed to help with old fashioned teleprinters and they are not often used. For example, **RTS** - Request To Send is a line that it used to ask permission to send data from the device at the other end of the connection, **CTS** - Clear To Send is a line that indicates that it is okay to send data and so on. Usually these are set by the hardware automatically when the receive buffer is full or empty.

You can use RTS and CTS as a hardware flow control. There is also a standard software flow control involving sending **XON** and **XOFF** characters to start and stop the transmission of data. For most connections between modern devices you can ignore these additional lines and just send and receive data. If you need to interface to something that implements a complex serial interface you are going to have to look up the details and hand-craft a program to interact with it. For the rest of this chapter we are going to work with Tx and Rx and ignore additional status and signaling lines.

Modern system-on-a-chip devices like the Pi usually have one or more serial devices or Universal Asynchronous Receiver/Transmitters (UARTs) built in. The Pi has two, a full-function UART and a mini-UART. The difference is the size of the buffers and support for features. The mini-UART has a problem in that it is tied to the system clock and, as this varies to deal with the demands of the processor, the mini-UART's baud rate changes. You can fix the system clock to a set frequency, but this is not a good idea. For this reason we will concentrate of the full UART, but the principles are the same for any UART.

There is a problem with making the connection to the Pi's RX and TX pins in that devices work at different voltages. PC-based serial ports usually use +13 to -13 and all RS232-compliant ports use a + to - voltage swing which is completely incompatible with the Pi and most other microprocessors which work at 5V or 3.3V. If you want to connect the Pi to a PC then you need to use a TTL to RS232 level converter. In this case it is easier to use the PC's USB port as a serial interface with a USB to TTL level serial level converter. All you have to do is plug the USB port into the PC, install a driver and start to transmit data.

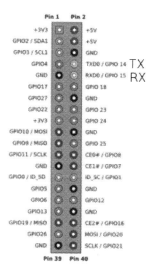

The full UART is brought out onto pin 8 TX and pin 10 RX, corresponding to GPIO 14 and GPIO 15 in mode ALT0. At the moment these are set to ALT0 when Linux boots up, but there are discussions about changing this, in which case you will have to explicitly set both GPIO lines to ALT0 to use the serial interface.

Remember when you connect the Pi to another device TX goes to the other device's RX and RX goes to the other device's TX pin. Also remember that the signaling voltage is 0 to 3.3V.

Linux gets in the way

Now we come to a difficult problem. Serial interfaces have long been the way that Linux, and Unix before it, connected to the outside world. As a result there is support for serial consoles built into the Kernel. When Linux boots up it generally configures at least one serial interface to work as a console.

What this means is that your program cannot simply connect to the serial interface because Linux is already using it. What happens when something connects to the serial interface is that Linux issues the prompt to log in and then presents the user with a command line interface.

If this is what you want to do then you can make a serial connection to the Pi either over the full UART serial interface or over a USB serial connection. This isn't difficult, but it is not what we are trying to do here. We want our programs to have full control of the serial interface so as to be able to send and receive what data they want to without any interference from the operating system.

What this means is that we have no choice but to alter the configuration of Linux so that it doesn't claim the serial interface.

At this point, if you know about the GPIO, you might be tempted to sidestep Linux altogether and simply resort to programming the UART directly via its control registers. While this is possible, you would still have to disable the Linux serial driver to avoid problems. Once you have stopped Linux from using the serial port as a login console the driver itself isn't a problem and you might as well use it as a way of controlling the serial port.

Unfortunately everything has become more complicated with the arrival of the Pi 3, which has introduced breaking changes into the latest version of Raspbian. These mean that most of the existing examples of using the serial port on the Pi no longer work.

Due to the Pi 3's support for Bluetooth. the full serial interface is now used by the built-in Bluetooth device and the console uses the mini-UART with all its clock problems.

By default a serial console is configured on all versions of the Pi. On the Zero and earlier this is **ttyAMA0** which is the full UART. On the Pi 3 it is **ttyS0** because the full UART is used for Bluetooth.

To allow for this difference to be transparent there are two new symbolic links which are used to refer to the UARTs according to their use.

On a Pi 3 there are two links:

```
serial0 -> ttyS0
serial1 -> ttyAMA0
```

On the Zero and earlier there is just one link

```
serial0 -> ttyAMA0
```

as there is no point in setting up ttyS0 because it uses the same GPIO pins as ttyAMA0.

You can check that serial0 has been defined using:

```
ls -l /dev
```

So if you always use serial0 you will be using the UART that is assigned to the console, be it running on a Pi 3 or any other Pi.

The only problem is that ttyS0 isn't a good UART to use for general purpose communications because its clock speed is linked to the core clock and this varies in speed unless you select a fixed frequency, which slows the Pi 3 down.

You can use the full UART, ttyAMA0, even on the Pi 3 if you are prepared to accept either a fixed clock frequency or disable Bluetooth.

To swap the use of the UARTs you have to edit boot/config.txt

```
sudo nano /boot/config.txt
```

and add the line:

```
dtoverlay=pi3-miniuart-bt
```

Save and reboot and on a Pi 3 the two serial ports will be redefined as

```
serial0 -> ttyAMA0
serial1 -> ttyS0
```

If you want to disable Bluetooth completely you can add:

```
dtoverlay=pi3-disable-btpi3-disable-bt
```

to the end of /boot/config.txt

Getting Rid of the Console

Whichever UART is assigned to serial0 Linux will use it as a console. This is exactly what you want if you plan to connect using a terminal program such as PuTTY or miniterm. If you do this you will see the usual logon appear and you can start using Linux as normal.

This isn't what you want to happen if you are writing a program to transfer commands and data to another device. To stop Linux responding you have to stop it using serial0 as a console.

There are a number of ways of doing this. The simplest is to use:

```
sudo raspi-config
```

Select Advanced and disable the serial console in the GUI that appears:

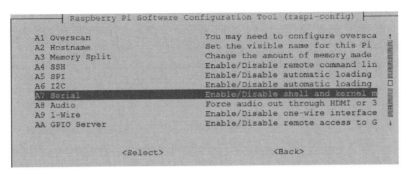

However, if you do this you will discover that any programs you write fail with an error that says there is no such device as serial0. The reason is that if Linux isn't using serial0 as a console, it simply doesn't set up the serial port. This seems a reasonable idea, but if you want to use it then the Linux driver for it has to be initialized. To make the system do this you have to add:

```
enable_uart=1
```

to /boot/config.txt and reboot.

Setting enable_uart to 0 disables the UART and setting it 1 enables it so you also need to remove any mention of serial0 in /boot/cmdline.txt using:

```
sudo nano /boot/cmdline.txt
```

You generally have to remove:

```
console=serial0,115200
```

Another, and arguably neater, way of doing the same job is to use the systemd systermctl command to stop the serial console service. For example, to stop ttyAMA0 you would use:

```
sudo systemctl stop serial-getty@ttyAMA0.service
```

After this your program is free to use the ttyAMA0 UART until the next time the system boots. If you want to disable the service for subsequent boots then use:

```
sudo systemctl disable serial-getty@ttyAMA0.service
```

Of course, if the service you want to make use of is ttyS0 use the commands to stop and disable that instead.

Neither of these commands change /boot/cmdline and so you probably won't have to modify enable_uart, but it is worth checking.

If you don't want to modify the operating system configuration, a reasonable approach is to execute the stop command from within the program. The proper way to do this is to learn about systemd and dbus, but a simpler way is to use the system command which can be used to run another program.

To disable the use of ttyAMA0 as a console use the system function:

```
system("sudo systemctl stop serial-getty@ttyAMA0.service");
```

before you open the file.

You should check for an error if the system function returns -1.

When you are trying to debug a serial port:

- If you get a Device not found error then the problem is most likely that you don't have uart=1 in the /boot/config.txt file.

- If the program works, but you don't get sensible results and you have set the baud rate etc correctly, the chances are you haven't disabled the Linux console.

Opening the Serial Port

The basic principle of Linux is that everything is a file - and so it is with the serial port. A file is just something you can read data from and write data to and this is also true of most devices. As a result Linux is fairly safe in treating the serial port as a file, but there are some important differences between a file on disk and a serial port that is being treated like a file.

To use the serial port we have to open it as a file in the usual way. The only thing that might be problematic is that you have to specify the device name in place of a filename and this can change. Indeed it changed in the latest version of Raspbian and so invalidated most of the examples of using the serial port. To work with the serial port you need to specify:

```
#include <unistd.h>
#include <fcntl.h>
#include <termios.h>
```

and to make error handling easy you might as well add:

```
#include <errno.h>
```

To open the serial port we use:

```
int sfd = open("/dev/serial0", O_RDWR | O_NOCTTY );
if (sfd == -1){
  printf ("Error no is : %d\n", errno);
  printf("Error description is : %s\n",strerror(errno));
  return(-1);
};
```

Notice the location of the device file, /dev/serial0, that we specify it is opened for read and write, O_RDWR, and the NOCTTY constant specifies that the serial port should not kill the process if a Ctrl-C is received.

The Linux driver does a lot of processing on the received data and as a result there are lots of settings that go well beyond the basic baud rate, stop bits, data bits and parity. However, if we assume that everything is set up reasonably, or equivalently if pin 8 and 10 have been connected together for a loopback test, we can already send and receive data:

```
char buf[]="hello world";
char buf2[11];
int count = write(sfd, buf, 11);
count=read(sfd,buf2,11);buf2[11]=0;
printf("%s",buf2);
close(sfd);
```

If you try this out using a loopback connection the chances are you won't see anything from the read. The reason is that by default the serial port echoes the output back to the input, which is okay for connections to a terminal, but for a loopback test you usually need to change the configuration. In principle this is the smallest program that can work with a serial port, but not if you are using a loopback.

Notice that we write to and read from the serial port as if it was a file, but of course it isn't and there are some differences. In particular, we can't read back more characters than we wrote in a loopback setup. The read and write function calls are also set up to be blocking - and this often isn't the best way to work. It is important that you know how to handle the fact that you might want to read data, but there might not be any data to be read, see later.

Setting Up

The default settings work for a loopback, but in most cases we need to talk to another device that often has exact specifications for the serial protocol - baud rate, data bits, parity and stop bits are the most common things we have to set.

The key to setting any parameters of any device that is being treated as a file, or indeed any file, is to use the **ioctl** function. This is low level and for the serial device it is easier and more common to use **termios** which in turn uses the ioctl function to get the job done.

To use termios to configure the serial port we simply fill in the details in a termios struct:

```
struct termios options;
```

You can look up all of the many possible settings for the stuct's fields. There are also functions that will work with the struct. There are a number of fields that can be set, although most of the time you only have to work with a few options:

Member	Description
c_cflag	Control options
c_lflag	Line options
c_iflag	Input options
c_oflag	Output options
c_cc	Control characters
c_ispeed	Input baud (new interface)
c_ospeed	Output baud (new interface)

The most common are to set the basic operation of the UART using the c_cflag.

Baud rate

To set the baud rate you can use the functions:

```
cfsetospeed(&options,speed); //for output speed
cfsetispeed(&options,speed);  //for input speed
```

where speed is one of:

```
B0 B50 B75 B110 B134 B150 B200 B300 B600 B1200 B1800
B2400 B4800 B9600 B19200 B38400 B57600 B115200 B230400
```

There is also a single speed setting function:

```
cfsetspeed(&options,speed);
```

The reason you use a function and not simply set the relevant bits is that the way the baud rate is set in different systems varies and the functions cover up the differences. Notice that most UARTS can only work at the same speed for input and output and you should set both to the same value unless you know better.

Data bits

To set the number of data bits you have to directly set a bit mask using **CSIZE** and values CS5, CS6, CS7, or CS8.

For example:

```
options.c_cflag &= ~CSIZE;
options.c_cflag |= CS7;
```

sets the number of data bits to 7. What is going on here is not hard to understand once you realize that the CS constants are multibit settings. So you first **and** a bitmask with the current value to zero just the bits in question, then you **or** the new value you want.

239

Parity

You can set parity by direct setting of the bits that control it.

For example:

```
options.c_cflag |= PARENB
options.c_cflag |= PARODD
```

enables parity and sets it to odd. Notice that as **PARODD** and **PARENB** are single bit settings. You don't have to use a bit mask to zero the location first, just OR the set bit with the value and it's done. To set the opposite of a single bit flag, i.e. to zero the bit in **cflag** you simply AND its NOT. That is, you can use &=~PARODD to set even parity and &=~PARENB to set no parity, i.e. to disable parity.

Stop Bits

The default is one stop bit. If you want to set two then you use;

```
options.c_cflag |= CSTOPB;
```

or **&=~ CSTOPB** if you want to explicitly clear the stop bit field to set one stop bit.

There are also two bits we always have to set in normal operation:

```
options.c_cflag |= CLOCAL;
options.c_cflag |= CREAD;
```

The first ignores the modem control lines and the second enables the read operation. The only other part of the struct that we generally need to modify is the **c_lflag** to set local options.

Raw Mode

There are two ways the driver handles input, canonical and raw. In **canonical** mode it works a line at a time, waiting until there is a full line of text, signaled by a carriage return or a line feed, before being sent. In **raw** mode characters are passed through as they arrive and they are not processed in any way.

For device to device communications raw is the mode you want to use. In addition you also generally want to stop any echo of input to output. You can also opt to handle the software interrupts, the signals, that the serial port generates - usually you don't want to.

To set raw mode with no echo and no signals you use:

```
options.c_lflag &= ~(ICANON | ECHO | ECHOE | ISIG);
```

Note as the flags are all single bit they can be ored together and applied in a single operation. You can do this with other single bit flags to simplify setting options.

There is a similar setting for raw output:

```
options.c_oflag |= OPOST;
```

A simpler way of setting all options so that you have raw mode on input and output is to use the function

```
cfmakeraw(pointer to termios);
```

This sets the following options:

```
c_iflag &= ~(IGNBRK | BRKINT | PARMRK | ISTRIP | INLCR |
                            IGNCR | ICRNL | IXON);
c_oflag &= ~OPOST;
c_lflag &= ~(ECHO | ECHONL | ICANON | ISIG | IEXTEN);
c_cflag &= ~(CSIZE | PARENB);
c_cflag |= CS8;
```

The final problem is that we also need to fill in values for all of the other fields in the termios struct and mostly we aren't interested in them. The standard technique is to first fill the termios struct with the current values set on the serial port and then simply modify the ones of interest.

The function:

```
tcgetattr(filedescriptor, pointer to termios)
```

will fill the struct with the current values corresponding to the serial port specified by the file descriptor.

The function:

```
tcsetattr(filedescriptor, when,pointer to termios)
```

does the reverse job and stores the values back in the device.

There is one last matter to be cleared up. When you change the configuration of the serial port it might already be in the middle of sending or receiving some data. You need to specify when you want the changes to take effect. This is what the **when** parameter specifies and you can usually set it to **TCSANOW** for an immediate change.

So now our standard algorithm is to get the attributes, modify the ones we want to and then set the attributes back in the device. For example to set raw mode. no echo, with 8n1 at 9600 baud you would use:

```
struct termios options;
tcgetattr(sfd, &options);
cfsetspeed(&options, B9600);
options.c_cflag &= ~CSTOPB;
options.c_cflag |= CLOCAL;
options.c_cflag |= CREAD;
cfmakeraw(&options);
tcsetattr(sfd, TCSANOW, &options);
```

If this program doesn't work and you can't set the parameters of the serial port, the reason is usually that Linux has not relinquished control of the port as a console.

Utility Functions

There are some useful utility functions you need to know about:

- `tcdrain(filedescriptor);`

waits until all of the data that has been written has been sent. The Linux UART driver will accept large amounts of data and send it for you while your program gets on with something else and this is true even in blocking mode. If you need to wait before sending any more data or reading a response this is the way to do it.

- `tcflush(filedescriptior,action)`

discards data written to the object referred to by fd but not transmitted, or data received but not read, depending on the value of action.

```
TCIFLUSH flushes data received but not read
TCOFLUSH flushes data written but not transmitted
TCIOFLUSH flushes all data waiting to be processed
```

- `tcsendbreak(filedescriptor,duration)`

transmits a continuous stream of zero-valued bits for a specific duration. A break is an "out of band" transmission needed to signal special conditions like a hard reset to some devices. It doesn't correspond to any transmitted character because it is out of specification for the number of bits, stop bit and parity specified - the line is simply held low for a given time. If duration is zero, it transmits zero-valued bits for at least 0.25 seconds, and not more that 0.5 seconds. If duration is not zero, it sends zero-valued bits for some implementation-defined length of time.

Sending Data

We have already used the write function without really discussing it in its simplest form.

You can use the standard file descriptor writing function to send data:

- `write(fd,buffer,len)`

writes len bytes of buffer to the file specified by the file descriptor.

What is less well known is that you can also use **dprintf**, which is the file descriptor version of printf to write to the file descriptor and a Posix standard since 2008.

- `dprintf(filedescriptor,formatstring,variablelist)`

For example:

```
char buf[] = "hello world";
int count = write(sfd, buf, 11);
```

can be written

```
char buf[] = "hello world";
dprintf(sfd,"%s",buf);
```

The dprintf function is very useful when you need to send the value of a numeric variable to a device over the serial connection. It works on most systems, including the Pi.

For example:

```
int total=100;
dprintf(sfd,"%d\n\r",total):
```

sends "100" followed by a newline and carriage return.

There is also the subtle point of when the writing functions return control to your program. It is usually said that writing data to a serial port is either **blocking**, i.e. it only returns when all the data written, or **non-blocking**, i.e. it returns at once. In fact, as the Linux device driver effectively implements a 4096 byte buffer in raw mode, there is little difference between the two modes for writing data in most cases.

Non-blocking mode can be set by opening the file using O_NONBLOCK in the open. That is, following:

```
int sfd = open("/dev/serial0", O_RDWR | O_NOCTTY|O_NONBLOCK );
```

if you select blocking raw mode then, as long as the data you are writing is less than 4096 bytes and the buffer is empty, the call to write returns immediately even though most of the bytes have still to be transmitted.

If you need to wait for all of the data to be sent then use:

```
tcdrain(filedescriptor);
```

In non-blocking raw mode, discussed in the next section, the same thing happens when you write data. However reading data is quite different.

In short, because the write is to a buffer the difference between blocking and non-blocking mode for write isn't important. In both cases a write can return before the data has actually been transmitted.

Reading Data

When programming a serial connection it is reading data that usually causes the most difficulty. You could say writing is easy, reading is hard. Sending data is easy because you just send the data and the device on the other end has the problem of processing it. Receiving data by contrast requires you to know that there is some data to receive. In short, the problem is finding out when the other device has sent you something to process.

It is often said that there are just two modes – blocking and non-blocking, when it comes to a serial read. In fact the situation is much more complicated. There are in fact four possible ways that a serial read can behave controlled by two parameters in the termios struct:

```
c_cc[VTIME]
c_cc[VMIN]
```

Roughly speaking **VTIME** sets how long to wait i.e. the timeout and **VMIN** sets the minimum number of characters before the call is considered satisfied. Note that both parameters are single byte char variables so the maximum value you can set is 255 characters for VMIN or 25.5 seconds for VTIME.

To understand how these work you have to keep in mind that the Linux serial driver will read data from the serial port as it becomes ready and store it in a fairly large buffer, irrespective of what your programming is doing. So when you go to read the serial port there might well be data waiting to be read.

The read call specifies the number of bytes to read but this doesn't determine what happens when there aren't enough bytes in the buffer to satisfy the read. That is, if you use:

```
read(sfd,buff,10);
```

then if there are more than 10 bytes in the serial buffer the call returns at once with 10 bytes - leaving the rest in the buffer for future reads. In other words, the byte count you specify in read determines what happens when there are more than that number of bytes in the buffer. It is the maximum number of bytes that will be read.

The question is what happens if there aren't 10 bytes in the buffer?

The answer depends on the setting of c_cc[VTIME] and c_cc[VMIN]:

- ```
  c_cc[VTIME]=0 and c_cc[VMIN]>0
  ```

  VMIN sets the number of characters to receive before the read is satisfied. There is no timeout and the call will wait forever if the number of characters is never received. The default is

  ```
  c_cc[VTIME]=0 and c_cc[VMIN]=1
  ```

  and this is usually called a blocking read.
  ```

- c_cc[VTIME]>0 and c_cc[VMIN]=0

  the read will be satisfied if a single character is available to read. If there is no character to read then the call will wait for the specified time in tenths of a second.

- c_cc[VTIME]>0 and c_cc[VMIN]>0

  now the time specified is an inter-character timer. The call waits for at least the number of characters to be received but will return if the time between characters exceeds the timeout. The timer is reset each time a character is received. It is very important to note that the timer is only started after the first character is received and this means that the call can block forever is no characters are received.

- c_cc[VTIME]=0 and c_cc[VMIN]=0

  the read will be satisfied immediately. The number of characters currently available or the number of characters requested will be returned. This is usually refereed to as non-blocking call and it is the way to set one up after the serial port has been opened.

To summarize, the number of bytes you specify in the read function sets the maximum number of bytes that will be read. The actual number of bytes read is returned by the read function. c_cc[VMIN] sets the minimum number of bytes that will satisfy the read function and c_cc[VTIME] sets the timeout to wait for each character to be received.

For example:

```
options.c_cc[VTIME]=10;
options.c_cc[VMIN]=5;
```

will cause read to return when five characters have been received or when more than 1 second has elapsed between characters being received. As already mentioned, this call will block indefinitely if no characters are received, i.e. there is no overall timeout.

You can now see that there isn't just blocking and non-blocking mode. You can adjust the time that the read waits and how many characters are required before it returns. The setting

```
options.c_cc[VTIME]=0;
options.c_cc[VMIN]=1;
```

corresponds to what is usually called a blocking call because the read will wait for any amount of time until at least one character is ready to read and the setting

```
options.c_cc[VTIME]=0;
options.c_cc[VMIN]=0;
```

corresponds to what is usually called a non-blocking read because it returns at once perhaps with no characters read.

The configuration c_cc[VTIME]>0 and c_cc[VMIN]>0, which will wait for at least c_cc[VMIN] with a timeout of c_cc[VTIME] between characters is useful because it corresponds to reading a burst of data. The device being read is assumed to send a block of data and then fall silent for a period. The end of the block is detected by the inter-character timeout. However, it has a problem in that there is no overall timeout. So if you start a read with c_cc[VTIME]>1 and c_cc[VMIN]>100, you could wait forever if the device doesn't send any data at all. It only needs to send one character to start the timeout but if this doesn't happen you don't recognize that no block is being sent. The solution to this problem is to not start a read until at least one character is available in the buffer.

To discover how many characters are in the buffer we need to use the lower level ioctl function. The **FIONREAD** command will return the number of characters waiting:

```
#include <sys/ioctl.h>
int bytes;
ioctl(sfd, FIONREAD, &bytes);
```

Following this bytes contains the number of characters you can read. Notice that this is a minimum number of characters because more could be received while you are setting up the read.

Polling For Data With Blocking

You can set up a software interrupt to signal when there is data to be read and use another thread to process it, but the majority of serial applications work best with a simple polling loop and you can do the job with some mix of blocking and non-blocking. For example, suppose you have just sent a command to a device and now you need to wait for it to respond. Suppose the response is a block of code always less than 100 bytes and after this has been transmitted nothing happens until the next command is sent to the device.

To do the job with a blocking call we can read one block of data at a time by setting c_cc[VTIME] and c_cc[VMIN] correctly. As we are only expecting fewer than 100 bytes we can set c_cc[VMIN] to 100 and be safe that the call to read will not return before reading all of the characters sent by the device.

Setting c_cc[VTIME]=1 means that if there is more than a one tenth of a second pause between bytes then the block is assumed complete and the read returns with the data. Of course, if the device pauses for more than 0.1 s and it hasn't finished then the block will be received incomplete. However, in many cases this is unlikely and when it does happen represents an error that needs a complete retry.

There is also the problem of what happens if the device doesn't send any data at all. In this case the timeout between characters is never triggered and the read call blocks forever. To avoid this problem we have to use **ioctl** to test for at least one character in the buffer before we start the read.

An example program using this method is:

```c
#include <stdio.h>
#include <stdlib.h>
#include <string.h>
#include <unistd.h>
#include <fcntl.h>
#include <termios.h>
#include <errno.h>
#include <sys/ioctl.h>
int main(int argc, char** argv) {
 system("sudo systemctl stop serial-getty@ttyAMA0.service");
 int sfd = open("/dev/serial0", O_RDWR | O_NOCTTY);
 if (sfd == -1) {
  printf("Error no is : %d\n", errno);
  printf("Error description is : %s\n", strerror(errno));
  return (-1);
 };
 struct termios options;
 tcgetattr(sfd, &options);
 cfsetspeed(&options, B9600);
 cfmakeraw(&options);
 options.c_cflag &= ~CSTOPB;
 options.c_cflag |= CLOCAL;
 options.c_cflag |= CREAD;
 options.c_cc[VTIME]=1;
 options.c_cc[VMIN]=100;
 tcsetattr(sfd, TCSANOW, &options);
 char buf[] = "hello world";
 char buf2[100];
 int count = write(sfd, buf,strlen(buf));
 usleep(100000);
 int bytes;
 ioctl(sfd, FIONREAD, &bytes);
 if(bytes!=0){
   count = read(sfd, buf2, 100);
 }
 printf("%s\n\r", buf2);
 close(sfd);
 return (EXIT_SUCCESS);
}
```

This will work with a loopback connection and you don't need to wait for the transmitted data to be received because you have a 0.1 second timeout between characters that effectively waits for the data. All that matters is that at least one character has been received. The pause of a tenth of a seconds before testing to see if there are any characters in the buffer is reasonable as you have the same inter-character timeout.

This works well in situations where you have a send-receive command-response setup, but it has some disadvantages. The first is that your program is halted while the block of data comes in. If it has nothing else to do this acceptable.

An alternative is to spin the data transfer off onto a different thread, but even in this case there is also the small problem of 0.1s wasted at the end of the transmission to confirm that the block has been sent. This is often acceptable as well.

Polling For Data With Non-blocking

An alternative way of doing the same job is to use a polling loop and read in the data a character at a time without blocking. The problem in this case is knowing when the block of data is complete. You can do this by arranging for the sending device to indicate the number of bytes to be transferred or by sending a flag byte to indicate the end of the block. However it is done, you have to have some way of knowing that a block is complete.

In this example the end of the block is marked by a null byte as if it was a string. The non-blocking read is created by setting c_cc[VTIME] =0 and c_cc[VMIN]=0 but you could do it another way.

```c
#include <stdio.h>
#include <stdlib.h>
#include <string.h>
#include <unistd.h>
#include <fcntl.h>
#include <termios.h>
#include <errno.h>

int main(int argc, char** argv) {
 system("sudo systemctl stop serial-getty@ttyAMA0.service");
 int sfd = open("/dev/serial0", O_RDWR | O_NOCTTY);
 if (sfd == -1) {
  printf("Error no is : %d\n", errno);
  printf("Error description is : %s\n", strerror(errno));
  return (-1);
 };

 struct termios options;
 tcgetattr(sfd, &options);
 cfsetspeed(&options, B9600);
 cfmakeraw(&options);
 options.c_cflag &= ~CSTOPB;
 options.c_cflag |= CLOCAL;
 options.c_cflag |= CREAD;
 options.c_cc[VTIME]=0;
 options.c_cc[VMIN]=0;
 tcsetattr(sfd, TCSANOW, &options);
```

```
char buf[] = "hello world";
char buf2[100];
char c;
int count = write(sfd, buf,strlen(buf)+1);

int i=0;
while(1){
  count = read(sfd, &c, 1);
  if(count!=0){
    buf2[i]=c;
    i++;
    if(c==0)break;
  };
};
printf("%s\n\r", buf2);close(sfd);
return (EXIT_SUCCESS);
}
```

Notice that the work is done in the while loop and also notice that we don't wait for the transmitted data to be available as a block. There is no overall timeout and if the transmitting device never sends a null then the loop never ends. In practice you would need to include an overall timeout for the loop. In this example we do send the null at the end of the string and so it should end as long as there isn't a transmission problem.

Receiving A Big Block

What if you want to receive a block that might be bigger than 511 characters but you still want an inter-character timeout? The answer is that you can write your own function that does the job.

The algorithm is simple. Peek at the number of bytes in the serial buffer. If it has reached the maximum size that you want to deal with, read the buffer. If it hasn't then wait for the specified timeout and peek at the number of characters in the buffer again. If it hasn't increased the timeout is up and you read as many characters as are available in the buffer. Otherwise you wait another timeout period to see if more data comes in.

The function is:

```c
int getBlock2(char buf[], int Toutms, int maxbytes) {
    if(maxbytes>=sizeof (buf)) return -1;
    int bytes = 0;
    int oldbytes = 0;
    struct timespec pause;
    pause.tv_sec = 0;
    pause.tv_nsec = Toutms * 1000;
    for (;;) {
        oldbytes = bytes;
        if (bytes >= maxbytes) break;
        nanosleep(&pause, NULL);
        ioctl(sfd, FIONREAD, &bytes);
        if (oldbytes == bytes)break;
    }
    memset(buf, '\0', sizeof (buf));
    if (bytes >= maxbytes)bytes=maxbytes;
    int count = read(sfd, buf, bytes);
    buf[count+1] = 0;
    return count;
}
```

Blocking Versus Non-blocking

This use of completely non-blocking reads is the typical way that serial port communications is handled. This is mostly because the range of behavior that you can program using blocking reads isn't properly appreciated. You don't just have a choice of blocking versus non-blocking. You can set a timeout between characters and a minimum number of characters to wait for and a maximum to return. When you don't know how much data is going to be sent, only an upper limit to a block of data, then blocking reads are simpler and preferable as long as you set a timeout and a minimum character size.

Notice that a blocking read doesn't load the processor because the thread is suspended while the driver waits for data. A polling blocking read, on the other hand, occupies a single core 100% of the time, but it can be doing other things as well as checking for data. If there isn't enough to do in the polling loop then a usleep or nanosleep call, see Chapter 3, will give the processor back to the operating system and so reduce the loading. However, using 100% of a core doesn't matter so much if you have other cores to keep the system working and it doesn't matter at all if you haven't got anything else for the core to do.

In more complicated situations you may have to use a separate thread to poll or wait for blocked calls, but this isn't necessary as often you might think. Neither is the use of a software interrupt to service incoming data, as most transactions are of a command- response nature.

Chapter 18

Connecting With The Web - Sockets

It is fairly easy to get the Pi on the Internet either via a wired connection or a USB WiFi device. However, there is the small matter of software. If you want get data out of a device the best idea is to allow it to serve a web page. If you want to get data into a device then what better than to get it to read a web page. Getting the Pi on the web doesn't require a browser or a server – in fact all you need is some socket code.

Sockets are general-purpose way of communicating over networks and similar infrastructure. Essentially they are a generalization of streams to things other than storage devices. The main problem is that they are called "sockets", which sounds strange. In addition, they are so general purpose that it can be difficult to see what you can do with them.

To send some web data, an HTML page or JSON data, most programmers think of a web server and that the next step is to install and configure Apache. This is usually far too big a solution to a small problem.

It is very easy to implement a simple web server or a web client using sockets and in this chapter you will discover how versatile they can be. All sockets do is transport data from one point to another, so you can use them to communicate using almost any standard protocol, like HTTP, or a custom protocol of your own devising.

Socket Basics

The basic steps in using a socket are fairly simple:

1. Create socket
2. Connect the socket to an address
3. Transfer data

Sockets connect to other sockets by their addresses. The simplest case is where there are just two sockets, or two endpoints, communicating. Once the connection is made the two sockets operate in more or less the same way. However, in general one of the sockets, the client, will have initiated the connection; and the other, the server, will have accepted it.

There is a conceptual difference between a client and a server socket. A server socket is setup and then it waits for clients to connect to it. A client socket actively seeks a connection with a server. Once connected, data can flow in both directions and the difference between the two ends of the connection becomes less.

The key idea is that a socket is implemented to make it look as much like a standard Linux file as possible. This conforms with a general principle of Linux that any I/O facility should follow the conventions of a file.

Socket Functions

The basic socket functions that you need to know are:

Create a socket

```
sockfd = socket(int socket_family, int socket_type, int protocol);
```

This returns a socket descriptor an int which you use in other socket functions.

The socket_family is where you specify the type of communications link to be use and this is where sockets are most general. There are lots of communications methods that sockets can use including AF_UNIX or AF_LOCAL which don't use a network but allow intercommunication between processes on the same machine. In most cases you are going to be using AF_INET for IPv4 or AF_INET6 for IPv6 networking.

The socket_type specifies the general protocol to be used. In most cases you will use SOCK_STREAM which specifies a reliable two-way connection - for IP communications this means TCP/IP is used. For some applications you might want to use SOCK_DGRAM which specifies that the data should be sent without confirming that it has been received. This is a broadcast mechanism that corresponds to UDP for IP communications.

The protocol parameter selects a sub-protocol of the socket type. in most cases you can simply set it to zero.

As we are going to be working with sockets that basically work with the web we will use AF_INET and SOCK_STREAM.

Connect a socket to an address

To connect a socket as a client of another socket you need to use:

```
int connect(int sockfd,const struct sockaddr *addr,
                              socklen_t addrlen);
```

The sockfd parameter is just the socket file descriptor returned from the socket function. The addr parameter points at a sockaddr struct which contains the address of the socket you want to connect to. Of course addrlen just specifies the size of the struct. Socket address type depend on the underlying communications medium that the socket uses, but in most cases, and certainly in this article, it is just an IP address. As addresses are used in many different socket functions it is worth dealing with how to construct an address as a separate topic.

Bind a socket to an address

To assign a server socket to the address it will respond to, use:

```
int bind(int sockfd, const struct sockaddr *addr,socklen_t addrlen);
```

The sockfd parameter is just the socket file descriptor returned from the socket function and addr is a pointer to an address struct.

Beginners often ask what the difference is between connect and bind. The answer is that connect makes a connection to the socket with the specified address whereas bind makes the socket respond to that address. Put another way, use connect with a client socket and bind with a server socket.

Reading and Writing

There isn't anything much to say about sending and receiving data from an open socket because it is just a file and you can use the standard read and write functions that you would use to work with a file. Of course there are some differences and some additional features that you need to work with a network, but this is the general principle.

Listen and Accept

There is one small matter that we have to deal with that takes us beyond simple file use semantics. If you have opened a socket and bound it to an IP address then it is acting as a server socket and is ready to wait for a connection. How do you know when there is a connection and how do you know when to read or write data? Notice this problem doesn't arise with a client socket because it initiates the complete connection and sends and receives data when it is ready.

The function:

```
        int listen(int sockfd, int backlog);
```

sets the socket as an active server. From this point on it listens for the IP address it is bound to and accepts incoming connections. The backlog parameter sets how many pending connections will be queued for processing. The actual processing of a connection is specified by:

```
int accept(int sockfd, struct sockaddr *addr, socklen_t *addrlen);
```

The accept command provides the address of the client trying to make the connection in the sockaddr structure. It also returns a new socket file descriptor to use to talk to the client. The original socket carries on operating as before. Notice that this is slightly more complicated than you might expect in that it is not the socket that you created that is used to communicate with the client. The socket you created just listens out for clients and creates a queue of pending requests. The accept function processes these requests and creates new sockets used to communicate with the client.

This still doesn't solve the problem of how the server detects that there are clients pending. This is a complicated question with many different solutions. You can set up the listening socket to be either blocking or non-blocking. If it is blocking then a call to accept will not return until there is a client ready to be processed. If it is non-blocking then a call to accept returns at once with an error code equal to EAGAIN or EWOULDBLOCK. So you can either use a blocking call or you can poll for clients to be ready.

A more complex approach would be to use another thread to call the poll() function which performs a wait with no CPU overhead while the file descriptor isn't ready, see Chapter 5 for an example.

A Web Client

We now have enough information to implement our first socket program, a web client. It has to be admitted that a web client isn't as common a requirement as a web server, but it is simpler and illustrates most of the points of using sockets to implement an HTTP transaction.

The first thing we have to do is create a socket and for the TCP needed for an HTTP transaction:

```
int sockfd = socket(AF_INET, SOCK_STREAM, 0);
```

To allow this to work you have to add:

```
#include <sys/socket.h>
```

Next we need to get the address of the server we want to connect to. For the web this would usually be done using a DNS lookup on a domain name. To make things simple we will skip the lookup and use a known IP address. Example.com is a domain name provided for use by examples and you can find its address by pinging it. At the time of writing it was hosted at:

```
93.184.216.34
```

This could change so check before concluding that "nothing works".

There are three fields in the address structure:

```
struct sockaddr_in addr;
```

sin_family is just set to:

```
addr.sin_family = AF_INET;
```

254

to indicate an internet IPv4 address. The next field is the **port number** of the IP address, but you can't simply use addr.sin_port = 80; because the bit order used on the Internet isn't the same as used on most processors. Instead you have to use a utility function that will ensure the correct bit order:

```
addr.sin_port = htons(80);
```

The function name stands for "host to network short" and there are other similarly named functions.

The actual address is defined in the **in_addr** field. This is a struct with only one field you should use and rely on that is **s_addr**. This is a 32-bit representation of an IP address. The format is fairly simple. Regard the 32-bit value as four bytes with each byte coding one value of the "dotted" IP address.

That is, if the IP address is w.x.y.z then w, x, y and z are the bytes of s_addr. For example, the IP address of example.com is 93.184.216.34 and converting each value into its byte equivalent in hex gives 5d.b8.d8.22, which would be the hex value we have to store in s_addr if it wasn't for the fact that the bytes are stored in reverse order. So, the hex equivalent of the IP address is 0x22d8b85d and this is used to initialize the address struct:

```
addr.sin_addr.s_addr = 0x22d8b85d;
```

To make all this work you need to add:

```
#include <sys/types.h>
```

and

```
#include <netinet/in.h>
```

With the address worked out and safely stored we can now make the connection:

```
connect(sockfd, &addr, sizeof (addr));
```

This will return 0 if it successfully connects and we do need to test for this condition. You will also get a type warning because the pointer to the addr structure isn't as defined in the function. In fact there are many variations on the addr structure which you could pass and it is the standard idiom to cast them to the function's pointer type:

```
connect(sockfd, (struct sockaddr *) &addr, sizeof (addr)
```

Finally we need to check for an error:

```
if(connect(sockfd,(struct sockaddr*)&addr,sizeof(addr))<0)return -1;
```

As long as there is no error then we can start to send and receive data. But what data? The answer is that it all depends on the protocol you are using. There is nothing about a socket that tells you what to send. It is a completely general I/O mechanism. You can send anything, but if you don't send what the server is expecting you won't get very far.

The web uses the HTTP protocol and this is essentially a set of text formatted headers that tell the server what to do and a set of headers that the server sends back to tell you what it has done.

The most basic transaction the client can have with the server is to send a GET request for the server to send a particular file. Thus the simplest header is:

```
char header[] = "GET /index.html HTTP/1.1\r\n\r\n";
```

which is a request for the server to send index.html. However, in most cases we do need one more header, HOST, which gives the domain name of the server. Why do we need to do this? Simply because HTTP says you should and many websites are hosted by a single server at the same IP address. Which website the server retrieves the file from is governed by the domain name you specify in the HOST header.

This means that the simplest set of headers we can send the sever is:

```
char header[] = "GET /index.htm HTTP/1.1\r\n
                           HOST:example.org\r\n\r\n";
```

which corresponds to the headers

```
GET /index.html HTTP/1.1
HOST:example.org
```

An HTTP request always ends with a blank line. If you don't send the blank line then you will get no response from most servers. In addition the HOST header has to have the domain name with no additional syntax - no slashes and no http: or similar.

With the headers defined we can send our first HTTP request using write as if the socket was just another file to write data to:

```
int n = write(sockfd, header, strlen(header));
```

and of course to use the strlen function we need to add:

```
#include <string.h>
```

The server receives the HTTP request and should respond by sending the data corresponding to the file specified, i.e. index.html. We can read the response just as if the socket was a file:

```
char buffer[2048];
n = read(sockfd, buffer, 2048);
printf("%s", buffer);
```

You can make this more complicated by checking the number of bytes read and reading more if the buffer is full. but this is a simple and direct way to get the HTML. In fact you get more than the HTML as you get the entire HTTP response including the response headers:

```
HTTP/1.1 200 OK
Cache-Control: max-age=604800
Content-Type: text/html
Date: Sun, 14 Aug 2016 15:30:44 GMT
Etag: "359670651+gzip+ident"
Expires: Sun, 21 Aug 2016 15:30:44 GMT
Last-Modified: Fri, 09 Aug 2013 23:54:35 GMT
Server: ECS (ewr/15F9)
Vary: Accept-EncodinX-Cache: HIT
x-ec-custom-error: 1
Content-Length: 1270

<!doctype html>
<html>
<head>
```

and so on...

Notice the blank line marking the end of the header and signaling that the data payload follows.

The complete program is:

```c
#include <stdio.h>
#include <stdlib.h>

#include <sys/socket.h>
#include <string.h>
#include <sys/types.h>
#include <netinet/in.h>

int main(int argc, char** argv) {
 int sockfd = socket(AF_INET, SOCK_STREAM, 0);
 struct sockaddr_in addr;addr.sin_family = AF_INET;
 addr.sin_port = htons(80);
 addr.sin_addr.s_addr = 0x22d8b85d;
 if (connect(sockfd, (struct sockaddr *) &addr,
                     sizeof (addr)) < 0)return -1;
 char header[] = "GET /index.html HTTP/1.1\r\n
                     Host:example.org\r\n\r\n";
 int n = write(sockfd, header, strlen(header));
 char buffer[2048];
 n = read(sockfd, buffer, 2048);
 printf("%s", buffer);
 return (EXIT_SUCCESS);
}
```

Of course, we can do much better than this simple example. For one thing each socket operation needs to be checked for errors. Here we only check for the mostly likely error that the sever refuses the connection.

Connecting Using A URL

There is also utility function that will perform DNS lookup for you or convert an IP address specified so you don't need to specify an IP address struct. Surprisingly this is almost an easier way to do things and it has become the standard way to set up a socket. The **getaddrinfo** function not only looks up the URL using DNS, it also constructs all of the structs you need to open a socket and connect. It will also return as many address specifications as you request, IPv4 and IPv6 for example.

The function specification is:

```
int getaddrinfo(const char *node,
                const char *service,
                const struct addrinfo *hints,
                struct addrinfo **res);
```

and you need to add

```
#include <netdb.h>
```

You pass it the IP address or the DNS name, i.e. either " 93.184.216.34" or "www.example.com", as node. The service can be specified as a port address "80" or as a service name "http". The **hints** struct is used to specify what sort of socket and address you are going to use. The result is a linked list of structs pointed at by addrinfo. The only slightly complication in using getaddrinfo is that you might have more than one result - one for IPv4 say and one for IPv6 - and then you have to work out which one to actually use.

The result struct contains structs that you need to both open the socket and to connect. For example, setting up the hints as:

```
struct addrinfo hints;
memset(&hints, 0, sizeof hints);
hints.ai_family = AF_INET ;
hints.ai_socktype = SOCK_STREAM;
```

asks for structs to be made for a TCP IPv4 socket.
We can now get the address details we need:

```
struct addrinfo *servinfo;
int status = getaddrinfo("www.example.com", "80",&hints,
&servinfo);
```

Notice that you could use the IP address as a string.

As long as this works the result should be a linked list with a single entry. In this case servinfo points to the first and only addrinfo struct. If there are any additional structs they are pointed at by:

```
servinfo->next
```

which is NULL if there is no next struct.

Using the single result is easy. To create the socket we use:

```
int sockfd = socket(servinfo->ai_family,
                    servinfo->ai_socktype,
                    servinfo->ai_protocol);
```

and to connect to the server we use:

```
connect(sockfd,
        servinfo->ai_addr,
        servinfo->ai_addrlen);
```

This is so much simpler that you tend to fall into the idiom of writing:

```
struct addrinfo hints;
memset(&hints, 0, sizeof hints);
hints.ai_family = AF_INET ;
hints.ai_socktype = SOCK_STREAM;
struct addrinfo *servinfo;
int status = getaddrinfo("www.example.com", "80",&hints,
&servinfo);
int sockfd = socket(servinfo->ai_family,
                    servinfo->ai_socktype,
                    servinfo->ai_protocol);
connect(sockfd,
        servinfo->ai_addr,
        servinfo->ai_addrlen);
```

whenever you need a socket connected to a given URL or IP address and port. The only minor complication is that you need to remember to free the linked list once you are finished with it using:

```
freeaddrinfo(servinfo);
```

A Server

A server is more or less the same as a client from an implementation point of view. The only real difference is that it has to wait around until a client connects before dealing with a transaction.

The first step is to create the socket and this follows the same pattern as for the client. We could simply set up the address structures and create a socket but now we know how to use getaddrinfo it is easier to use this to do the job automatically and flexibly:

```
struct addrinfo hints, *server;
memset(&hints, 0, sizeof hints);
hints.ai_family = AF_INET;
hints.ai_socktype = SOCK_STREAM;
hints.ai_flags = AI_PASSIVE;
getaddrinfo(NULL, "80", &hints, &server);
```

The AI_PASSIVE flag assigns the current system's IP address. You can easily get address structures for alternative addresses such as IPTv6 using this but for simplicity we just ask for an IPv4 address. Notice the specification of port 80 for an HTTP server socket. After the call to getaddrinfo, the structs we need to create sockets are ready to be used:

```
int sockfd = socket(server->ai_family,
                    server->ai_socktype,
                    server->ai_protocol);
bind(sockfd, server->ai_addr,
             server->ai_addrlen);
listen(sockfd, 10);
```

You can see how easy getaddrinfo makes everything. The call to bind assigns the socket the IP address of the machine on port 80 and listen starts things going with a queue of 10 pending clients.

We can now use accept to wait for a client to connect:

```
struct sockaddr_storage client_addr;
socklen_t addr_size = sizeof client_addr;
int client_fd = accept(sockfd,
                       (struct sockaddr *) &client_addr,
                       &addr_size);
```

At this point our program is blocked waiting for a client to connect to the socket. If you want to keep processing things then you need to use a socket in non-blocking mode, see later.

For the moment we can assume that when accept returns there is a new socket descriptor in client and details of the client in clien_addr. Again for simplicity we are not going to check to see who the client is just serve them a web page.

The client will first send the server an HTTP GET packet, assuming they do want to GET a web page. We can read this in using:

```
char buffer[2048];
int n = read(client_fd, buffer, 2048);
printf("%s", buffer);
```

The data in the GET headers tell the server which file is required and you can do some string handling to process it to get the name. In this case we are going to send the same HTML file no matter what the client asked for. To do this we need some HTTP headers defining what we are sending back and some HTML to define the page we are sending. The simplest set of headers that work is:

```
char headers[] = "HTTP/1.0 200 OK\r\n
        Server: Cpi\r\n
        Content-type: text/html\r\n\r\n";
```

which corresponds to sending

```
HTTP/1.0 200 OK
Server: CPi
Content-type: text/html
```

with a blank line to mark the end of the headers.

Notice that we have swapped to HTTP 1.0 because this is simpler and works with a smaller set of headers. If you want to support HTTP 1.1 then you need to specify the Content-Length header and the Connection header.

Some sample HTML:

```
char html[] =
"<html><head><title>Temperature</title></head><body>
{\"humidity\":81%,\"airtemperature\":23.5C}</p></body></html>\r\n";
```

is a typical small page for a small server reporting back temperature and humidity say. The html could be anything as long as it is not too big.

Now we can assemble the data and send it to the client:

```
char data[2048] = {0};
snprintf(data, sizeof data, "%s %s", headers, html);
n = write(client_fd, data, strlen(data));
close(client_fd);
```

If you put all of this together and run the program you will find that the server waits until a client, any web browser, connects. The web page will then be displayed in the browser. Of course this only works once.

To make the whole thing continue to work we have to put the entire client handling code into a loop:

```
for (;;) {
  int client_fd = accept(sockfd,
      (struct sockaddr *) &client_addr,
      &addr_size);
  int n = read(client_fd, buffer, 2048);
  printf("%s", buffer);
  fflush(stdout);
  n = write(client_fd, data,  strlen(data));close(client_fd);
}
```

The only problem with this loop is that **accept** is a blocking call which means you can't include any additional processing in the loop. Sometimes this doesn't matter. For example, if this was a processing loop for a sensor then the sensors could be read after a client connected and the web data served.

If this isn't the case we need to make the call to accept non-blocking. The simplest way of doing this is to use the getaddrinfo to add a non-blocking parameter to the structs it creates:

```
hints.ai_family = AF_INET;
hints.ai_socktype = SOCK_STREAM ;
hints.ai_flags = AI_PASSIVE|| SOCK_NONBLOCK;
getaddrinfo(NULL, "80", &hints, &server);
```

Note that this only works under Linux - if you want Unix compatibility then use ioctl via the fcntl function:

```
fcntl(sockfd, F_SETFL, O_NONBLOCK);
```

Following this the call to accept will return immediately and the value of client_fd is negative if there is no client waiting:

```
for (;;) {
  int client_fd = accept(sockfd,
      (struct sockaddr *) &client_addr, &addr_size);
  if (client_fd > 0) {
   int n = read(client_fd, buffer, 2048);
   printf("%s", buffer);
   fflush(stdout);
   n = write(client_fd, data, strlen(data));
   close(client_fd);
  }
}
```

Notice that this polling loop is a bad idea if the machine is a general purpose system as it uses 100% of one core's time. However, if the system is dedicated to doing a single job, this is the most logical and effective solution. In this case the polling loop also implements other repetitive and essential tasks.

In a more general context, the problem of how to handle incoming client connects has two solutions that divide opinion on which is better. Servers like Apache create a new thread for each client that has to be served. This is efficient but handling lots of threads and cleaning up after threads terminate can be a problem. Node.js, on the other hand, uses a single thread to deal with all client requests and manages things using events. Event handling is basically an elaboration on the polling loop shown above and it is claimed that event-based servers can be faster than thread-based ones. Use whichever method suits your application.

The complete listing for the server with non-blocking calls is:

```c
#include <stdio.h>
#include <stdlib.h>
#include <sys/socket.h>
#include <string.h>
#include <sys/types.h>
#include <netinet/in.h>
#include <netdb.h>
int main(int argc, char** argv) {
 struct addrinfo hints, *server;
 memset(&hints, 0, sizeof hints);
 hints.ai_family =  AF_INET;
 hints.ai_socktype = SOCK_STREAM;
 hints.ai_flags = AI_PASSIVE || SOCK_NONBLOCK;
 getaddrinfo(NULL, "80", &hints, &server);
 int sockfd = socket(server->ai_family,
          server->ai_socktype, server->ai_protocol);
 bind(sockfd, server->ai_addr, server->ai_addrlen);
 listen(sockfd, 10);
 struct sockaddr_storage client_addr;
 socklen_t addr_size = sizeof client_addr;
 char headers[] = "HTTP/1.0 200 OK\r\nServer:CPi\r\nContent-type:
                   text/html\r\n\r\n";
 char buffer[2048];
 char html[] = "<html><head><title>Temperature</title>
           </head><body>{\"humidity\":81%,
            \"airtemperature\":23.5C}</p></body></html>\r\n";
 char data[2048] = {0};
 snprintf(data, sizeof data,"%s %s", headers, html);
 for (;;) {
  int client_fd = accept(sockfd,
   (struct sockaddr *) &client_addr, &addr_size);
  if (client_fd > 0) {
   int n = read(client_fd, buffer, 2048);
   printf("%s", buffer);
   fflush(stdout);
   n = write(client_fd, data, strlen(data));
   close(client_fd);
  }
 }
 return (EXIT_SUCCESS);
}
```

The ESP8266 provides a low cost and relatively easy way to get a Pi onto WiFi without using a USB port. This is a particularly attractive proposition for the Pi Zero, which only has a single micro USB connector. As we will make a lot of use of the Pi's serial port, it is assumed that you know roughly how it works. In particular, it is assumed that you are familiar with the material in Chapters 17 and 18 on the serial port and sockets.

The Amazing ESP8266

Before we get on to the details of using the ESP8266 we need to find out what makes it special. It is remarkably low cost, $5 or less, but it is a full microprocessor with GPIO lines, RAM and built in WiFi. It is built by a Chinese company Espressif Systems, but there are a number of copies on the market. The proliferation of devices and software revisions makes it difficult to work with, but it is well worth the effort.

While you can set up a development system yourself and program the ESP8266 to do almost anything, it comes with built-in software that allows it to be used as a WiFi module for other processors. This is how we are going to use it to give WiFi capability to the Pi, and especially to the Pi Zero which lacks a full size USB connector for a WiFi dongle.

The ESP8266 connects to the outside world using the serial port. The Pi controls it and transfers data using a system of AT commands. These were commonly used to control modems and other communication equipment and they still are used in mobile phone modems. In essence the ESP8266 looks like a modem that connects to WiFi. The module that is used in this chapter is the ESP-01 which is widely available from many different sources but they all look like the photo:

There is another version, the ESP-07, which comes with a screen RF stage and other advantages and this should also work.

A bigger problem is that there are new versions of the firmware and some of these might not work in exactly the same way. However, it should be easy to make the changes necessary.

Connecting the ESP8266 ESP-01

There a number of minor problems in using the ESP8266. The first is that it comes with an 8-pin male connector which is not prototype board friendly. The best solution to this is to use some jumper cables - female to male - to connect it to the prototype board or use female-to-female cables to connect directly to the Pi.

You can power the ESP8266 directly from the Pi's 3.3V supply, but only if you are using a Pi 3 or Zero. Early Pis before the B+ just didn't have the power.

When transmitting, the ESP8266 takes a lot of current, 300mA or so, and this means there isn't a lot left over to power other things. You can use a separate 3.3V power supply if you need more power. Of course, you can use this to power both the ESP8266 and the Pi and in some situations this would be an advantage.

You can use one of the many low cost prototyping board power supplies with no problems:

The pinout of the ESP-01 is usually shown from the component side, but in fact the pins that you want to connect to are on the other side. To make things easier the two views are given in the diagram:

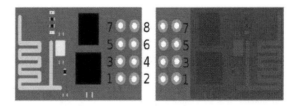

266

The pin functions are:

1 Ground   connect to ground
2 TXO   the serial tx pin
3 GPIO2   ignore
4 CHPD   chip enable connect to 3.3V
5 GPIO0   ignore
6 RST   reset leave unconnected
7 RXI   the serial rx pin
8 VDD   supply voltage connect to 3.3V

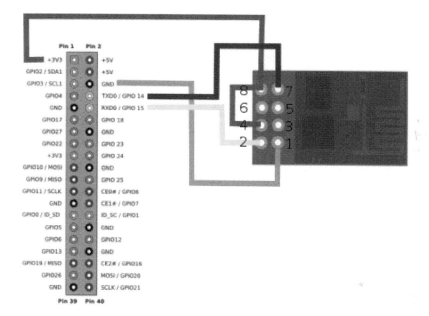

From the pinouts you should be able to work out the way the ESP8266 has to be connected. If we use P0 as Tx from the Pi and P1 as Rx to the Pi we have to connect ESP-01 pin 7 to P0, pin 2 to P1 and ESP-01 pins 8 and 4 to the external power supply. To make it all work we also have to connect ESP-01 pin 1 to the ground of the external power supply ground and to the ground of the Pi, as shown:Of course this arrangement is particularly useful for the Pi Zero as you can now have a low cost WiFi connection without having to use up the one and only USB socket.

AT Commands

The key idea in using the ESP8266 is that the Pi has to send an AT command, literally the characters AT, followed by other command strings. The command has to end with \r\n for the ESP8266 to take notice of it.

You can find a fill list of commands at the Espressif web site, but the most important are:

AT	Attention
AT+RST	Reset the board
AT+GMR	Firmware version
AT+CWMODE=	Operating Mode
	1. Client 2. Access Point 3. Client and Access Point
AT+CWJAP=	Join network
AT+CWLAP	View available networks
AT+CWQAP	Disconnect from network
AT+CIPSTATUS	Show current status as socket client or server
AT+CIPSTART=	Connect to socket server
AT+CIPCLOSE	Close socket connection
AT+CIFSR	Show assigned IP address when connected to network
AT+CIPMUX=	Set connection
	0. Single Connection 1. Multi-Channel Connection
AT+CIPSERVER=	Open the Socket Server
AT+CIPMODE=	Set transparent mode
AT+CIPSTO=	Set auto socket client disconnect timeout from 1-28800s
+IPD	Data

This is just a very general overview and omits the commands that allow the device to work as an access point. It is assumed that client mode is the more common application, but it isn't difficult to extend this example to access point operation.

Setup

We need a function to set up the hardware ready to communicate with the device:

```
int initWiFi() {
 system("sudo systemctl stop serial-getty@ttyAMA0.service");
 sfd = open("/dev/serial0", O_RDWR | O_NOCTTY);
 if (sfd == -1) {
  printf("Error no is : %d\n", errno);
  printf("Error description is : %s\n", strerror(errno));
  return -1;
 }
 struct termios options;
 tcgetattr(sfd, &options);
 cfsetspeed(&options, B115200);
 cfmakeraw(&options);
 options.c_cflag &= ~CSTOPB;
 options.c_cflag |= CLOCAL;
 options.c_cflag |= CREAD;
 options.c_cc[VTIME] = 1;
 options.c_cc[VMIN] = blocksize;
 tcsetattr(sfd, TCSANOW, &options);
};
```

The model of ESP8266 used worked at 115200 baud by default. Newer models and updated firmware are reported to work at 9600 baud. If this is the case you need to modify the data rate and/or change the ESP8266's baud rate.

The read mode is set to a tenth of a second timeout between characters and a minimum read of 511 characters if there are no timeouts, the maximum. The plan for the rest of the functions is to use dprintf to send data and a blocking read that times out when the device has sent a burst of data. If you want to know more about the way the serial interface is set up then see Chapter 18.

Attention!

To start with the easiest, but possibly least useful, command let's implement some functions that test that we have a connection to the device - always a good thing to start with.

In this section we develop the first of a number of functions that send a command to the device and get back a response. To do this we need a few other functions to help and these are reused in other AT functions. Once you have one AT function the rest are very similar, so it is worth spending some time following how this most simple AT function works.

There isn't much point in moving on until you have tested that the connection works. To do this send the string AT\r\n and the ESP8266 should reply with a single "OK", which proves that the serial interface is working.

The most basic AT function is simply:

```
int ATWiFi() {
  dprintf(sfd, "AT\r\n");
  return 0;
}
```

This is the most basic form of function that will do the job, but it isn't really practical. We need to check that it works and get some feedback by reading the data from the device.

It makes sense to create a function that reads a block of data. It uses a blocking read to get as much data from the device as possible. The timeout is 0.1 seconds, which is enough time for more than 500 characters at 115200 baud and 100 at 9600 baud. Typical responses are a few hundred bytes, so using a buffer 512 bytes in size is reasonable.

The following function attempts to read a block of data from the device:

```c
int getBlock() {
  int bytes;
  struct timespec pause;
  pause.tv_sec = 0;
  pause.tv_nsec = 100000000;
  nanosleep(&pause, NULL);
  memset(buf, '\0', sizeof (buf));
  ioctl(sfd, FIONREAD, &bytes);
  if (bytes == 0)return 0;
  int count = read(sfd, buf, blocksize - 1);
  buf[count] = 0;
  if (DEBUG) {
   printf("%s", buf);
   fflush(stdout);
  }
  return count;
}
```

It first uses nanosleep to pause for 0.1 seconds and then it checks to see if there is any data in the serial buffer. If there isn't it returns without waiting. This means that there is an inter-character timeout of 0.1 second even if there are no characters to be read. Next the read function attempts to read a full buffer of data. Notice that there might not be a full buffer when the call is made, but as long as the data is coming in with gaps shorter than 0.1 second between characters it will continue reading until the buffer is full. Notice that a zero byte is added to the end of the buffer so that it can be treated like a valid C string.

If the AT command has been successful it returns a string containing "OK". One of the problems of working with AT commands is that they don't have an exact syntax and there is no formal "end of message" signal. By observation, any successful command does end with "OK" and if you can't find "OK" in the response then you either haven't read it all or there has been an error.

With all of this we can now finish the ATWiFi function:

```c
int ATWiFi() {
 dprintf(sfd, "AT\r\n");
 return getBlock();
}
```

The return value is the number of bytes read which could be zero. If the constant DEBUG is a 1 then the string is printed to stdout and you can examine it.

Put all this together with a main program:

```c
#include <stdio.h>
#include <stdlib.h>
#include <string.h>
#include <unistd.h>
#include <fcntl.h>
#include <termios.h>
#include <errno.h>
#include <sys/ioctl.h>
#include <time.h>
#define blocksize 255
#define DEBUG 1
int sfd;
char buf[blocksize];
int initWiFi();
int ATWiFi();
int getBlock();
int main(int argc, char** argv) {  initWiFi();
 ATWiFi();
 return (EXIT_SUCCESS);
}

int initWiFi() {
 system("sudo systemctl stop serial-getty@ttyAMA0.service");
 sfd = open("/dev/serial0", O_RDWR | O_NOCTTY);
 if (sfd == -1) {
  printf("Error no is : %d\n", errno);
  printf("Error description is : %s\n", strerror(errno));
  return -1;
 }
 struct termios options;
 tcgetattr(sfd, &options);cfsetspeed(&options, B115200);
 cfmakeraw(&options);
 options.c_cflag &= ~CSTOPB;
 options.c_cflag |= CLOCAL;
 options.c_cflag |= CREAD;
 options.c_cc[VTIME] = 1;
 options.c_cc[VMIN] = blocksize;
 tcsetattr(sfd, TCSANOW, &options);
};
```

```
int getBlock() {
 int bytes;
 struct timespec pause;
 pause.tv_sec = 0;
 pause.tv_nsec = 100000000;
 nanosleep(&pause, NULL);
 memset(buf, '\0', sizeof (buf));
 ioctl(sfd, FIONREAD, &bytes);
 if (bytes == 0)return 0;
 int count = read(sfd, buf, blocksize - 1);
 buf[count] = 0;
 if (DEBUG) {
  printf("%s", buf);
  fflush(stdout);
 }
 return count;
}
int ATWiFi() {dprintf(sfd, "AT\r\n");
 return getBlock();
}
```

When you run this program then you should see:

```
AT
OK
```

printed on the serial console. If you don't there are five possible reasons:

1. You have connected the wrong pins - check

2. The power supply you are using is inadequate - check/replace

3. The serial console isn't working - check you can see any message

4. The baud rate is wrong - try 9600

5. The ESP8266 is broken - try another

Some Utility Functions

Assuming that you have managed to make the AT command work it is time to move on to other AT commands. The first useful command is to find the Version number of the firmware. This is more or less the same as the AT function, but the command is AT+GMR and we get back more data - hence the longer wait time:

```
int getVersionWiFi() {
 dprintf(sfd, "AT+GMR\r\n");
 return getBlock()
}
```

The device in use returned:

```
AT+GMR
AT version:0.60.0.0(Jan 29 2016 15:10:17)
SDK version:1.5.2(7eee54f4)
Ai-Thinker Technology Co. Ltd.
May  5 2016 17:30:30
OK
```

The manual says that it should return AT, SDK and the time it was compiled, so we get a little extra with this third party device.

Another useful function is Reset. The device often gets stuck and then a reset is all that you can try. This is a software reset; another option is to use a GPIO line to connect to reset pin 6. By controlling this line you can force the device to hard reset. The soft reset command is AT+RST and all you get back in theory is "OK", but in practice the device sends a few hundred bytes of configuration data.

```
int resetWiFi() {
 dprintf(sfd, "AT+RST\r\n");
 return getBlock();
}
```

The final utility function is to set the serial connection parameters to 115200, 8 bits, 1 stop bit, no parity, no flow control:

```
int setUARTWiFi() {
 dprintf(sfd, "AT+UART_CUR=115200,8,1,0,0\r\n");
 return getBlock();
}
```

If you change the baud rate to something other than what is in use you will, of course, lose communication with the device until you reconfigure the serial connection.

Configuring WiFi

The first thing we need to configure is the operating mode. The ESP8622 can operate as an access point, i.e. it can allow other devices to connect to it. However, in most cases you will want it to work in client mode, i.e. connecting to your existing WiFi.

Mode

A function to set its operating mode is:

```
int modeWiFi(int mode) {
 dprintf(sfd, "AT+CWMODE_CUR=%d\r\n", mode);
 return getBlock();
}
```

In this case the command is:

```
AT+CWMODE_CUR=n
```

where n is 1 for client, 2 for access point and 3 for both. If you want to make the change permanent then change CUR to DEF and the setting is stored in flash memory. Older devices do not support CWMODE_CUR. Simply change it to CWMODE, which is deprecated.

To set client you would call:

```
modeWiFi(1);
```

and see OK sent back.

Scan

The scan function is one that everyone wants to try out, but in practice it isn't very useful. Why would you want a list of WiFi networks? There are some applications for this function, but not as many as you might think. In most cases you simply want to connect to a known WiFi network, which is what we do in the next section.

The scan command is easy - just send AT+CWLAP and the device sends you a complete list of WiFi networks. The problem is that scanning takes a long time and often hangs for a few seconds. Clearly we can't simply read a single block of data. We need a more powerful reading function that retrieves multiple blocks with an overall timeout. While it is doing this it might as well also scan the incoming data for a target like "OK" to use as a signal that it can stop reading blocks;

```
int getBlocks(int num, char target[])
 int I
 struct timespec pause;
 pause.tv_sec = 1;
 pause.tv_nsec = 0;
 for (i = 0; i < num; i++) {
  nanosleep(&pause, NULL);
  getBlock();
  if (strstr(buf, target))return i;
 }
 return -1;
}
```

Notice that we try to retrieve a maximum of num blocks and wait 1 second between trying each. If a block contains the target string then we return with the number of blocks read. The getBlock function is used to get each block and it displays what it has retrieved if DEBUG is set to 1. In a more sophisticated application you would probably want to concatenate the received blocks into a single larger buffer for further processing.

Now we can retrieve multiple blocks we can implement the scan function:

```
int scanWiFi()
 dprintf(sfd, "AT+CWLAP\r\n");
 return getBlocks(20, "OK");
}
```

In this case the function is set to retrieve a maximum of 20 blocks, which could mean waiting as long as 20 seconds for the function to exit. However, in most cases it exits after only a small number of blocks because it detects an "OK".

The getBlocks function is so useful that you might as well go back and change the call to getBlock to getBlocks(20, "OK") which will improve the reliability of the program.

Connecting to WiFi

Our final and most useful functions connect the device to a known WiFi network. All you have to do is supply the SSID and password. There are other versions of the command that allow you to specify the connection more precisely, but this general form is the most useful. Connection to a network takes a while and there is quite a lot of data sent back, so we need to use a long timeout in the getBlocks function introduced in the scan function:

```
int connectWiFi(char ssid[], char pass[])
 dprintf(sfd, "AT+CWJAP_CUR=\"%s\",\"%s\"\r\n",ssid, pass)
 return getBlocks(20, "OK");
}
```

Notice the way the dprintf function is used to insert the SSID and password into the command. If you have an older device you might need to change CWJAP_CUR to the deprecated CWJAP command. There is also a CWJAP_DEF command that will save the connection in the flash memory.

The connection is made with:

```
connectWiFi("myWiFi","myPassword");
```

After a few seconds you should see:

```
AT+CWJAP_CUR="myWiFi","myPassword"
WIFI DISCONNECT
WIFI CONNECTED
WIFI GOT IP
OK
```

Once you are connected and the "WIFI GOT IP" message has been received you can ask what the IP address is:

```
int getIPWiFi() {
 dprintf(sfd, "AT+CIFSR\r\n");
 return getBlocks(10, "OK");
}
```

Of course, if you really need to know the IP address within a program you need to extract it from the string. The device replies with:

```
IP address:
AT+CIFSR
+CIFSR:STAIP,"192.168.253.4"
+CIFSR:STAMAC,"5c:cf:7f:16:97:ab"
OK
```

This makes it very easy to get the IP address even without the help of a regular expression.

Getting a Web Page

Now we have enough functions to tackle the two standard tasks in using the TCP stack - getting and sending data as a client and as a server.

First we tackle the problem of acting as a client. This isn't as common a requirement as you might expect because most of the time devices like the Pi are used to supply data to other servers, not the other way round. However, it is worth seeing how it is done.

It doesn't matter if you are implementing a client or a server, either way you make use of sockets which represent the basic TCP connection. What you do with this connection is up to you. For example, if you send HTTP headers on an appropriate port, you can fetch or deliver a web page, i.e. HTTP over TCP. However, what data you actually send and receive over a socket connection is up to you and/or the protocol you are trying to use. For more information on socket programming see the previous chapter.

The first thing we have to do is set up a socket connection between the client, i.e. the Pi, and the server.

```
int getWebPageWiFi(char URL[], char page[]) {
    dprintf(sfd, "AT+CIPSTART=\"TCP\",\"%s\",80\r\n", URL);
    if (getBlocks(10, "OK") < 0) return -1;
```

You pass the URL to the function as an IP address or as a full URL, but the device looks up domain names using a fixed set of DNS servers. It is recommended that you use an IP address, especially when testing. The CIPSTART command opens a socket to the specified IP address and port.

You can also specify a TCP or UDP connection:

```
AT+CIPSTART=type, IP, port
```

In this case we open port 80 on the specified IP address or URL. If it works you will get back a message something like:

```
Connect
AT+CIPSTART="TCP","192.168.253.23",80
CONNECT
OK
```

Now we have a socket open we can send some data to the server and wait for some data to be sent back to us. This can be a problem as you can't anticipate the amount of data you get back from the web server.

For this example the web page is served by a small sensor that returns a JSON temperature and Humidity reading. The sensor is another Pi running the web server is described in the next section.

To send data over a socket you use CIPSEND, which will send any data you specify to the server. As already made clear, what you send is a matter of what protocol you are using over the socket. In this case it is HTTP and we are going to send headers corresponding to a GET request for index.html

```
char http[150]
sprintf(http, "GET %s HTTP/1.1\r\nHost:%s\r\n\r\n",page, URL);
```

This time we can't just send the string using dprintf because we need to include the length of the string in the header we send to the server.

The headers we are sending are:

```
GET /index.html HTTP/1.1
Host:192.168.253.23
```

Remember, an HTTP request always ends with a blank line.

To send this request we use the CIPSEND command which specifies the number of characters that are to follow:

```
dprintf(sfd, "AT+CIPSEND=%d\r\n", strlen(http));
```

Now we have to send the number of bytes/ characters that we specified in the CIPSEND. but first we wait for a ">" to indicate that the device is ready to receive the data:

```
if (getBlocks(10, ">") < 0) return -1;
dprintf(sfd, "%s", http);
return getBlocks(10, "</html>");
}
```

What happens next depends on the server. As a result of the HTTP GET the server will now send data over the WiFi link and the device will send this over the serial connection as soon as it gets it. Notice that this data is not a direct response to a command and so the device prefixes it with:

```
+IPD,len:
```

The +IPD makes it clear to the client that is a packet of data sent from the server. The len value gives the number of characters sent after the colon. You could use this to work out when to stop reading data, but for simplicity we scan for "</html>" which is usually, but not always, the final tag at the end of a web page.

In principle what your program should do next is sit in a polling loop looking for +IPD. It should then read the digits between the comma and the colon and convert this to an integer. Finally it should then read exactly that number of characters from the serial port:

```
+IPD,17:HTTP/1.0 200 OK
+IPD,99:Server: BaseHTTP/0.6 Python/3.2.3
Date: Thu, 14 Jul 2016 16:42:37 GMT
Content-type: text/html
+IPD,127:<html><head><title>Temperature</title></head>
<body><p>{"humidity":0,"airtemperature":0}
</p></body></html>CLOSED
```

You can see that there are three "packets" of data - 17 characters, 99 characters and finally 127 characters. In principle you could process the +IPD characters as they come in and work out how many characters to read. However, you still wouldn't know how many packets to expect.

The complete function is:

```
int getWebPageWiFi(char URL[], char page[]) {
 dprintf(sfd, "AT+CIPSTART=\"TCP\",\"%s\",80\r\n", URL);
 if (getBlocks(10, "OK") < 0) return -1;
 char http[150];
 sprintf(http, "GET %s HTTP/1.1\r\nHost:%s\r\n\r\n",page, URL);
 dprintf(sfd, "AT+CIPSEND=%d\r\n", strlen(http));
 if (getBlocks(10, ">") < 0) return -1;
 dprintf(sfd, "%s", http);
 return getBlocks(10, "</html>");
}
```

A Web Server

The most common use for an internet connection on a small device like the Pi is to allow another device to request data. It is fairly easy to create a web server running on the ESP8266, but don't expect Apache or anything advanced. All you can reasonably do is accept a connection and send a web page or two back to the client.

The key differences between client and server mode is that in server mode the device constantly "listening" for clients to make TCP connections on the port.

When the device receives a connection it reads all of the data the client sends and passes it on via the serial port to the Pi. This means that in server mode the Pi has to be constantly on the lookout for new data from the ESP8266. You can do this using an interrupt, but for simplicity this example uses a polling loop.

There is another difference between client mode and server mode - there can be multiple TCP connections from as many clients as try to connect. The solution to this problem is that the ESP8226 assigns each TCP socket connection an id number and this is what you need to use to make sure you send the data to the right place.

Let's see how it all works.

Assuming we are already connected to WiFi and have an IP address, we can set up a server quite easily. First we need to use the command CIPMUX =1 to set the device into multiple connection mode. You cannot start a server if CIPMUX=0, the default single connection mode. Once multiple connections are allowed you can create a server using CIPSERVER=1,port.

In this example we are using port 80. the standard HTTP port, but you can change this to anything you want:

```
int startServerWiFi() {
 char temp[blocksize];
 char id[10];
 dprintf(sfd, "AT+CIPMUX=1\r\n");
 if (getBlocks(10, "OK") < 0) return -1;
 dprintf(sfd, "AT+CIPSERVER=1,80\r\n");
 if (getBlocks(10, "OK") < 0) return -1;
```

If you run just this part of the program you will see the response:

```
AT+CIPMUX=1
OK
AT+CIPSERVER=1,80
no change
OK
```

Now we just have to wait for a client to make a connection and send some data. This is done simply by reading the serial input and checking for "+IPD" in an infinite polling loop:

```
for (;;) {
 if (getBlocks(1, "+IPD") < 0)continue;
```

If we don't get a block containing "+IPD" we simply move on to the next iteration. There should be a call to nanosleep just before we do getBlocks to reduce the load on the processor . This is particularly important if you are running this on a single core Pi Zero.

If we have received a block containing "+IPD", the body of the loop processes it. As this is C string processing it is not elegant. The received data has the format:

```
+IPD,id, rest of data
```

We now need to extract the id so we can use it to communicate with the client. This is just some standard string handling, but it is still messy:

```
char *b = strstr(buf, "+IPD");
b += 5;
strncpy(temp, b, sizeof (temp));
char *e = strstr(temp, ",");
int d = e - temp;
memset(id, '\0', sizeof (id));
strncpy(id, temp, d);
```

The algorithm is:

- Find "+IPD" and trim the string to remove it and the comma
- Find the next comma and extract the characters from the start of the string to the next comma.

Now we have the id we can communicate with the client, but first we need something to send. As with all HTTP transactions, we have to send some headers and then some data. There are a lot of possible headers you could send, but a reasonable minimum that works with most browsers is:

```
char data[] = "HTTP/1.0 200 OK\r\n
                Server: Pi\r\n
                Content-type: text/html\r\n\r\n
        <html><head><title>Temperature</title></head>
        <body><p>
          {\"humidity\":81%,\"airtemperature\":23.5C}
        </p></body></html>\r\n";
```

Of course, in a real application, the HTML part of the data would be generated by the program or read from a file. You can include time stamps and lots of other useful information, but this is simple and it works. Remember to include a blank line at the end of the headers. This is vital as the browser will ignore everything sent to it if you don't.

Now we want to send the data to the client. This is just a matter of using the CIPSEND command again, only this time with the id specified as the first parameter:

```
CIPSEND=id,data length
```

and we wait for the response ">" before sending the data: Notice that we don't have to open a TCP socket as we did in the case of acting as a client. The TCP socket has already been opened by the client connecting to the server and when the transaction is complete we can close it:

```
dprintf(sfd, "AT+CIPSEND=%s,%d\r\n", id, strlen(data));
if (getBlocks(10, ">") < 0) return -1;
```

Now, at last, we can send the data to the client:

```
dprintf(sfd, "%s", data);
if (getBlocks(10, "OK") < 0) return -1;
```

and wait for it to complete.

Finally we close the connection and complete the loop to wait for another connection:

```
dprintf(sfd, "AT+CIPCLOSE=%s\r\n", id);
if (getBlocks(10, "OK") < 0) return -1;
}
}
```

Try it out with a main program something like:

```
int main() {
 initWiFi();
 modeWiFi(1);
 connectWiFi("ssid","pass");
 getIPWiFi();
 startServerWiFi();
}
```

You should now be able to connect to the IP address that is displayed and retrieve the web page that displays:

```
{"humidity":81%,"airtemperature":23.5C}
```

There are a lot of WiFi commands that haven't been covered here, but now that you have seen examples of most of the basic types and encountered the typical problems that occur you should be able to implement any that you need.

There is still going to be the occasional unexplained crash and in this case the best solution is to use the soft reset command. It is also worth mentioning that the server program as presented does not actually handle multiple simultaneous connections. It has to finish dealing with one connection before it can deal with a second. If you want to do this you need to create a new thread every time that a connection is made or you need to implement an event queue so that you can deal with each request in turn.

Complete Listing

```c
#include <stdio.h>
#include <stdlib.h>
#include <string.h>
#include <unistd.h>
#include <fcntl.h>
#include <termios.h>
#include <errno.h>
#include <sys/ioctl.h>
#include <time.h>

#define blocksize 255
#define DEBUG 1int sfd;

char buf[blocksize];int initWiFi();

int ATWiFi();
int getBlock();
int getBlocks(int num, char target[]);
int getVersionWiFi();
int resetWiFi();
int setUARTWiFi();
int modeWiFi(int mode);
int scanWiFi();
int connectWiFi(char ssid[], char pass[]);
int getIPWiFi();
int startServerWiFi();
int getWebPageWiFi(char URL[], char page[]);/*

int main(int argc, char** argv) {
 initWiFi();ATWiFi();
 connectWiFi("ssid", "password");
 getIPWiFi();
 startServerWiFi();
 return (EXIT_SUCCESS);
 }
```

```c
int initWiFi() {
 system("sudo systemctl stop serial-getty@ttyAMA0.service";);
 sfd = open("/dev/serial0", O_RDWR | O_NOCTTY);
 if (sfd == -1) {
  printf("Error no is : %d\n", errno);
  printf("Error description is : %s\n", strerror(errno));
  return -1;
 }
 struct termios options;
 tcgetattr(sfd, &options);
 cfsetspeed(&options, B115200);
 cfmakeraw(&options);
 options.c_cflag &= ~CSTOPB;
 options.c_cflag |= CLOCAL;
 options.c_cflag |= CREAD;
 options.c_cc[VTIME] = 1;
 options.c_cc[VMIN] = blocksize;
 tcsetattr(sfd, TCSANOW, &options);
};

int ATWiFi() {dprintf(sfd, "AT\r\n");
 return getBlock();
}

int getVersionWiFi() {
 dprintf(sfd, "AT+GMR\r\n");
return getBlock();
}

int resetWiFi() {
 dprintf(sfd, "AT+RST\r\n");
 return getBlock();
}

int setUARTWiFi() {
 dprintf(sfd, "AT+UART_CUR=115200,8,1,0,0\r\n");
 return getBlock();
}

int modeWiFi(int mode) {
 dprintf(sfd, "AT+CWMODE_CUR=%d\r\n", mode);
 return getBlock();
}

int scanWiFi() {
 dprintf(sfd, "AT+CWLAP\r\n");
 return getBlocks(20, "OK");
}
```

```c
int connectWiFi(char ssid[], char pass[]) {
 dprintf(sfd, "AT+CWJAP_CUR=\"%s\",\"%s\"\r\n", ssid, pass);
 return getBlocks(20, "OK");
}

int getIPWiFi() {
 dprintf(sfd, "AT+CIFSR\r\n");
 return getBlocks(10, "OK");
}

int getWebPageWiFi(char URL[], char page[]) {
 dprintf(sfd, "AT+CIPSTART=\"TCP\",\"%s\",80\r\n", URL);
 if (getBlocks(10, "OK") < 0) return -1;
 char http[150];
 sprintf(http, "GET %s HTTP/1.1\r\nHost:%s\r\n\r\n", page, URL);
 dprintf(sfd, "AT+CIPSEND=%d\r\n", strlen(http));
 if (getBlocks(10, ">") < 0) return -1;
 dprintf(sfd, "%s", http);
 return getBlocks(10, "</html>");
}

int startServerWiFi() {
 char temp[blocksize];
 char id[10];
 dprintf(sfd, "AT+CIPMUX=1\r\n");
 if (getBlocks(10, "OK") < 0) return -1;
 dprintf(sfd, "AT+CIPSERVER=1,80\r\n");
 if (getBlocks(10, "OK") < 0) return -1;
 char data[] = "HTTP/1.0 200 OK\r\n
                 Server:Pi\r\n
                 Content-type: text/html\r\n\r\n
  <html><head><title>Temperature</title></head>
  <body><p>
  {\"humidity\":81%,\"airtemperature\":23.5C}
  </p></body></html>\r\n";
 for (;;) {
  if (getBlocks(1, "+IPD") < 0)continue;
  char *b = strstr(buf, "+IPD");
  b += 5;
  strncpy(temp, b, sizeof (temp));
  char *e = strstr(temp, ",");
  int d = e - temp;
  memset(id, '\0', sizeof (id));
  strncpy(id, temp, d);
  dprintf(sfd, "AT+CIPSEND=%s,%d\r\n",id, strlen(data));
  if (getBlocks(10, ">") < 0) return -1;
  dprintf(sfd, "%s", data);
  if (getBlocks(10, "OK") < 0) return -1;
  dprintf(sfd, "AT+CIPCLOSE=%s\r\n", id);
  if (getBlocks(10, "OK") < 0) return -1;
 }
}
```

```
int getBlock() {
 int bytes;
 struct timespec pause;
 pause.tv_sec = 0;
 pause.tv_nsec = 100000000;
 nanosleep(&pause, NULL);
 memset(buf, '\0', sizeof (buf));
 ioctl(sfd, FIONREAD, &bytes);
 if (bytes == 0)return 0;
 int count = read(sfd, buf, blocksize - 1);
 buf[count] = 0;
 if (DEBUG) {
  printf("%s", buf);
  fflush(stdout);
 }
 return count;
}

int getBlocks(int num, char target[]) {
 int i;
 struct timespec pause;
 pause.tv_sec = 1;
 pause.tv_nsec = 0;
 for (i = 0; i < num; i++) {
  nanosleep(&pause, NULL);
  getBlock();
  if (strstr(buf, target))return i;
 }
 return -1;
}
```

Index

18427279R00162

Printed in Great Britain
by Amazon